ARISTOCRACY IN PROVENCE

THE MIDDLE AGES

a series edited by
EDWARD PETERS
Henry Charles Lea Professor
of Medieval History
University of Pennsylvania

ARISTOCRACY IN PROVENCE
THE RHÔNE BASIN AT THE DAWN
OF THE CAROLINGIAN AGE

PATRICK J. GEARY

upp

UNIVERSITY OF PENNSYLVANIA PRESS · PHILADELPHIA

1985

First published in the United States of America in 1985
by the University of Pennsylvania Press, Philadelphia

First published in the Federal Republic of Germany
in 1985 by Anton Hiersemann, Stuttgart

Photosatz in Sabon-Antiqua und Druck: Sulzberg-Druck GmbH, Sulzberg im Allgäu. Bindearbeit: Großbuchbinderei Ernst Riethmüller, Stuttgart.

ISBN 0-8122-7999-9

Printed in the Federal Republic of Germany

TABLE OF CONTENTS

PREFACE IX
INTRODUCTION 1
CHAPTER I: The Testament and its Transmission 12
   Vienne and Grenoble 12
   The Cartulary of Grenoble 18
   The Carolingian Forgery 21
   The Testament 27
   The Identity of the Testator 33
CHAPTER II: Edition and Translation 36
   The Text 38
   The Translation 39
CHAPTER III: Land and Lordship 80
   Land 81
   Dependents 90
   Landholding 97
   Conclusions 99
CHAPTER IV: The Aristocracy: Kinship and Power 101
   Ethnic/Identity 101
   Kinship Patterns 115
   Officeholding 119
CHAPTER V: The Revolt of the Provence 126
   Neustrian Maiors of the Palace 131
   Connections between Neustria and the Rhône Valley . 138
   Conclusions 144
CHAPTER VI: Conclusion 149
BIBLIOGRAPHY OF PRIMARY SOURCES 153
BIBLIOGRAPHY OF SECONDARY SOURCES 155
INDEX 165

PREFACE

The early medieval aristocracy has, over the past thirty years, proven one of the most significant and fruitful fields of research for European scholars. The structure of the early medieval nobility has long interested German historians, and recently it has attracted the attention of American and British as well. The specific questions that have dominated German scholarship — the origins of the Frankish nobility; the relationship between king and aristocracy in the Merovingian period; and the development of the so-called Imperial Aristocracy — have recently begun to merge with broader questions of social structure of the type pursued by French social historians in the tradition of Marc Bloch and, most recently, Georges Duby. Likewise, the study of the nobility is now understood as inseparable from the examination of the relationships between these elites and the rest of society: the free, the semi-free, and slave populations that comprised the vast majority of the medieval population. As the pioneering works of Karl Bosl and others have demonstrated, the social and economic structures of the agricultural world form the necessary horizons in which to understand nobles, for whom land and lordship were of paramount importance.

In general, these investigations have been pursued through two closely related types of studies: the first, based largely on newly refined prosopographical methodology, comprises examinations of the horizontal relationships among European aristocratic groups and explores these complex interrelationships among aristocratic clans across Europe. The second includes more vertically oriented regional studies which examine the complexities of regional societies. Ideally, of course, one should attempt both: that is, the regional aristocratic groups of the early Middle Ages must be understood within their local context as well as within the structures of kinship and politics which connected them to other regions of Europe.

The present study investigates both the horizontal and vertical structures of the Provençal aristocracy and is intended as the first in a series of investigations into the structure and self-perceptions of aristocratic groups in the Rhône valley during the Early Middle Ages. When I first began the project on the advice of Professor Georges Duby, my original intention was to trace the relationships between the aristocracy of the lower Rhône and other areas of Europe between the ninth and eleventh centuries. However, I quickly realized that in order to understand this later period it was first necessary to investigate the region during the first half of the eighth century, the moment when Arnulfing (or Carolingian) control was first established there. Professor Jean-Pierre Poly suggested that I take a look at the testament of Abbo, and from that moment I found myself increasingly drawn into the problems raised by this unique document. At first I envisioned a brief article, then a section of a larger book, and then, ultimately, a separate volume as I began to realize that the testament and other related documents not only illuminate the society of the Rhône region, but also bear directly on some of the most significant issues of seventh- and eighth-century social history.

Thousands of testaments must have been prepared by the churchmen and aristocrats of the Merovingian period living under Roman law and wishing to direct the disposition of their property upon their deaths. Of these not even a dozen have survived the ravages of time, and only that of Abbo presents the testamentary dispositions of a layman. Moreover, the testament was written at the very moment at which the Carolingian subjugation of the Rhône region had been accomplished, a subjugation in which Abbo had played an important rôle. In its dispositions, therefore, it preserves an image of both the old and the new structures of the Provençal society, an image closely related to that of other areas of Francia, particularly Bavaria and Alemannia to the east and Burgundy and Neustria to the north. This text thus presents a unique opportunity to examine the transformation of European aristocratic society during the final decades of the rise of Carolingian power.

I hope that the present attempt to reinterpret this transformation will serve as a modest contribution to the growing number of studies which have recently come to be called "micro-histories", that is, attempts to re-create, through the analysis of one unique document or event, the underlying structures and forces of the world in which it had meaning. The minute analysis of the specific document, in this case the *Testamentum Abbonis*, is not an end in itself, but merely a means to understand the broader issues which can be seen through it.

As is always the case when attempting the social history of the Merovingian period, the paucity and intractability of the sources are such that my results must remain tentative and my conclusions mere hypotheses. Much will be found in my methods and inferences that will strike some readers as too speculative. Nevertheless, to shrink from the attempt to understand the society which has left these tantalizing fragments is to abnegate what Lucien Febvre recognized as "the supreme, the idea, the final purpose of the historian": "To recompose, through thought, for each of the periods he studies, the intellectual material of the people of this period; to reconstitute, by a powerful effort simultaneously of scholarship and of imagination, the universe, the entire universe, physical, intellectual, and moral, of each of the generations which preceded him ..."[1] I have attempted, in my work, to meet this challenge, ever mindful of Febvre's warning that such an historical construct will necessarily be incomplete and imperfect, and of his admonition to eschew the sorts of historical anachronisms which threaten such efforts to understand the past.

If I have to any extent succeeded in reconstituting something of the world of the eighth century, it is largely due to the kindness of a great many scholars in Europe and in North America who have been extraordinarily generous in offering detailed assistance, criticism and advice: to acknowledge all here would be impossible, and the many scholars who have assisted on specific points are acknowledged in the notes. I do wish to express my particu-

---

[1] Lucien Febvre, "De Linné à Georges Cuvier," in *Combats pour l'histoire* (Paris: 1965), p. 334.

lar gratitude to Professor Georges Duby, who first set me on this study, as well as to Professors John Baldwin, Thomas Bisson, Giles Constable, Walter Goffart, Otto Gerhard Oexle, Jean-Pierre Poly, Giovanni Tabacco, Priv. Doz. Michael Borgolte, and Dr. Martin Heinzelmann, who were extremely helpful at preliminary stages of the project; and especially to Professors Bernard Bachrach, Karl Bosl, Karl Brunner, Edward Champlin, Hugo Ott, Friedrich Prinz, Franz Staab, Giuseppe Sergi, Gisella Wataghin Cantino, Karl Ferdinand Werner, Herwig Wolfram, and Dr. Anton Scharer, all of whom have read and commented on all or large portions of the manuscript. Professors Jo Ann McNamara and John E. Halborg assisted me in revising the translation of the manuscript. To acknowledge the criticism and assistance of these scholars is not to imply that all approve of or agree with my conclusions – far from it. However, without their interest and assistance its deficiencies would have been greater.

In the course of my research I have received support from Princeton University, the Austrian Institute, the German Academic Exchange Service, the American Philosophical Society, and the University of Florida. The final draft was completed during a semester as Gastprofessor at the University of Vienna, in the course of which I had the opportunity to devote my seminar to the *Testamentum Abbonis*. For their hospitality, advice and support I am particularly grateful to Professor Heinrich Fichtenau and his colleagues and students in the Institut für österreichische Geschichtsforschung.

Finally, I wish to acknowledge my debt to the scholar who first introduced me to the Mediterranean world of the early Middle Ages, Professor Robert Lopez, who once remarked in the course of a seminar a decade ago that, while he fully expected his students to find some errors in his work, he hoped we would not accuse him of being not only wrong but also foolish. I sincerely hope that he will apply the same sense of generous criticism to the work of his student as he reads this volume which, with gratitude and admiration, is dedicated to him.

ABBREVIATIONS

BM²	*Regesta imperii*, ed. J. F. Böhmer and Engelbert Mühlbacher.
AASS	*Acta Sanctorum*
DArn.	*Diplomata maiorum domus e stirpe Arnulforum*
DKar.	*Diplomatum Karolinorum*
DM.	*Diplomata regum Francorum e stirpe Merowingica*
LS.	*Les diplômes originaux des merovingiens*, ed. Ph. Lauer and Ch. Samaran
MGH	*Monumenta Germaniae Historica*
Dipl.	*Diplomatum*
Epist.	*Epistolae*
SS	*Scriptores in folio*
SSRL	*Scriptores rerum Langobardicarum et Italicarum*
SSRM	*Scriptores rerum Merovingicarum*
SS rer Germ.	*Scriptores rerum Germanicarum in usum scholarum separatim editi*
MIÖG	*Mitteilungen des Instituts für österreichische Geschichtsforschung Geschichtsforschung*
PL	*Patrologia Latina* ed. J. P. Migne

ARISTOCRACY IN PROVENCE

INTRODUCTION

On the fifth of May, 739, one Abbo, a wealthy landowner in the mountainous areas to the east of the Rhône and in lower Provence, established as his heir the monastery of Novalesa which he had founded thirteen years previously. The properties bequeathed to Novalesa were scattered over a region of roughly 34,500 square kilometers, an enormous and diverse area of mountains, valleys, and coastal regions which had, in late Antiquity, made up the Roman provinces of the Viennensis, Narbonensis II and Alpes maritimae, and which today include the French départments of the Var, Bouches-du-Rhône, Vaucluse, Drôme, Isère, Savoie, Hautes-Alpes, Alpes-de-haute-Provence, and Alpes-Maritimes, as well as the Italian province of the Piemonte. As in the eighth century, this is a region of extremely varied geography, vegetation, and economy. The dominant features are the Alps to the east commanded by the Barre des Écrins (4104 m), the Grande Casse (3852 m) and numerous peaks such as Mont Cenis and the Grande Chartreuse well above 2,000 meters. On the western boundary flows the Rhône, not the longest but certainly the most varied and forceful of France's great rivers. Itself starting as a mountain torrent in the Swiss Alps, through its entire course it is fed by mountain streams as it rushes to the sea. North of the Massif Pelvoux, which forms a sort of north-south divider in the Alps, the Rhône receives the Isère, itself fed by the Arly to the north and the Drac to the south. Below the Massif the Rhône is augmented by the Eygues, the Ouvèze and, most important, the Durance, which drains the lower Alps through the Ubaye, the Blèone, the Verdon and the Guil.

North of the Massif Pelvoux the Alps are higher, but the area receives greater precipitation and, most important for its scattered population, the valleys penetrate to the very bases of the mountains, making possible the support of a great number of isolated but prosperous settlements, dependent on pasturage in the lush mountain valleys and upland meadows for their support. The extremes of weather at these altitudes necessitated, well into the nineteenth century, the great annual transhumance, that seasonal migration of people and flocks which were both symptom of, and escape from, their isolated and precarious existence.

South of the Massif Pelvoux the Alps are not as imposing, but the relief becomes more irregular, valleys are less frequent, and the thinner vegetation is typical of the more Mediterranean flora of the Provençal Alps. Here population is less dense and clustered along the upper valleys of the Verdon and the Durance, engaged likewise in pasturage and, where possible, the traditional Mediterranean cultivation of vines and olive groves.

From the heights of the Alps, the region falls to the Rhône itself, at Avignon only 13 m above sea level. In the interior of Provence, the population is likewise scattered, but here the problem is the arid climate and the poverty of soil, with communities living on virtual islands of fertile and well-watered land surrounded either by parched, limestone hills or, around Arles, by the brackish semi-land of the Camargue.[1]

Through generations, by means of inheritances, purchases, exchanges, and grants, Abbo and his ancestors had acquired property throughout this varied region of mountains, valleys, and rugged Mediterranean coastlands, and all of it passed now to the new monastery on the eastern slopes of the Alps. Not much is known of Abbo from other sources, and the testament provides little information on his public life. Nevertheless, if the testator remains in considerable obscurity, this single document can serve as a window through which one glimpses the complex history of a most crucial region of Europe, the lower Rhône, at what was certainly a decisive moment in Western history: the decades that saw the rise and triumph of the Carolingians in the Frankish realm.

On the political scene, during this period took place the final disintegration of the Merovingian dynasty and its supporters and the rise of the Arnulfings or Carolingians who, by the 740s, had established effective control over the kingdom of the Franks and over most of its tributaries. The success of this family has long been studied in terms of astute political perception and ability on the part of its members, in terms of innovation in military tactics and equipment, and has been explained in part by suggestions of weakness, if not of degeneracy, in the Merovingian royal family.[2]

However, the rise of the Carolingians was not merely a political phenomenon: it was part of a process of sweeping social changes involving the aristocracy of the Frankish

---

[1] On the relationship between Provence and its inhabitants through history, see E. Baratier, G. Duby, E. Hilde-Sheimar, *Atlas historique de la Provence* (Paris: 1969). On the Alpine regions of Europe in the Early Middle Ages as a cultural and social unit see the important remarks of Karl Bosl in *Die Grundlagen der modernen Gesellschaft im Mittelalter: eine deutsche Gesellschaftsgeschichte des Mittelalters* vol. 1, Monographien zur Geschichte des Mittelalters 4/1 (Stuttgart: 1972), pp. 21–23, and the bibliographical material in note 10, p. 22.

[2] As introduction to the enormous literature on the rise of the Carolingians, one can consult the first volume of Wattenbach-Levison, *Deutschlands Geschichtsquellen im Mittelalter. Vorzeit und Karolinger* (Weimar: 1952) and the bibliography in Heinz Löwe, *Deutschland im fränkischen Reich, Gebhardt Handbuch der deutschen Geschichte* 9th edition vol. I (Stuttgart: 1970), pp. 90–216, and, most recently, Josef Semmler, "Zur pippinidisch-karolingischen Sukzessionskrise 714–723" *Deutsches Archiv* vol. 33, 1 (1977) pp. 1–36. On possible effects of military innovations see Lynn White Jr., *Medieval Technology and Social Change* (Oxford: 1962) pp. 1–38, and, most recently, Pierre Contamine, *La guerre au moyen âge*, La nouvelle Clio vol. 24 (Paris: 1980) pp. 315–320. The old myth which explained the decline of the Merovingian family as the result of genetic degeneracy has largely been put to rest by recent scholarship referred to above as well as by J. M. Wallace-Hadrill, *The Long-Haired Kings* (New York: 1962), especially pp. 231–248. Eugen Ewig provides an excellent overview of the relationship between the early Carolingians and the Church in vol. III/1 of the *Handbuch der Kirchengeschichte* (ed. Hubert Jedin), *Die mittelalterliche Kirche, erster Halbband: Vom kirchlichen Frühmittelalter zur gregorianischen Reform* (Freiburg: 1966) pp. 9–19.

heartlands of Neustria and Austrasia as well as that of the peripheral areas of the realm: Aquitaine, Thuringia, Bavaria, Frisia, and Provence.[3] The Carolingians rose to power along with the Austrasian aristocracy from which they emerged, and consolidated their position at the expense of the Neustrian families which had previously controlled the more Romanized parts of Francia. At the same time, the struggles between the Austrasians and Neustrians had given regional groups the opportunity to establish themselves as largely autonomous powers in their *regna* or subkingdoms. In the course of the suppression of these independent groups by Pepin II and his son Charles Martel, numerous old aristocratic factions and families of diverse origins disappeared, at least temporarily, from the European scene. In their place, or as an amalgam of these older groups, emerged the so-called "Imperial Aristocracy," a group of aristocratic clans loyal to the Carolingians by which Europe was to be ruled for the next two centuries.

The later disintegration of this unified Europe and the emergence or reemergence of regional groups in the late ninth and tenth centuries have long challenged historians to examine the relationship between these new territorial principalities, their aristocracies, and the earlier *regna* of the seventh and eighth centuries. The old interpretation of the disintegration of the Empire which viewed territorialization as the reemergence of ethnic duchies reasserting their individuality in opposition to Frankish domination was laid to rest in Germany by the work of Gerd Tellenbach, although as late as 1948 the Belgian historian Jan Dhondt could still argue that "The Carolingian empire, in effect, constituted a real conglomerate of diverse nationalities which had kept alive the sentiment of their individuality and which tried without cease to escape from the Frankish empire."[4] Even more recently, Michel Rouche can trace in Aquitaine and Provence a continuous sense of mutual cultural and institutional antagonism between Franks and Romans.[5]

Significantly, both Dhondt and Rouche based their arguments on the Midi of France which they insisted had a quite particular history because of the strong and continuing

---

[3] Again, the literature on early medieval aristocracy is enormous and rapidly growing. Of primary importance are Gerd Tellenbach, *Königtum und Stämme in der Werdezeit des deutschen Reiches* (Weimar: 1939); the articles of Eugen Ewig collected and edited by Hartmut Atsma in *Spätantikes und fränkisches Gallien, Beihefte der Francia* vol. 3, 1 and 2, (Munich: 1976 and 1979); Karl Schmid, "Zur Problematik von Familie, Sippe und Geschlecht, Haus und Dynastie beim mittelalterlichen Adel," *Zeitschrift für die Geschichte des Oberrheins* vol. 105 (1957) pp. 1–62; and the work of Karl Ferdinand Werner, especially his "Bedeutende Adelsfamilien im Reich Karls des Großen, in *Karl der Große: Persönlichkeit und Geschichte*, ed. Helmut Beumann vol. I (Düsseldorf: 1965) pp. 83–142. Translated in *The Medieval Nobility*, ed. T. Reuter (Amsterdam: 1978) pp. 137–202.

[4] Jan Dhondt, *Études sur la naissance des principautés territoriales en France (IXe–Xe siècle)* (Bruges: 1948).

[5] Michel Rouche, "Les Aquitains ont-ils trahi avant la bataille de Poitiers? Un éclairage événementiel sur les mentalités," *Le Moyen Age* vol. 74 4eme serie 23 (1968) pp. 5–26.

Roman traditions there. Elsewhere, the work of Tellenbach, Eugen Ewig, Karl Schmid and others has stressed the futility of looking for continuity between fifth-century peoples and the tenth-century territorial principalities which happened to carry the same names. In the course of the seventh century, these scholars argue, the sense and importance of old ethnic differences separating Franks, Romans, Burgundians, and Alemanni, disappeared at the politically relevant level of the aristocracy. References to these groups in eighth and ninth century sources have only a territorial meaning, and new opposition groups which play a prominent rôle in the Carolingian period had no real continuity with the *Stämme* of the fifth and sixth centuries.

For Gerd Tellenbach and his school, this loss of ethnic identity in the aristocracy is the result of the diffusion throughout the West of the "imperial aristocracy," a relatively small group of magnates drawn almost entirely from Austrasian supporters of the Carolingians and dependent upon the new dynasty for its rise and power. These families, who constituted a new aristocracy in the eighth century, gradually formed local, particularist connections in the regions into which they had been sent by the successors of Charles the Great, and with their followers constituted the political elites of the new territorial principalities of the 880s and later. Since these families, drawn from Austrasia, intermarried extensively and served the Carolingians as administrators of outlying areas, they in no sense continued the old ethnic traditions of the local populations. These populations, lacking a significant aristocratic element in politics or official (ecclesiastical) culture, quickly lost their ethnic traditions of origin which lingered on only in the personality-principle of law, but not in any broader sense.

Most recently, this notion of an Austrasian "imperial aristocracy," dependent on the Carolingian dynasty which used it to control the Frankish kingdoms, has been called into question by Karl Ferdinand Werner and Karl Brunner who, using the methods of the Tellenbach school, have demonstrated the complexity of the Carolingian aristocracy.[6] True, some families had risen to prominence as a result of their cooperation with the Carolingians, but the Carolingians themselves owed their rise to an alliance with equally old or older families, some from Austrasia, but others from Neustria, from Gallo-Roman stock, or from families which had risen as supporters of the Merovingians. These aristocratic groups have to be viewed more as partners than as agents of the Carolingians, and increasingly the political history of the eighth and ninth centuries is being rewritten in terms of partnership and opposition rather than in the traditional terms of Carolingian dynastic policy.

If these families did not owe their prominence and power to the whim of the Carolin-

---

[6] Werner, "Bedeutende Adelsfamilien"; in addition to the studies of Werner and Brunner, among the most significant of these new studies of Matthias Werner, *Adelsfamilien im Umkreis der frühen Karolinger. Die Verwandtschaft Irminas von Oeren und Adelas von Pfalzel*. Vorträge und Forschungen, Sonderband 28 (Sigmaringen: 1982).

gians, then not only must the traditional history of Carolingian politics and administration be reexamined, but also the origins, composition, and activities of this aristocracy have to be considered anew from a social and cultural perspective. If the local aristocracy from which the autonomous dukes and counts of the tenth century emerged was not merely a nobility of service dependent on the Carolingians, then the question of its pre-Carolingian origins, its real power bases, and its relationship with other aristocratic groups must be reconsidered. Increasingly study is focusing on the Merovingian period, particularly on the crucial seventh and eighth centuries, and scholars are reexamining the diffusion of Frankish aristocratic kin groups prior to Carolingian rule.

This examination is being conducted not only at the level of the international aristocracy or within the traditional Frankish heartlands of Neustria, Austrasia, and Burgundy, but, increasingly, within the context of regional studies. The structural relationships between the aristocracy, the unfree and semi-free levels of society, and the church are being approached at the level of smaller, cohesive regions within the Frankish world. Among the pioneering studies of this sort are those of Karl Bosl for Franconia,[7] Wilhelm Störmer for Bavaria,[8] Franz Staab for the Rhineland,[9] Matthias Werner for the Ardennes,[10] and Michel Rouche for Aquitaine.[11] Although these regions vary greatly in their cultural, political, and economic traditions and structures, in each the power of aristocratic groups appears based on local ties as well as on wider contacts and alliances with or against the Carolingians.

Thus scholars are trying to reassess the sense of identity and group solidarity through the Carolingian period – to see the tenth century as a continuation of the seventh. The results point to a revised image of the emergence of territorial principalities which again emphasizes a continuity, not with some sort of "primeval Germanic" past, but with a dynamic, evolving sense of ethnicity and solidarity; a sense far removed both from the fantasies of past (and present) nationalist ideologues and from an exclusively territorial and political sense. Such a revision involves not only a reappraisal of the relationship between the Carolingians and their partners and enemies, but a reassessment of ethnic identity and of aristocratic kinship structures in the early Middle Ages.[12]

---

[7] Karl Bosl, *Franken um 800. Strukturanalyse einer fränkischen Königsprovinz* (Munich: 1969).

[8] Wilhelm Störmer, *Früher Adel: Studien zur politischen Führungsschicht im fränkisch-deutschen Reich vom 8. bis 11. Jahrhundert*, 2 vols. (Stuttgart: 1973).

[9] Franz Staab, *Untersuchungen zur Gesellschaft am Mittelrhein in der Karolingerzeit* (Wiesbaden: 1975).

[10] Matthias Werner, *Der Lütticher Raum in frühkarolingischer Zeit: Untersuchungen zur Geschichte einer karolingischen Stammlandschaft* (Göttingen: 1980).

[11] Michel Rouche, *L'Aquitaine des Wisigoths aux Arabes 418–781: Naissance d'une région* (Paris: 1979).

[12] Karl Brunner, *Oppositionelle Gruppen im Karolingerreich* (Vienna: 1979). See especially the conclusions, pp. 194–197.

Economy

Simultaneously with these changes in the political and social composition of the European aristocracy important transformations occurred in Europe's economy: the nature of landholding and the organization of estates seems to have been changing, as were the commercial relationships between the interior of Francia and the Mediterranean world.

The great Carolingian polyptychs provide a glimpse of estate organization and management once thought to have been a continuation of Roman agricultural traditions, if not of "millennial types of agrarian civilization."[13] In particular, the division of great estates into a reserve cultivated directly by unfree or semi-free labor and into the tenures of individual peasants, *mansus* (or *mansi*) in the texts of Northern Europe, were seen to be characteristics of European agricultural organization inherited from the late Roman Empire. Increasingly, however, the Carolingian polyptychs are being interpreted, not as evidence of continuity, but rather as documents prepared during a process of estate reform and restructuring. François Louis Ganshof, Adriaan Verhulst,[14] and others have argued that those very elements which typify the classic medieval manor are innovations resulting from a complex of cultural, political and geographical factors at work in the late Merovingian period. Verhulst asserts that "the classic domanial structure, or, at least, certain of its essential elements, originated during the course of the seventh and eighth centuries in certain regions of Northern France where certain human conditions (sufficiently dense establishment of royal domains, expansion of the arable) and certain geographical conditions (attractive soils, their composition and relief) favorable to their development were united to an extent reached at this time nowhere else."[15]

While Walter Goffart does not deny the importance of this period in the formation of classic manorial organization, he suggests that continuity with Roman taxation and managerial traditions should not be dismissed.[16] He points out that already in the mid-sixth century certain characteristics of the bipartite manor, particularly the mention of weekly labor services owed by holders of *colonicae* and the term *in domnico*, possibly referring to the landlord, appear in Northern Italy.[17] Moreover, discussing the relationship between

---

[13] Marc Bloch, *Les caractères originaux de l'histoire rurale française* 2nd ed. 2 vols. (Paris: 1960–61).

[14] François Louis Ganshof, "Quelques aspects principaux de la vie économique dans la monarchie franque au VIIe siècle. *Caratteri del secolo VII in occidente*. Settimane di studio del centro italiano di studi sull'alto medioevo V (Spoleto: 1958) pp. 73–101; Adriaan Verhulst, "La genèse du régime domanial classique en France au haut moyen âge," *Agricoltura e mondo rurale in occidente nell'alto medioevo*, Settimane di studio del centro italiano di studi sull'alto medioevo XIII (Spoleto: 1966) pp. 135–160.

[15] Verhulst, p. 159.

[16] Walter Goffart, "From Roman Taxation to Mediaeval Seigneurie: Three Notes", *Speculum* vol. 47 (1972) pp. 165–187; 373–394.

[17] *Ibid.*, p. 386.

the Roman tax unit, the *condoma*, which he defines as "human units of agrarian lease,"[18] and the *mansus*, he argues that the latter must be seen not as a term describing social conditions, "the timeless familial basis of rural life,"[19] but rather as referring to land which was the source of specific obligations to the lord. For him, the process described by Ganshof and Verhulst was a Merovingian adaptation of Roman fiscality. In particular this adaptation involved the continued use of Roman fiscal terminology and concepts employed by estate owners and their agents who looked upon themselves increasingly "as estate managers rather than collectors of treasure."[20]

Goffart further hints that Étienne Fornial may be correct to interpret this process as the result of the general constriction of the Frankish economy.[21] This constriction of long distance commerce has been throughout the century the major topic of discussion among historians of early medieval economy ever since Henri Pirenne first suggested that Muslim control of the Mediterranean destroyed the commercial vitality of Merovingian Francia and led directly to the stagnation of its economy, the weakening and collapse of the dynasty, and the creation of those economic, political and social structures which are characteristically medieval.[22]

Today few if any scholars accept the Pirenne Thesis in its entirety. Muslems did not object to carrying on commerce with non-Muslims; contact between the East and the West did not end in the latter half of the seventh century; the economy of western Europe never actually sank to the level of a natural economy; the types of imports on which Pirenne placed particular emphasis were peculiarly susceptible to manipulation for political purposes and their supply had more to do with short term diplomatic pressures than with long term hostilities between Arabs and Franks. Moreover, internal factors which had been part of the Western half of the Empire since its inception are increasingly recognized as more significantly linked to the changes in its trade than the presence of Muslim pirates on the Mediterranean. The lack of exports, the gold drain, the structure of western agriculture have all rightly been pointed out as contributing to the West's decreasing ability to hold its own in East-West trade.

And yet, as Peter Brown has pointed out, in spite of weaknesses of perspective and data, Pirenne's "historical testament" cannot be entirely dismissed. When all is said and done, even admitting that the trade between East and West, particularly in slaves, continued throughout the ninth century and allowing that perhaps the turn to a silver coinage may have been more a symptom of economic health than of illness, one cannot deny that very fundamental changes in the nature of the West's involvement in the Mediterranean world

---

[18] *Ibid.*, p. 185.

[19] *Ibid.*, p. 186.

[20] *Ibid.*, p. 392.

[21] *Ibid.*, p. 392, n. 208, citing Étienne Fournial, *Histoire monétaire de l'occident médiéval* (Paris: 1970) p. 5.

[22] The classic statement is his *Mahomet et Charlemagne* (Paris–Brussels: 1937).

did take place between 650 and 750. Whether one sees these changes as evidence of internal weakness or as important growth in new directions, one must recognize these decades as a time of important realignment not only in commerce and communications but in culture and society as well.[23]

In no area of Europe were these monumental changes felt more strongly than in the Rhône watershed. Well into the first decades of the eighth century the region from the Alps to the Rhône and south to the sea had maintained its traditional political and legal structures established during the late Empire. With its *patricii* and *rectores*, the representatives of the Frankish king whose officers continued Romano-Ostrogothic traditions; with its twin commercial and ecclesiastical "capitals" of Marseille and Arles; with its aristocracy which, in its naming patterns, preserved the onomastic traditions of the great Gallo-Roman families such as the Syagrii and Aegidii who had dominated the region since the fourth century; the valley in the beginning of the eighth century was a continuation of an earlier, Roman world.

The first decades of the century saw the end of all of these traditions. The last *patricius* disappeared no later than 751 and possibly even ten years earlier as did the last mention of a *rector*. In their place one finds rather counts reminiscent of the more northern parts of Francia. The ports of Marseille and Fos, which had long been the primary centers of Mediterranean commerce connecting the upper reaches of the Rhône and central Francia with Italy, Byzance, and the East, lost their importance for three centuries. In the words of Henri Pirenne, "By the ninth century Provence, once the richest country of Gaul, had become the poorest."[24] The urban continuity so strong in the region, as evidenced by the bishop lists of its dioceses reaching back into the earliest period of Gallic Christianization, was broken in most of its cities for at least fifty years. Finally, these decades saw the last appearances of the old and glorious Gallo-Roman names and hence, apparently, of the old perceived continuity in the aristocracy which had dominated the region for over four hundred years.

True, even in the Carolingian period Provence, with its Roman law, Romance language, and rich physical heritage of Roman roads, cities, buildings, aqueducts, and place names continued to preserve more of the old ways than perhaps any other region of

---

[23] The best collection of the most outstanding responses to the Pirenne thesis, including the classic articles on the subject by Robert Lopez and Maurice Lombard is that edited by Paul Egon Hübinger, *Bedeutung und Rolle des Islam beim Übergang vom Altertum zum Mittelalter* (Darmstadt: 1968). See also Alfons Dopsch, *Die Wirtschaftsentwicklung der Karolingerzeit vornehmlich in Deutschland* vol. 2 (3rd edition, Darmstadt: 1962), pp. 186–252. On the continuing significance of Henri Pirenne's reflections on the discontinuity of the eighth century, see Peter Brown, "*Mohammed and Charlemagne* by Henri Pirenne," *Society and the Holy in Late Antiquity* (Berkeley: 1982), pp. 63–79.

[24] Henri Pirenne, *Medieval Cities* (Garden City: s. d.), p. 20.

Europe north of the Alps. But in other ways, from the most humble aspects of daily life and material culture to the most elevated levels of culture and politics, important changes had taken place. One can conceive of the region, with its mighty river and important coast, as having two axes, one horizontal and Mediterranean oriented to the lands and peoples of the civilized world, the other vertical and terrestrial, oriented towards the Frankish barbarian kingdom. From the beginning of the eighth century the region was dominated by its fluvial axis, an orientation which would not change again until well into the eleventh century.

Thus the Rhône basin is an ideal area in which to observe the monumental changes of the seventh and eighth centuries. It experienced all of the politcal, social and economic turmoil of the age: revolution, occupation by Saracens, pacification by Charles Martel. When one speaks of the decline of Frankish trade with the East, one is speaking of the decline of its principal ports – Marseille and Fos. When one speaks of the disappearance or absorption of the old Gallo-Roman aristocracy one is speaking of its Syagrii and Aegidii. And yet the most important study of the region in the Merovingian period, that of Rudolf Buchner, omits this period altogether aside from an account of the various revolts and a brief discussion of the ports of Marseille and Fos in the early eighth century.[25] Buchner justifies this silence quite reasonably since "into the thirties of the eighth century we are informed by chance mentions in a couple of saints' *vitae*, by more or less uncertain conclusions based on coin finds and a few obscure allusions in charters, so that our overall image remains extremely defective."[26]

This image could have been improved had Buchner been able to accept as genuine one particular document which purports to have been written at the end of the 730s: the testament of Abbo. In 726 Abbo, who described himself as *rector* of Maurienne and of Susa, had founded the monastery of Novalesa on his family's property. His testament dates from thirteen years later in 739. In the document Abbo makes the monastery of St. Peter at Novalesa his heir and, aside from a few miscellaneous bequests to individuals and to the churches of St. Jean of Maurienne and the cathedral of Gap, he leaves all his property to his monastery. The dispositions of the testament are very detailed: in each bequest Abbo states from whom he had acquired the property and usually under what conditions it was being held. In addition, the text contains references to the revolt in Provence which had shortly before been crushed (738), alludes to Roman law as it still functioned in the region, and in numerous incidental details provides a view of the society, economy and governance of the lower Rhône valley from the time of Abbo's grandparents in the second half of the seventh century until 739. For its wealth of information on the economy, society and politics of the region during these decades, the testament might well be an unparalleled and priceless source.

---

[25] Rudolf Buchner, *Die Provence in merowingischer Zeit* (Stuttgart: 1933).
[26] *Ibid.*, p. 19.

That is, of course, if it is neither a formal nor a material forgery. Buchner thought that it was, and dismissed the document in a footnote: "On the use of Abbo's Testament, I renounce it entirely, since it is probably a pancarte of the holdings of Novalesa from a later period."[27] Although he made no effort to demonstrate that the document was a catalogue of later Novalesan properties, he based his statement on good authority: Engelbert Mühlbacher before him had rejected the testament along with the Carolingian confirmation within which it is preserved.[28] Apart from the falsification of the Carolingian document, the actual testament was rejected on two grounds. First, Mühlbacher understood the date of the document, *"anno vigesimo primo gubernante inlustrissimo nostro Karolo regna Francorum,"* as the twenty-first year of the rule of Charlemagne, hence 789, a clear impossibility. Second, he concluded that the holdings of Novalesa in the eighth century simply could not have been as extensive as the testament made out, so that it had to be a pancarte.

In fact, as we shall see, the testament is genuine – its authenticity, never doubted in France and in Italy, has recently been recognized in Germany as well. Once rehabilitated, it can then be used as a window into the early eighth century, the period when Charles Martel was effectively ruling the kingdoms *('regna')* of the Franks (the actual meaning of the datation formula given above). What this book proposes to do then is to look through this window and to describe the society, economy and government of the Rhône valley which can thus be perceived. Our description will attempt to recognize the characteristics of the region on the eve of the Carolingian conquest as well as to place the region in the broader context of Continental history at the end of the Merovingian period. In particular we shall try to examine such questions as landholding, lordship, kinship, ethnic and political allegiance, and the relationship between Provence and the rest of Francia. Our purpose is not to resolve the classic debate concerning the Pirenne thesis, nor to describe the role of ethnicity in early medieval Europe, nor to determine with absolute certainty the extent to which Charles Martel restructured and renewed the Frankish aristocracy. However, we shall touch on each of these issues and try to provide a clearer image of them in this particular region.

Although the testament of Abbo is not the only source for examining the Rhône valley during this period, it is the principal one. For this reason we shall proceed as follows: First, we shall work into the text itself – that is, we shall examine the reasons and the means by which it was transmitted, the problems of its formal and technical characteristics. The edition of the testament in Chapter Two is provided in order to correct previous errors of editors and to supply the reader with the text to which we shall constantly refer. The accompanying translation is intended both to present the editor's sense of the text and to

---

[27] *Ibid.*, p. 31 note 6.

[28] J. F. Böhmer, *Regesta imperii* I. *Die Regesten des Kaiserreichs unter den Karolingern 751–918* neu bearbeitet Engelbert Mühlbacher 2nd edition (Innsbruck: 1899) (hereafter BM[2]) 491 (467) DKar. 310.

make accessible to students one example of an early eighth-century private act. Beginning in Chapter Three, we shall interpret the text in ever-widening scope as we consider progressively the economy, society and governance of the region. For much of this examination, the testament will be our only direct witness for practices in the region; for other aspects it will be possible to supplement the testament with additional sources. Thus, while we never quite lose sight of the testament, our final goal is not simply an explication of this text, however significant, but an understanding of the men and women who inhabited the world in which it originated.

CHAPTER I
THE TESTAMENT AND ITS TRANSMISSION

The survival of Abbo's testament is not the result of chance but rather directly the result of a selection and preservation process which took place during the period of the Gregorian reform. Such processes explain the preservation of most fragments which remain from the vast archival collections that must have existed in the Early Middle Ages: documents deemed useful in the eleventh and twelfth centuries, whether for politcal, economic or liturgical purposes were recopied or preserved; others were ignored and allowed to disappear. Thus the period can be seen as a sort of filter, similar to that of the late Roman transition from papyrus to vellum, when texts not considered interesting enough to be recopied on the more durable material were lost not by conscious design but by lack of interest in their preservation. In the reform period, the preservation of administrative documents was directly related to attempts to reform and reconstitute the patrimony of cathedrals and monasteries, an essential material aspect of the Gregorian movement often ignored in favor of the more spectacular but often ephemeral aspects of spiritual reform. As reformers and their opponents attempted to demonstrate claims to ecclesiastical properties they necessarily became something of historians, searching out and collecting old charters which might demonstrate the justice of their cause. However, since they were by no means disinterested historians, they were often compelled to reconstruct documents no longer extant or to fabricate from whole cloth documents recording privileges granted orally if at all, or, more frequently, to amend whatever documents they did find to their own purposes.

Abbo's testament was preserved in just such circumstances, and the validity of using it to examine the eighth century cannot be assumed before examining how it alone, of what must have been hundreds of early medieval testaments from the Rhône valley, survived not only the first three centuries of its existence but the winnowing process of the reform as well.

Vienne and Grenoble

The testament survived because it was deemed valuable by Hugo of Châteauneuf d'Isère who became bishop of Grenoble in 1079.[1] Hugo was a young noble who had risen quickly in the Church because of his close adherence to the radical reformers of the late

---

[1] On Hugo there exists a nineteenth-century biography, Albert du Boys, *Vie de saint Hugues, évêque de Grenoble* (Grenoble: 1837) based largely on the *Vita S. Hugonis, AASS Aprilis I*, 37–46. Most recently see Bernard Bligny, *L'église et les ordres religieux dans le royaume de Bourgogne aux XIe et XIIe siècles* (Grenoble: 1960), esp. pp. 70–73 and *passim*.

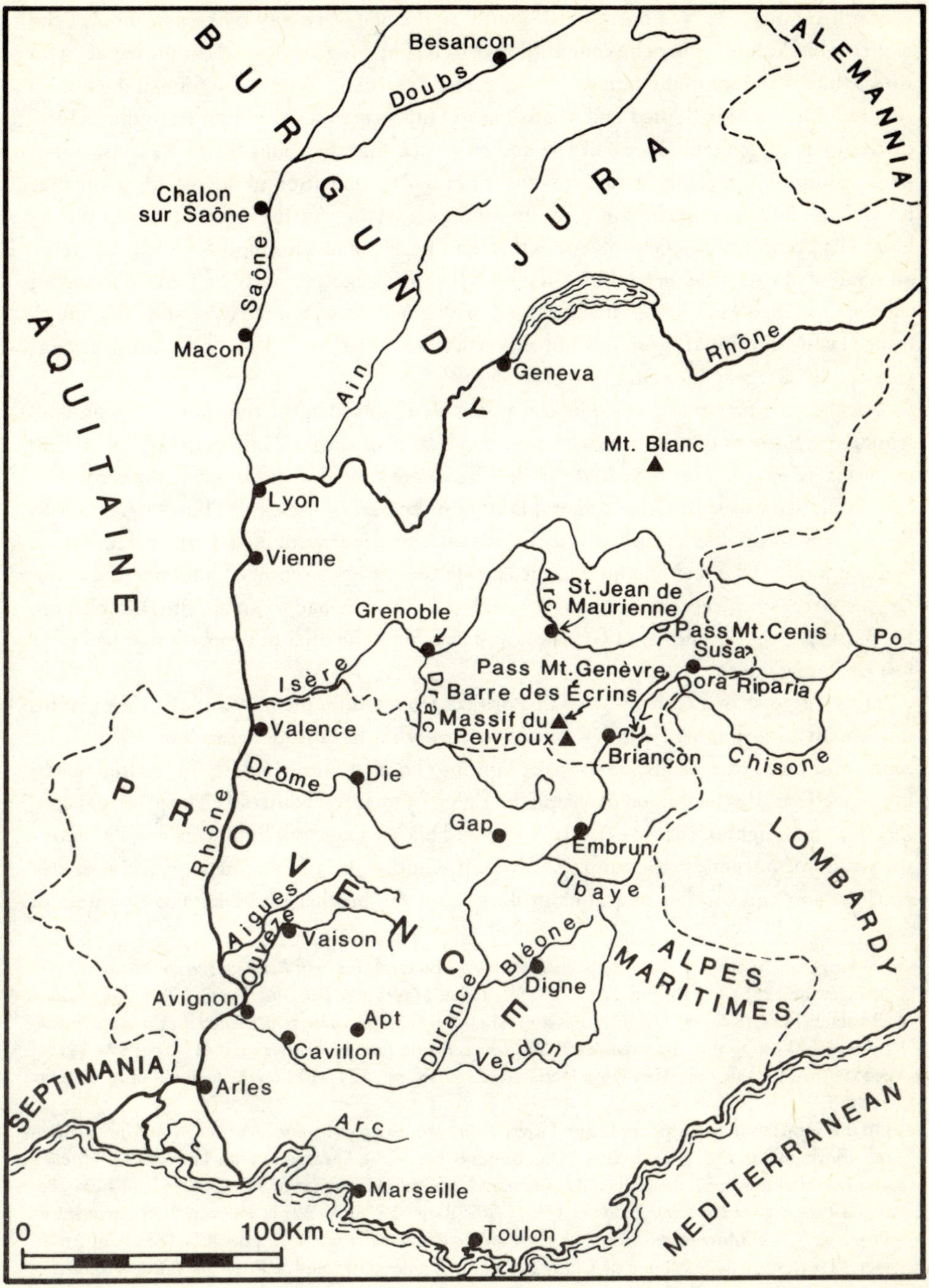
BURGUNDY
ALEMANNIA
JURA
AQUITAINE
PROVENCE
LOMBARDY
ALPES MARITIMES
SEPTIMANIA
MEDITERRANEAN
Besancon
Doubs
Chalon sur Saône
Saône
Macon
Ain
Geneva
Rhône
Mt. Blanc
Lyon
Vienne
Grenoble
Arc
St. Jean de Maurienne
Pass Mt. Cenis
Susa
Po
Pass Mt. Genèvre
Dora Riparia
Barre des Écrins
Massif du Pelvroux
Isère
Drac
Valence
Briançon
Chisone
Drôme
Die
Gap
Embrun
Ubaye
Rhône
Aigues
Ouvèze
Vaison
Bléone
Digne
Durance
Avignon
Apt
Cavillon
Verdon
Arles
Arc
Marseille
Toulon
0
100Km

eleventh century. He was born in 1053 and by the age of twenty-two was canon of the cathedral of Valence where he caught the eye of bishop Hugo of Die, apostolic legate, who took Hugo with him to the synod of Avignon held in 1080.[2] During the council the bishop of Grenoble, Pontius II, died and according to Hugo's *vita*, a delegation from the chapter of Grenoble came before Hugo of Die and requested that the young canon be consecrated their bishop. Whatever the actual reasons for Hugo's nomination to the see, it is clear that his election and subsequent consecration marked a victory for the reform party in the region. His predecessor in Grenoble, Pontius, had been a staunch supporter of the Emperor and had died excommunicated by Gregory VII. The Gregorian party had little support in the region: Hugo's metropolitan, Garmond of Vienne, was so tainted by simony that Hugo refused consecration at his hands but rather went instead directly to Rome and was consecrated by Gregory himself.[3]

For the next fifty-two years, Hugo was heavily involved in the reform movement, particularly in his own diocese which he found in a state of spiritual and material dissipation upon his accession. Not only had the diocese existed for decades in what the reformers could only view as spiritual and moral laxity on the part of the clergy, but owing both to the growth of aristocratic power in the region and the destructions perpetrated by the Saracen pirates who had operated in the Alps in the previous century,[4] he found the material resources of the episcopal fisc sadly depleted. Thus he had to go about reestablishing the patrimony of the church of Grenoble and clarifying the titles to property that had been lost or in dispute for years.

Hugo faced strong opposition to this project from within the laity and the clergy of his diocese. In addition, his efforts in the defense of what he considered to be the legitimate rights and properties of his see brought him into conflict with similarly motivated neighboring ecclesiastics bent upon asserting the rights of their own dioceses. The principal conflict with his neighbors arose between Hugo and his own metropolitan, Garmond's successor Guido of Burgundy, the future Calixtus II. Guido was an extremely powerful aristocrat, the son and brother of counts in Burgundy, the brother of Willelmia, Countess of

---

[2] On Hugo of Die see Robert L. Benson, *The Bishop-Elect: A Study in Medieval Ecclesiastical Office* (Princeton: 1968) p. 218 and 223–224; W. Lühe, *Hugo von Die und Lyon, Legat von Gallien* (Breslau: 1898); Bligny, *L'Église*, passim; Theodor Schieffer, *Die päpstlichen Legaten in Frankreich vom Vertrag von Meersen (870) bis zum Schisma von 1130* (Berlin: 1935), pp. 89–141.

[3] *AASS* April I, p. 39. Schieffer, *Die päpstlichen Legaten*, pp. 121–122 on the Council of Avignon in 1080.

[4] On the Saracens in the Alps see Bruno Luppi, *I saraceni in Provenza in Liguria e nelle Alpi occidentali* (Bordighera: 1952); O. Vehse, "Das Bündnis gegen die Sarazenen vom Jahre 915," *Quellen und Forschungen* aus italienischen Archiven und Bibliotheken 19 (1927) 181–204; Jean-Pierre Poly, *La Provence et la société féodale, 879–1166* (Paris: 1976) 3–29; E. Duprat, "Les Sarrasins en Provence," *Les Bouches-du-Rhône: Encyclopédie départementale* I, ii, pp. 147–163; Paul Amargier, "La capture de S. Maïeul de Cluny et l'expulsion des Sarrazins de Provence," *Revue Bénédictine* vol. 73 (1963) pp. 316–323.

Maurienne and mother of Queen Adelaïde, wife of Louis VI the Fat. While a supporter of the reform, Guido was not a member of the radical faction close to Gregory. He was, however, adamant in his efforts to reassert his rights over the patrimony of the Church of Vienne, and his efforts in this pursuit brought him into head-on conflict with Hugo over the rights to the archdeaconry of Sermorens, which lay on the border between the two dioceses.[5] As the archbishop and the bishop proceeded to reaffirm their authority over their respective dioceses and to clarify their rights over areas that had long remained contested, they could not ignore the region which formed the *pagus* of Sermorens, and their conflict developed into a protracted legal battle in which words were at times supported by arms, and which involved ultimately the bishops of neighboring dioceses, the apostolic legate Hugo of Die, and, finally, Popes Urban II and Pascal II.[6]

The origins of the dispute lay in the different means by which the opposing parties understood the history of their region and in particular the period of disruption caused in the tenth century by the establishment of Saracens in the mountain passes near Grenoble. This long Muslim presence was accompanied by periodic raids on religious institutions and destruction of property and records and was, from the perspective of Hugo, the major event in his diocese's history which accounted for the weakened temporal and spiritual state in which he had found it. In particular his policy was to reestablish his rights as they had been before the arrival of the Saracens, a difficult task since the archives of the diocese were largely dispersed or destroyed. The disputed status of Sermorens was a case in point. Both Hugo and Guido recognized that the archdeaconry was, at the end of the eleventh century, under the authority of the bishop of Grenoble. However Guido disputed the right of the bishop of Grenoble to the area.

According to Hugo's certainly partial account,[7] the resulting dispute went as follows. Guido summoned Hugo to Vienne to settle the disagreement, but the two were unable to resolve the issue. They therefore decided to meet at Romans and to have the dispute arbitrated by neighboring bishops; Pontius of Belley and Landricus of Mâcon represented Hugo and Gontardus of Valence and Guido of Geneva took the part of Guido. Hugo pre-

---

[5] See Jules Marion's introduction to the *Cartulaires de l'église cathédrale de Grenoble dits Cartulaires de Saint-Hugues* (Paris: 1869) pp. xxxiii–xxxix, and Alfons Becker and Dietrich Lohrmann, "Ein erschlichenes Privileg Papst Urbans II. für Erzbischof Guido von Vienne (Calixt II.)" *Deutsches Archiv* vol. 38 (1982) pp. 66–111. Michel Colardelle has summarized the archeological evidence on the importance of the region in the eleventh century in the catalogue of the exposition *Des Burgondes à Bayard: Mille ans de moyen âge recherches archéologiques et historiques* (Grenoble: 1981), p. 133.

[6] Marion, *Ibid.* summarizes the dispute in pp. xxxiii–xl. More recently see the two studies by Noël Didier, "Étude sur le patrimoine de l'église cathédrale de Grenoble, de la fin du Xe au milieu du XIIe siècle", *Annales de l'Université de Grenoble* vol. 13 (1936) pp. 5–87 and "Notes sur la fortune immobilière de l'église cathédrale de Grenoble du Xe à la fin du XIIe siècle." *Annales de l'Université de Grenoble* vol. 22 (1947), pp. 9–49; Bernard Bligny, *L'Église*, p. 72.

[7] Edited by Marion, pp. 49–57.

sented written and oral testimony[8] to demonstrate that Grenoble had held the disputed area for over a century. This Guido did not deny but asserted rather that his predecessor Barnuinus had granted it to Bishop Isarnus of Grenoble as a temporary measure to help his suffragan survive the losses incurred at the hands of the Saracens. However as proof Guido could offer no written evidence.[9] Seeing that they held an advantage the canons of Grenoble pushed the arbiters to announce a decision, but Guido, fearing that things would go against him, refused to hear it. Instead, gathering a group of *milites* whose assistance he had previously enlisted ostensibly to preserve the Peace of God, he invaded and occupied the territory in 1094.

Hugo immediately appealed to Pope Urban II who, as was normal in such cases, referred the case to his legat, Hugo's old friend and supporter Hugo of Die, Archbishop of Lyon. The legate convoked his court at Baon and provisionally returned Sermorens to Hugo while reserving a final judgment for the next synod to be held in France. Guido ignored the injunction and appealed to Rome for a standard confirmation of all the privileges of the Church of Vienne. However, at the cost of 500 *solidi* spread through the curia (of which Hugo claims to have heard from Guido himself[10]), Guido managed to have the name of the disputed archdeaconry secretly inserted into the document just before it was issued by Urban. Thus Guido was able to present to the apostolic legate nothing less than a papal confirmation of his rights to Sermorens with which he intended to oppose the claims of Grenoble.

As soon as Hugo learned of the deception he complained to the Pope concerning the ruse that had been perpetrated by Archbishop Guido. Urban then wrote to his legate Hugo to instruct him to settle the matter and to assure him that he had not purposely conceded anything to the archbishop of Vienne which he was not previously known justly to have possessed. He also wrote a letter to Hugo of Grenoble to make similar assurances.

At the next round in the affair, this time at the Council of Autun, Guido did not attempt to press the validity of his papal confirmation, but produced instead a "very old" charter which purported to record that Archbishop Barnuinus had granted Bishop Isarnus the Church of Saint Donatus and the Archdeaconry of Sermorens as a conditional benefice with the stipulation that it be returned after the Saracens had left the diocese of Grenoble.[11] Bishop Hugo, of course, after an examination of the document, objected on the grounds that it was a forgery and should be put aside. He based his argument on the asser-

---

[8] *Ibid.*, p. 49 "Ubi et scriptis et aliis testimoniis ostendimus ..."

[9] *Ibid.*, "... responsum est nullum exinde scriptum habere, sed solum uulgi rumorem sufficere."

[10] *Ibid.*, 50: "Pro cuius impetratione, sicut ipse nobis postea confessus est, quingentos solidos in Romana curia dispensauit."

[11] *Ibid.*, 52: "... cum insultatione scripturam quasi multa vetustate contritam protulit, quę continebat quod Barnuinus, Viennensis archiepiscopus, Isarno Gratianopolitano episcopo, ęcclesiam Sancti Donati et Salmoriacensem pagum concessisset, donec Gratianopolitanę ęcclesię pax a persecutione paganorum, qua tunc vastabuntur, redderetur."

tion that Barnuinus and Isarnus had lived almost a century apart. (Barnuinus was Archbishop ov Vienne from 885–898, Isarnus was bishop of Grenoble ca. 960.) Hugo had apparently been busy collecting charters in support of his position, because he further showed that Isarnus' predecessor, Bishop Alcherius, already possessed Sermorens and that the Church of Saint Donatus had been received, not from the Archbishop of Grenoble, but from kings Boso and Louis of Provence. At this point Guido fell back on his papal confirmation which apparently failed to impress the assembled bishops. Finally he agreed to convoke his cathedral canons and to allow Hugo to examine and to judge the claims of Grenoble against Vienne. Hugo accepted, but upon his arrival in Vienne for that purpose Guido refused to discuss the case.

When Urban II summoned a council at Piacenza in 1095, Hugo hoped to attend and to ask the pope and the assembled bishops to settle the dispute. He had traveled as far as Milan when he met his metropolitan, who urged him not to go on to the council but offered rather to submit to a final settlement before the papal legate. Hugo agreed and started for home expecting that the archbishop would join him at Lyon as agreed upon. Naturally, Guido failed to appear at the appointed time and Hugo, realizing that he had been tricked yet again, rushed back across the Alps and arrived at Piacenza the last day of the council. After he had presented his case before the pope and the assembled bishops, Urban again dissociated himself from the fraudulently obtained confirmation and wrote to Guido expressing his displeasure, informing the archbishop that by the decision of the council he had reinvested Hugo with Sermorens and ordering him to return the archdeaconry and to allow Hugo to hold it without interference. Guido ignored the decision. Again Hugo traveled to Italy and obtained from Urban release from obedience to his metropolitan for himself, his clergy, and the laity of the archdeaconry.

Shortly after these exchanges, Urban began his famous journey through southern France, during which he would preach the First Crusade.[12] He stopped at Valence to consecrate the new cathedral, and since both Guido and Hugo were in attendance, he took the opportunity to order their appearance in Romans a few days later for a final resolution of the conflict. Hugo arrived burdened with a collection of ancient charters demonstrating the justice of his claims *(antiquis cartarum testimoniis onustus)*.[13] Guido brought with him a more eloquent defense: armed retainers who occupied the fortifications of the town in order to intimidate the pope. From this position of military superiority Guido announced that if the pope should speak against him he would remain in the archbishop's custody. Effectively intimidated, Urban postponed his judgment and was allowed to go. Only later, on

---

[12] See A. Fliche, "Le voyage d'Urbain II en France," *Annales du Midi* 49 (1937) 42–69 and René Crozet "Le voyage d'Urbain II et ses négociations avec le clergé de France 1095–1096", *Revue historique* 179 (1937) 270–310, and Alfons Becker, *Papst Urban II*, Vol. I: *Herkunft und kirchliche Laufbahn. Der Papst und die lateinische Christenheit*, Schriften der *Monumenta Germaniae Historica* vol. 19, I (Munich: 1964).

[13] Marion, p. 55.

25 November, 1095, when he was safely in Auvergne, did the Pope reconfirm the rights of Hugo, release him from obedience to his metropolitan, and invite the Count Guigo III of Albon to use his influence on the archbishop in order to bring about a renunciation and re- turn of the archdeaconry.[14]

This introduction of a secular power had its effect, but only temporarily. Hugo received the archdeaconry. However, about a year later, Hugo fell ill while on another trip to Italy. Guido took advantage of his rival's absence again to seize the archdeaconry and the pro- cess of appeals to the pope, appointment of adjudicators, and judgments continued another ten years. Finally in 1107 Pope Pascal II settled the dispute by compromise: each prelate received an equal portion of the disputed property and both were warned that if either disturbed the other he would lose his half to his opponent.[15]

Throughout this protracted dispute Hugo was at a considerable disadvantage. Not only was he disputing the word of his metropolitan, and a powerful one at that, but because of the turbulence of the previous two centuries in the region written evidence which he needed to refute the claims of the archbishop and to demonstrate the justice of his own cause was lacking. In order to overcome this handicap, Hugo had early set about to re- search the history of his see, to collect the names and episcopal years of his predecessors, and to assemble ancient documents that might prove his right to Sermorens and to other disputed properties. Considerable fragments of this collection are preserved in Ms Lat. 13879 of the Bibliothèque nationale, the so-called "Cartulary A of Saint Hugo."

The Cartulary

The manuscript, which dates from the first years of the twelfth century, contains acts and documents relating to the dispute between the bishop and his metropolitan written at probably three separate times and later bound together as one.[16]

Quires 2–9 were probably written first and may have formed part of the documenta- tion which Hugo prepared to press his case before Pascal II since the documents include his evidence, his account of the preceeding stages of the dispute, bishop-lists of Grenoble and Vienne, and the bulls of Urban II. Folia 10^v–36^r contain some sixteen charters gathered in Lyon, the diocese of Grenoble, and elsewhere which were written prior to the dispute and

---

[14] Urban's bull was included in Hugo's account, p. 57.

[15] ed. Marion, pp. 1–3.

[16] I am indebted to Professor Erika Laquer for her assistance in preparing the description of the man- uscript. It contains 90 folia quires as follows: q^1 fol. 0–9; q^2 fol. 10–19; q^3 fol. 20–27; q^4 fol. 28–37; q^5 fol. 38–47; q^6 fol. 48–57; q^7 fol. 58–67; q^8 fol. 68–79; q^9 fol. 80–89. The manu- script is written in folia of 21 lines to the page until folio 75^v. From fol. 75^v to the end each page contains 22 lines. The documents contained in q$^{2-9}$ are rubricated. Over-all dimensions of the manuscript are aproximately 25 cm × 17 cm.

which Bishop Hugo undoubtedly hoped would show the strength of his contention that Sermorens was under the jurisdiction of Grenoble. In fact, only four of these documents date from the period prior to the Saracen arrival in the region, and their evidence is somewhat vague on the rights of Grenoble in the disputed region. Sermorens had been a *pagus* separate from that of Grenoble and Vienne in the ninth and tenth centuries, and the charters Hugo had been able to collect which mentioned it did little to strengthen his general case: a diploma of Charles III the Fat dated 885 confirms property of St. Stephen's of Lyon in the *pagus*, but indicates nothing of Grenoble's rights in the area; a private donation of 830 mentions three locations – Bossieu, Rosière and Arsilio – as being in the *pagus* of Grenoble, but grants them likewise to the Church of Lyon. Two charters of the early tenth century recorded donations at Thodure in the *pagus* of Grenoble to the Cathedral, but were useful primarily for establishing the years of the Bishops Isarnus and Isaac. The remaining charters are all later and hence could not in themselves contradict Guido's assertion that the disputed property had been granted to Grenoble on a temporary basis by his predecessor in the tenth century. All of these documents were copied seriatim, each preceded by a rubricated explanation of its significance for the case. Folia 36^v–37^v, which end the fourth quire are blank, indicating that these three quires probably formed a single pamphlet in the bishop's dossier.

Quires five and six contain one document, the testament of Abbo, to which we shall return shortly. The text runs from fol. 38^r–57^r. Fol. 57^v is blank, again suggesting that these two quires once formed a separate entity.

Quire seven contains Hugo's account of the first part of his dispute with Guido and the bulls of Urban II. This account is incomplete in its present condition, since it was apparently followed by a quire now lost: Folio 67^v indicates that the first word of the next quire should have been "adiuraui", while in fact quire eight begins with a new document, a record of a judicial assembly held in 912 before Louis III the Blind.[17] This quire contains, in addition, more charters supporting Hugo's case as well as a comparative bishop's list establishing the relative chronology of bishops of Grenoble and archbishops of Vienne, the purpose obviously being to demonstrate that the document produced by Archbishop Guido was a forgery since Bishop Isarnus and Archbishop Barnuinus were not contemporaries. Much of this comparison was made possible through the consultation of the Archiepiscopal archives of Lyon, to which Hugo no doubt had ready access thanks to his friend and patron Hugo of Die.[18]

Folio 74^v contains only three lines and folio 75^r is blank. Folio 75^v to the end of the manuscript contains more documents supporting Grenoble's claims and concerning the

---

[17] *Ibid.*, pp. 58–59, ed. René Poupardin, *Recueil des actes des rois de Provence (855–928)* (Paris: 1920) no. 52 pp. 96–97.

[18] For example: "Ebbo, Gratianopolitanus episcopus [855–870] fuit contemporaneus Agilmari archiepiscopi, sicut in catalogo libro Lugdunensis ecclesię repperit tempore Karoli filii Lotarii imperatoris," Marion, p. 63.

Church of St. Donatus which Hugo also claimed and which he was eventually granted as part of the compromise settlement, even though it was clearly within the Archdiocese of Vienne. The similarity of the hands suggests that these folia were apparently copied as one, although the fact that these last folia contain 22 lines each would suggest that they were done at a slightly later date than the preceding sections.

The first quire, clearly attached to the others when they were bound sometime in the twelfth century, contain the judgment of Pascal II and related documents. These folia are not rubricated and were not attached until after the entire proceedings were united.

From this brief examination of the manuscript, one can suggest that folia $38^r–57^r$, that is, quires five and six, which contain Abbo's testament, originally formed a self-contained pamphlet which had been included in Hugo's documentation because he hoped that it could be used to argue that the castle of Vinay and the vill of Quincieux belonged both to the pagus of Sermorens and to the diocese of Grenoble. The rubric heading on fol. 38^r reads: *"Hęc carta que est de monasterio noualisię dicit quod castrum de uinnaco et uilla quintiacum que est in mandamento sancti georgii, in pago salmoriacensi et in episcopatu gratianopolitano sunt."* In fact, once more the evidence in support of Hugo offered in the document is weak (and, as we shall see, suspect). The testament mentions the locations of Vinay and Quincieux in the pagus of Grenoble, but it neither identifies them as depending on the Cathedral of St. George, nor does it mention the pagus of Sermorens.

Just how Hugo came into possession of this testament is easy to imagine. The most direct route between Grenoble and Milan, to which he frequently traveled as in 1094 to meet Urban II at Piacenza, took him to Briançon and then over the pass at Susa and on down the valley of the Dora Riparia.[19] He must then have passed nearby Novalesa itself which had been reoccupied for almost a century and he would have been acquainted, too, with the members of that community living in Breme. Thus he would have had the opportunity to search in their archives as well any references to the status of his diocese prior to the Saracen raids.

However, while we can understand how Hugo came to know the document and why he preserved it, we cannot conclude that the document was genuine. In fact, the form in which it is found in the cartulary is clearly at least a formal if not a material forgery: it is contained in a forged diploma of Charles the Great.

Did Hugo or his chancery forge the document? One cannot *a priori* dismiss the possibility: at least one other charter in his dossier is clearly interpolated, the charter of Louis the

---

[19] On Roman and medieval routes through the region see E. Baratier, *Atlas historique de Provence*, and Gisella Wataghin Cantino, "Il valico del Moncenisio in età romana: dati archeologici e ipotesi di lavoro," *Le reseau routier en Savoie et en Piemont: Aspects historique et contemporain, Bulletin du Centre d'études franco-italien* vol. 8 (1981), pp. 27–33. This route was also used by those traveling to other points further north and west: Hugo of Die died at Susa on his return to Lyon following the council of Guastalla in 1107. Lühe, *Hugo von Die*, pp. 118–119; Uta-Renate Blumenthal, *The Early Councils of Pope Paschal II 1100–1110* (Toronto: 1978) p. 39.

Blind found on folio 75[r].[20] Moreover, Hugo was clearly not above remembering and preserving a memory of the past in such a way as to strengthen the position of the bishop vis à
vis other powers even if this meant forging documents, as is clear in his dealings with the
Count of Albon. Here, he invented a mythical past for the region in which comital power
had its origin in an episcopal concession – certainly a fiction.[21] Finally, one must consider
the possibility that, if not forged in its entirety, Hugo interpolated the document to better
suit his own purposes. All of these possibilities must be considered in turn.

The Carolingian Forgery

The Carolingian diploma explains that two monks, Gislarannus and Agabertus, had
been sent by Abbot Frodoinus of Novalesa to request that Charles renew the testament of
Abbo. The original, according to the text, had been carried throughout the region for use
at various court proceedings so often that it was in a very poor state. Since the monks did
not dare to renew the document themselves, they had decided to ask Charles to do it for
them. After much thought, he decided to comply and ordered his notaries to renew it. He
did this, he says, not "from the customs of previous kings, but only out of necessity," and
ordered that it be sealed with a lead bull.

Although the authenticity of this diploma has never been seriously questioned by
French scholars working on the history of Novalesa and the *Testamentum*, it has been recognized as a forgery for over a century in German and Italian scholarship.[22] The reasons
for this judgment are several and conclusive.

---

[20] René Poupardin, *Recueil*, no. 30 pp. 55–57 points out that the elements of the forgery, which was
based on genuine material, probably date from the late eleventh century. This would suggest that
Hugo or someone close to him had prepared it in order to argue for the independence of the Bishop
of Grenoble *vis à vis* the Archbishop of Vienne.

[21] ed. Marion, pp. 93–96. As Robert Latouche points out in *Les origines de l'économie occidentale*
(Paris: 1970) p. 272, nothing in this historical prologue can be believed.

[22] BM² 491 (124) In the nineteenth century the document was used by local historians debating
whether or not Abbo was *patricius* of Provence without consideration of whether or not the confirmation was genuine: J.-H. Roman, *Abbon et Valchin. Étude sur un point controversé de l'histoire du VIIIe siècle* (Paris: 1885); *Ibid.*, *Legs faits par Abbon dans son testament dans les pagi de
Briançon, Embrun, Chorges et Gap* (Grenoble: 1901). In this century Maurice Chaume in his *Les
origines du duché de Bourgogne* 2 vols. (Dijon: 1925–32), vol. I, p. 35; Paul Amargier, in "La
Provence au miroir des monumenta de la Novalaise," *Provence historique* vol. 27 (1977)
pp. 251–256; and Jean-Pierre Poly in *La Provence et la société féodale* have never questioned the
authenticity of the Carolingian diploma. On the other hand, G. Tabacco, in his "Dalla Novalesa a
S.-Michele della Chiusa," *Monasteri in Alta Italia dopo le invasioni saracene e magiare (sec.
X–XII)*, XXXIIo Congresso storico subalpino, Deputazione Subalpina di Storia Patria (Turin:
1966) pp. 481–526 was aware of the German opinion and corrected it. However neither the
French nor German scholars seem to have noted Tabacco's work on the question. All references to
the *Testamentum* will be to paragraph numbers of the edition and translation found in Chapter II.

First, while royal and imperial diplomas do often repeat more or less verbatim portions of other royal diplomas and occasionally even extensive sections of private charters, the integral repetition of an earlier private charter was unknown in the royal chancery.[23] Second, the *intitulatio* "*Karolus imperator augustus piissimus a Deo coronatus magnus pacificus imperator Romanum gubernans imperium, qui et per misericordiam Dei rex Francorum et Langobardorum,*" is inauthentic, but only in one detail. The authentic *intitulatio* used by Charles between May 29, 801, and his last diploma of May 9, 813, begins "*Karolus serenissimus augustus a Deo coronatus ...*" The words of the Novalesa diploma, "*imperator augustus piisimus*" recal the text of the imperial acclamation as recorded in the *Liber pontificalis,* "*Karolo piissimo augusto ...*" Since the *Liber pontificalis* was known in Novalesa and was one of the sources for the author of the *Chronicon Novaliciense* in the eleventh century (the period when, as we shall see, the forgery was made), it is possible that the use of *piisimus* in place of *serenissimus* may reflect its influence. Alternative sources for the terminology could be the *signum* line of a genuine diploma or private diplomatic usage of an unofficial imperial title in datation formulae.[24]

The *publicatio* (*Igitur notum sit omnium fidelium nostrorum magnitudinum presentium scilicet et futurorum*) follows authentic Carolingian usage. However, such a *publicatio* should follow an *arenga*, without which *igitur* is meaningless. Such an arenga is entirely missing, as are parts of the *narratio* and *dispositio*. The entire eschatol is lacking.[25]

Aside from the verbatim repetition of the testament, the most glaringly anachronistic element of the diploma is the *corroboratio* formula, "*subter plumbum sigillari iussimus*". While metal *bulla* were not entirely unknown in early Carolingian diplomas, the use of lead for such *bulla* is not recorded. The only surviving references are to gold *bulla* in the diplomas of Louis the Pious and Lothair. Only one diploma of Charles mentions a *bulla* (DKar. 211), and this is transmitted only by a late thirteenth-century copy in which the word *bulla* may have been inserted by error for *anulus*. In any case the formula, "*more*

---

[23] Theodor von Sickel, *Acta regum et imperatorum Karolinorum digesta et enarrata. Die Urkunden der Karolinger, gesammelt und bearbeitet* 2 vols. (Vienna: 1867) I *Lehre von den Urkunden der ersten Karolinger (751–840)* p. 129, 200. An example of the extensive repetition of a private charter in a diploma of Charles is *DKar.* 169, the confirmation of donations made to Kremsmünster by Tassilo III. The list of properties being confirmed is taken from the foundation charter of Tassilo, but the charter itself is not integrally copied into the confirmation.

[24] On the imperial title see most recently Herwig Wolfram, *Intitulatio* II: *Lateinische Herrscher- und Fürstentitel im neunten und zehnten Jahrhundert* (Wien–Köln–Graz: 1973), pp. 19–58. On *piissimus* and *serenissimus* see pp. 32–37. On the possible use of the *Liber Pontificalis* by the author of the *Chronicon* see Carlo Cipolla, ed., *Monumenta Novaliciensia vetustiora*, vol. 2 (Rome, 1980), p. 108, n. 3. For the evaluation of the Carolingian forgery the author has profited from the suggestions of Mr. Harald Krahwinkler.

[25] *BM*² 491 (167). See also Harry Bresslau, *Handbuch der Urkundenlehre für Deutschland und Italien* vol. 2 (Berlin: 1958), p. 302 note 2.

nostro eam subscribere et de bulla nostra iussimus sigillare" of the genuine diploma does not resemble that of the Novalesa forgery: *"et subter plumbum sigillari iussimus."*[26]

On the other hand, while clearly irregular, the document is not extremely wide of the mark and was certainly prepared using genuine diplomata of Charles the Great. This is evident from the near conformity of the diplomatic elements discussed above. Moreover, whoever prepared the document was not so far removed from chancery traditions that he did not realize how unusual such a confirmation would appear. Hence he had Charles make the apology that the integral repetition was not *"ex consuetudine anteriorum regum … sed solummodo propter necessitatem".*[27]

The combination of these authentic and spurious elements allows an accurate estimation of the date at which the forgery took place. First, Hugo of Châteauneuf d'Isère can be absolved of complicity in at least this part of the forgery. The *Chronicon novaliciense* written around the middle of the eleventh century provides a summary of the charter which makes it clear that it was known before it reached Grenoble:

> At that time blessed Frodoinus, wishing that the testament of this church be renewed which the late Abbo patricius of this church had made in the time of Theodoric king of the Goths, sent two monks, Agabertus and Gislaramnus to the Emperor Charles the Great that he might concede that the testament be renewed by his own imperial order. He, graciously agreeing, had ordered all which he had asked.[28]

The mention of a lead seal provides another terminus. Such corroboration *formula* first appears in imperial diplomas with those of Otto III at the end of the tenth century. The first extant is a diploma issued at Pavia on October 1, 998 on behalf of Bobbio and reads *sigilo plombeo sigilari precepimus.*[29] Other variations in Otto's diplomas include *plumbeo sygillo in calce iussimus insigniri,*[30] *sigilli nostri plumbea inpressione iussimus insigniri,*[31] and *sigilloque nostro plumbeo sigillari precepimus.*[32] Since the *Chronicon* was written around the middle of the eleventh century, the appearance of this particular formula in the forgery must date from the first half of the eleventh century.

---

[26] Sickel, I, pp. 199–200. Bresslau, II, p. 564, n. 4 and his more complete examination of metal seals in "Zur Lehre von den Siegeln der Karolinger und Ottonen," *Archiv für Urkundenforschung* I (1908), pp. 255–370. On DKar. 211 see p. 257, note 1.

[27] Bresslau, *Ibid.*

[28] Cipolla, vol. 2, Lib. III, c. xvii, p. 186: "Eo tempore beatus Frodoinus volens testamentum ipsius aecclesie renovari, quod quondam Abbo patricius de ipsa ęcclesia fecerat, tempore Theoderici Gothorum regis, misit duos monachos, Agabertum scilicet et Gislaramnum ad Karolum magnum imperatorem, ut sibi suo imperiali precepto testamentum ipsud renovari concęderet, qui benigne illi annuens, cuncta quae illi pętiit, impetrare valuit."

[29] DO III, 303.

[30] DO III, 304.

[31] DO III, 306.

[32] DO III, 311.

Such a date for the composition of the forgery is entirely consistent both with the internal history of Novalesa around the year one thousand and with the development of interest in the use of private charters to defend legal claims in the region at that time. In the early tenth century Novalesa had been abandoned by its monks who feared for their safety after the arrival of Saracen pirates in the area.[33] The community was dispersed, but many of its members found their way to Turin and later to Breme where in the eleventh century the monks were still to be found. After the expulsion of the Saracens, the monastery had been returned to the community, but it was never again the wealthy and powerful community it had been before its abandonment. In spite of repeated efforts, it was never able to reestablish control over its previous possessions in the Rhône watershed. The rupture in the continuity of its lordship and the development of new power bases in the local aristocracy both reduced the ability of the monastery to regain its former position, and the lack of a powerful royal or imperial power in the area, the traditional source of Novalesa's protection, left it relatively powerless. Thus, around the beginning of the eleventh century the monastery faced the same problem that Hugo would face in Grenoble at the end of the century: how to demonstrate and to reassert its ancient rights after almost a century of confusion and chaos.

The original source of the monastery's material wealth had been the extensive inheritance it had received from its founder, Abbo, in 739. The Carolingian dynasty, which looked to Novalesa as an important royal monastery securing the pass into Italy, had confirmed these properties in the eighth and ninth centuries.[34] Carolingian confirmations had not of course enumerated all the estates to which the monastery held title. However, as long as lordship was an ongoing state of affairs, such a detailed enumeration was unnecessary. The testament, which recorded these original bequests, still existed in the eleventh century, as did the foundation charter of 729, both removed from Novalesa before its de-

---

[33] See Tabacco, pp. 495–501. *Chronicon Nov.* IV, 17. Professor Gisella Wataghin Cantino, who is currently excavating the monastery of Novalesa, has informed the author that no evidence of destruction has been found. The poor conditions in which the monastery was found when the monks returned can better be explained by the effects of the particularly harsh winter weather in the region on any structure so long abandoned. On the excavations at Novalesa see the following reports published by Professor Wataghin Cantino: "Prima campagna di scavo nella chiesa dei SS. Pietro e Andrea dell' abbazia di Novalesa. Rapporto preliminare," *Archeologia medievale* vol. 6 (1979), pp. 289–317; "Seconda campagna di scavo nello chiesa dei SS. Pietro e Andrea dell'abbazia della Novalesa. Rapporto preliminare: Le fasi preromaniche," *Atti del V Congresso nazionale di archeologia cristiana. Torino, Valle di Susa, Cuneo, Asti, Valle d'Aosta, Novara, 22–29 settembre 1979* (Rome: 1981), pp. 1–10; the third report is in press.

[34] In particular, the genuine diplomas of Karlmann *BM²* 127 (124) and Charles the Great *BM²* 222 (216). The diploma of Karlmann also mentions a previous diploma of Pippin I, *BM²* Verlorene Urkunden 381. Two other diplomas of Charles must have also existed for Novalesa: *BM²* Verlorene Urkunden 382, 384.

struction. However, a private testament of the eighth century had no legal value in the eleventh. The monks were thus compelled to contaminate a genuine Carolingian diploma with the testament in order to establish a juridically valid claim to their former possessions.[35]

This need to obtain confirmation of ancient private charters was by no means unique to Novalesa. Goswin Spreckelmeyer has quite rightly compared the situation at Novalesa with that of the Church of Arles at the end of the tenth century.[36] In 992 Arles obtained from Count William the Liberator the confirmation of the testament of Caesarius of Arles within the count's own will.[37] Here the circumstances were not unlike those at Novalesa: William had not only ended Saracen control of the eastern parts of Provence and had thus restored order, but he had also begun a new family of counts in Provence.[38] Thus, in a doubly altered situation of restoration and reform the bishop and chapter were eager to secure confirmation of their older rights. Since William enjoyed real autonomy in Provence from the nominal king of Burgundy-Arles according to whose regnal years he dated his charters, a verbatim confirmation of the sixth century bishop's testament by him was considered the surest protection of the Church as it reestablished its rights to lordship. In Italy, the monks of Novalesa apparently thought along similar lines, but in that instance an imperial confirmation by Charles the Great, who had been a strong supporter of Novalesa, and was seen by Otto III as his great predecessor, was probably thought to have similar weight in obtaining from the new dynasty its support.

The Carolingian charter is then a formal forgery of the early eleventh century based on a genuine Carolingian diploma and was produced in order to reestablish Novalesa's rights, the enjoyment of which had been interrupted in the previous century. But what of the testament itself?

The authenticity of the testament has been questioned because of its transmission within the forged Carolingian diploma, because of its manner of dating, and because of its content. As we have seen above, the fact that the Carolingian diploma was an eleventh-century forgery in no way affects the possible value of the testament itself. Mühlbacher, however, dismissed it on two further grounds. First, he found the dating, *Anno uigesimo primo gubernante inlustrissimo nostro Karolo regna Francorum in inditione VIIa*, impossible. Second, he considered the vast amount of property indicated in the testament too extensive for the early eighth century and concluded that the document was rather a later

---

[35] Goswin Spreckelmeyer, "Zur rechtlichen Funktion frühmittelalterlicher Testamente," *Recht und Schrift im Mittelalter*. Vorträge und Forschungen XXIII ed. Peter Classen (Sigmaringen: 1977) p. 108.

[36] *Ibid.*, 108.

[37] D. G. Morin, "Le testament de S. Césaire d'Arles et la critique de M. Bruno Krusch," *Révue Bénédictine* 16 (1899) 97–100.

[38] Poly, *La Provence*, pp. 1–57.

pancarte.[39] Both of these criticisms are entirely unfounded but have unfortunately continued to be repeated and expanded upon in Germany and in Italy.

Mühlbacher's objections to the dating of the testament are simply based on a fundamental, erroneous assumption. He presumed that the *Karolus* was Charles the Great and thus understood the date to be the seventh year of his reign, 789 – a clear impossibility.[40] Without any doubt the *Karolus* is Charles Martel, who appears later in the testament along with the Merovingian Theudoric IV.[41]

Mühlbacher's error is hence incomprehensible. That the testament, written during the *interregnum* following the death of Theudoric, rather than being dated *post mortem*, is dated according to the mayor of the palace is, as Ulrich Nonn has pointed out, unusual, but not by any means inadmissable.[42] The decision to date the testament from 717/18, when Charles had definitively triumphed over his Neustrian enemies, indicates rather the close political ties between Abbo and Charles and the significance of the Neustrian power struggle for Provence, topics which will be discussed below in Chapter V.

In addition to the hasty assumptions of Mühlbacher, the authenticity of the testament has been denied by Luciano Gulli on the basis of a series of fantastic and superficial arguments aimed primarily at demonstrating that the foundation charter of Novalesa is a forgery. In 1959 Gulli attempted to demonstrate that the foundation charter, the testament, and all of the Carolingian diplomas for Novalesa were forgeries, even though the foundation charter of 726 and the diploma of Carlmann from 769 both are to be found in the original in the Archivio di Stato in Turin.[43] Gulli's errors, which he repeated in his article "Abbone" in the *Dizionario biographico degli Italiano*,[44] kindly attributed by Giovanni Tabacco to his "inesperienza,"[45] included: a superficial and impossible criticism of the regnal years of Theoduric IV; a misunderstanding of the office of *patricius* in the Merovingian period; an ignorance of the fact that in the eighth century the Susa valley belonged to the Frankish kingdom; an inadequate knowledge of Merovingian *formulae* and

---

[39] *BM²* 491 (167).

[40] *DKar* 310.

[41] *DKar* 310. Giovanni Tabacco, in his excellent discussion of the series of misunderstandings and errors that has surrounded the interpretation of both the foundation charter of Novalesa and the testament, suggests charitably that the date given by Mühlbacher was a typographical error ("Dalla Novalesa," p. 485 note 13). However, since 789 was the twenty-first year of Charles the Great's reign, it would appear that Mühlbacher, and not the typesetter, was responsible for the error.

[42] Ulrich Nonn, "Merowingische Testamente. Studien zum Fortleben einer römischen Urkundenform im Frankenreich", *Archiv für Diplomatik* vol. 18 (1972), pp. 1–129, here pp. 34–35. Nonn is to be credited with having finally brought the authenticity of the testament to the attention of German scholars.

[43] "A proposito della più antica tradizione novalicense," *Archivio storico italiano* vol. 117 (1959), pp. 306–318.

[44] (Rome: 1960), pp. 42–43.

[45] "Dalla Novalesa", p. 482 n. 5.

terminology; a confusion over the identities and dates of the bishops appearing in the foundation charter; an uncritical and vaguely founded rejection of the testament and the Carolingian diplomas; and an imperfect understanding of the literature on Carolingian diplomatics. The fundamental weaknesses of Gulli's attempt at scholarship were pointed out the following year by F. Cognasso,[46] but the damage was already done: Heinz Löwe accepted Gulli's condemnation of the testament along with the foundation charter in his 1963 revision of Wattenbach-Levison.[47]

Mühlbacher was not, however, bothered only by the dating of the testament. He dismissed it as "in reality a pancarte of the holdings of the monastery, which at that time could not have been so wide-reaching."[48] This second judgement is likewise without foundation. That the content of the testament is indeed genuine can be shown through an internal criticism of the text. If it were a pancarte or collection of properties claimed by Novalesa collected to resemble a testament, then the forgery would be the work of a brilliant and learned jurist whose intimate knowledge of late Roman testamentary form as well as of the economic, social and political situation of Provence in the early eighth century is nothing less than astounding. That such a person was at work in the early eleventh century is simply impossible.

The Testament

The most obvious criteria of authenticity are the extensive and accurate use of legal forms and terminology in the testament. Legal historians have long recognized the importance of the document in this regard.[49] In order to consider properly the legal elements and language of the text, however, it is essential to distinguish between those elements which would have come from the testamentary *formula* used by Abbo, or rather his clerk Hytbertus, to prepare the testament, and those elements which indicate a living use of Roman law.

As Ulrich Nonn has shown in great detail, the text is closely in accordance with late Roman testamentary form.[50] In fact, this latest Merovingian will is the one which remains

---

[46] F. Cognasso, "Attorno alla fondazione della Novalesa", *Bollettino storico bibliografico subalpino* vol. 58 (1960), pp. 362–64.

[47] p. 410.

[48] *DKar.* 310 p. 467.

[49] See most recently J. Gaudement, "Survivances romaines dans le droit de la monarchie franque du Vème au Xème siècle," *Revue d'histoire du droit* vol. 23 (1955) pp. 149–206, and Paolo Frezza, "Giurisprudenza e prassi notarile nelle carte italiane dell'alto medioevo e negli scritti di giuristi romani," *Studia et documenta historiae et iuris* vol. 42 (1976) pp. 197–245; *Ibid., L'influsso del diritto romano giustinianeo nelle formule e nelle prassi in Italia*, Ius romanum medii aevi pars I, 2, c ee (Milan: 1974).

[50] Nonn, "Merowingische Testamente," especially pp. 59–108.

closest to Roman legal traditions. The *formulae* employed in the testament are perfectly regular for Merovingian testaments: the *invocatio* is the same which appears in the testaments of Remigius, Aridius, Adalgisel and Irmina.[51] The initial dating follows the schema *"sub die NN anno NN"* as in the testaments of Aridius, Bertram, Adalgisel and Hadoindus.[52] Abbo's inclusion of the indiction, while unusual in a private charter before the mid ninth century, is not unknown in inscriptions from the region of Lyon in the Merovingian period.[53] The *intitulatio* is in conformity with the majority of the other Merovingian testaments,[54] as is the *formula "sana mente"*[55] and the "internal reason" *formula, "cogitans casus humani fragilitatis,"* which appears in slightly different versions in the testaments of Bertram, Hadoindus, Widerad, in the *formulae Marculfi* and elsewhere.[56] The testamentary declaration is common to all documents Nonn studied, *"testamentum condidi."*[57] The particulars concerning the scribe, *"quem NN scribendum"* or in the *testamentum Abbonis "scribendo rogavi"* are similar to those in the wills of Bertram, Adalgisel, Hadoindus, Irmina and Widerad.[58] Likewise conforming to normal Merovingian procedure are the testamentary directives,[59] the correction notice,[60] the penalty *formula*,[61] and the *adiuratio*.[62]

In some aspects, this latest Merovingian testament preserves more archaic forms than many of the other, older texts. The codicil clause, which is often lacking in late Merovingian testaments, is fairly well preserved in Abbo's testament although it was poorly tran-

---

[51] *Ibid.*, 59–60. The *invocatio* "In nomine Patris et Filii et Spiritus Sancti" par. 1.

[52] *Ibid.*, Anfangsdatierung, 60–61. Nonn points out pp. 34–35 that Abbo's dating is unusual in using the year 717/18 that Charles Martel defeated the Neustrian opposition, but that, as Cipolla had recognized before, the date is quite acceptable.

[53] *Ibid.*, p. 61. Nonn points out that the *apprecatio*, "feliciter" is indeed unusual (par. 1).

[54] *Ibid.*, p. 62. Normally the name would be followed by a title: here it is lacking: Abbo filius Felici (par. 1). In 726 Abbo had termed himself *"rector"*. The failure to use a title might indicate that he had ceased to serve in that capacity during the suppression of the revolt and was not yet, if indeed he ever was, *"patricius"*. However, the lack may be simply a question of individual style.

[55] *Ibid.*, pp. 3–5 "Handlungsfähigkeit." "Sana mente atque consilio." 20, 4–5.

[56] *Ibid.*, p. 64 "Innere Begründung."

[57] *Ibid.*, pp. 64–65 "Testamentserklärung."

[58] *Ibid.*, pp. 65–66 "Angaben über Schreiber."

[59] *Ibid.*, pp. 74–77 "Testamentarische Verfügungen." See below p. 29.

[60] *Ibid.*, pp. 78–79 "Korrekturvermerk" "et si qua karaxatura, aut litteratura in hanc paginam testamentis mei reperteque fuerint, nos eas fieri rogauimus." par. 61.

[61] *Ibid.*, pp. 100–104, "Poen." "Et si quis sperat hoc temerario contra hanc uoluntatem meam quem promptissimam deuotionem conscribere rogaui insidiator extiterit, et sese noluerit, iram cęlestem incurrat, et ad communionem omnium ęcclesiarum excommunicatus appareat, et insuper inferat ad ipsum sanctum locum heredem meam sociantem fisco auri libras quinquaginta, et quod repetit et uindicare non ualeat," 37, par. 63.

[62] *Ibid.*, pp. 104–107. "dum et non semel, sed sepius cum requisiuimus et humiliter preco domnis principibus, uel omnium potestatibus et episcopis, per Patre et Filio et Spiritu Sancto, ... ut hunc uoluntatis nostrę ... ut in nullo permittatis conuellere nec irrumpere ..." par. 62.

scribed.[63] The installation into inheritance follows the oldest Merovingian form also found in the testaments of Remigius, Caesarius, Bertram and Hadoindus: *"Tu, sacrosancta ęc-clesia ... heres michi es tu, heredem meam te esse volo ac iubeo."*[64] The dissociation clause which varies in position and wording in Merovingian testaments, appears here in its proper position according to Roman usage after the installation.[65] The *caput generale* appears likewise in the proper place for late Roman testaments and, with a simple word order transformation, appears complete.[66] The signature, which is in the form *"testamentum a me factum"* and not, as in other Merovingian testaments, simply *"testamentum meum"* and which lacks the term *relegit* thus conforms more closely to Roman testamentary form than do the other, more northern, Merovingian testaments.[67] Even in those aspects in which Abbo's testament deviates from Roman usage, as in the five witnesses instead of seven required since the sixth century, it probably follows still older Roman traditions.[68]

This brief summary of Nonn's exhaustive study of all extant Merovingian testaments and testamentary formularies indicates that the document is certainly not a pancarte but rather a genuine testament from the Merovingian period drawn up with the sort of intimate knowledge of Roman legal procedure impossible for a monk of the early eleventh century to have obtained. The same conclusions can be reached by examining the non-formulaic legal allusions and references in the text.[69]

Abbo makes three explicit references to Roman law as it was apparently still in use in the early eighth century, aside from those references which are part of testamentary tradition. The first appears in paragraph 44 in which he arranged the disposition of property which he and his cousin Honorata have held in common. Presumably Honorata was the heir of their grandparents Maurinus and Dodina and Abbo was the legatee. According to

---

[63] *Ibid.*, pp. 66–68. "Kodizillarklausel" Nonn points out that the words "ius civile" have been omitted in the transcription: "quod testamentum meum, si quo casum (iure civili) et iure pretorio, uel quale cuius lege adinuentionis quę quomodo valere nequiuerit, ac si ab intestato ad uicem codicellorum eum ualere uolo ac iubeo." par. 1.

[64] *Ibid.*, pp. 68–70 "Erbeneinsetzung."

[65] *Ibid.*, pp. 70–72, "Enterbungsklausel" Nonn points out that the classical formulation, "ceteri alii omnes exheredes sunto" was misunderstood quite early and in place of the third person plural imperative "sunto," one finds Abbo and elsewhere such phrases as "cęteri cętereuę exheredis sint tote." par. 1.

[66] *Ibid.*, pp. 72–74. "quos quas liberas liberosue esse decreuero, liberi libereue sint omnis, et quęque per hoc testamentum meum dedero, legavero, dare iussero, id ut fiat detur, prestetur fidei heredes mei commito." (par. 1)

[67] *Ibid.*, pp. 82–85 "Unterschrift des Erblassers."

[68] *Ibid.*, pp. 85–88. "Zeugenunterschriften" esp. p. 86.

[69] I am most grateful to Professor Edward Champlin for his assistance in understanding the legal aspects of the text. Specific legal and technical vocabulary indicating late Roman usage will be discussed in Chapters II and III.

the *lex Falcidia*,[70] which Abbo invokes, his amount of the estate could not exceed three quarters. Abbo's legacy had apparently exceeded this limit, thus making him or his heirs liable for claims against the amount in excess of three quarters which could be pressed by Honorata or her heirs. The estate had never been divided, but rather the two cousins had concluded a *pactum*[71] according to which an inventory of the estate had been made and certain portions of the excess legacy were to pass to Honorata. This *pactum* is now executed by Abbo so that no future claims can be made against Abbo or his heir, the monastery of Novalesa.

The second reference is to the *"lex de ingratis et contumacis libertis"*, in paragraph 45. Abbo orders that all *liberti* pay *obsequium et impensionem* to his heirs *"iuxta legis ordine"*. If they fail to do so, a *judex* is to be summoned and, according to the law, they are to lose their freedom. The reference is apparently to the *Codex Justinianus*, 6, 7, *de libertis et eorum liberis*, 2 & 3. In particular, the explicit mention of the summoning of the judge is closer to the Justinian than the Theodosian Code, 4, 10, 1–2. However, the mention of a *iudicium* in the *Leges Burgundionum* (XL, 1) would indicate that Abbo need not have been familiar with the *Codex Justinianus*.[72]

The third reference to Roman law occurs in paragraph 49. Abbo's uncle, Bishop Semforianus of Gap, had been Abbo's legal tutor following the death of his father Felix. Apparently Abbo and Semforianus had each inherited portions of the estate, but the estate had not been divided. Semforianus had desired to make a donation of his half to the Church of Gap and had done so. However, Abbo explains that this donation had been void. The reason suggested by Cipolla,[73] that the donation was void because of the prohi-

---

[70] On the lex Falcidia in general see W. W. Buckland, *A Text-Book of Roman Law from Augustus to Justinian* (Cambridge: 1966) pp. 342–43. On the later role of the *lex* see Max Kaser, *Das römische Privatrecht* II *Die Nachklassischen Entwicklungen, Rechtsgeschichte des Altertums im Rahmen des Handbuchs der Altertumswissenschaft* III Teil III Bd. II Abschnitt (Munich: 1971), § 298 VI, pp. 561–562

[71] On the increasing use of *pacta* in late Roman law see Ernst Levy, *West Roman Vulgar Law: The Law of Property* (Philadelphia: 1951) p. 172, 198, as well as his *Pauli Sententiae. A Palingenesia of the Opening Titles as a Specimen of Research in West Roman Vulgar Law* (Ithaca, N. Y.: 1945) pp. 42–43; and his *Weströmisches Vulgarrecht: Das Obligationenrecht* (Weimar: 1956) pp. 34–59.

[72] Cipolla, pp. 31 and 32, notes, following Savigny, suggests that Abbo knows the Justinian Code, although in a manner "meno determinato." The *Leges Burgundionum* offer possibly a closer parallel: Si quis Burgundio mancipio iuris sui libertatem donaverit, ... nec prius ad pristinam conditionem manumissor potuerit revocare, nisi forte talia in damnum et contumeliam absolutoris sui admisisse in iudicio convincatur ... MGH *Legum Sectio* I tom. II, 1, p. 72.

[73] *Ibid.*, p. 32 note 1. The form in which Roman law was transmitted in Provence and the lower Rhône in the Merovingian period has been the subject of considerable debate, particularly in the question of whether the so-called *Fragmenta Gaudenziana* reflect Roman Vulgar Law of that region or of northern Italy. See in particular G. Vismara, *Fragmenta Gaudenziana. Ius Romanum medii aeui* (Milan: 1978).

bition in Cod. V, 37, 16, against a tutor alienating the property of the pupil, is probably not germane. Instead, Abbo is basing his objection on the fact that the estate had not yet been divided between the two coheirs: *"et facultates nostras indiuisas remanserunt."* Until an actual division had taken place, transfer of the property could not take place without the consent of both owners, who were each half owners of the totality. Hence Semforianus' donation was prohibited by law, *"et lex hoc prohibit."*

Taken together these three references to Roman law indicate its continued importance and vigor in the early eighth century. Specific laws, such as that of freedmen, can be invoked, the law is administered before a public *iudex*, and even the niceties of Falcidian law and the law of inheritance continue in force. These indications of an intimate knowledge of Roman law, together with the close conformity of the document to Roman testamentary form, are further evidence that the testament is essentially genuine.

However, if the form is genuine, the content was probably interpolated, both in the late eleventh century by Hugo and, possibly, in the earlier part of that century by the monks of Novalesa. The extent to which these interpolations were made cannot be judged with complete accuracy, but the strict form within which properties are described and bequeathed minimalizes the possible distortions such interpolations cause in the general image conveyed of the region in the early eighth century. At most the interpolations may have added certain place names to those actually bequeathed by Abbo. Cases of possible interpolation can be identified by examining the form of the individual bequests.

The actual dispositions of the testament follow the dissociation clause and then consist of the following general sections:

1. Bequests of properties scattered throughout the region identified by *pagus*.[74] These specific bequests generally are identified by the *pagus* in which they are found, by place names in the locative case referring to locations at which are found particular *colonicae*, by the source of the property (allodial, purchase, etc.), by a formulaic enumeration of appurtenances, and then by the formula *tu heres mea ut habeas uolo ac iubeo*. As a variation, the bequest may be described by the name of the freedperson or slave who holds or inhabits the property, the nature of the holding, and the injunction that he or she is to continue to hold the property and belong to the monastery of Novalesa.

2. An annex in which Abbo settles with his cousin Honorata the title to the property which they had inherited in indivision from their maternal grandparents followed by a general admonition to his freedpersons that they continue to pay his heir *obsequium* and *impensionem* under pain of returning to slavery.[75]

3. More donations (of the type described in Section 1 above) in the pagus of Grenoble, followed by the enfranchisement of a *seruus*.[76]

---

[74] par. 2–43. The use of the term *pagus* rather than *comitatus*, frequent from the 9th century, is further evidence of the text's authenticity.

[75] par. 44.

4. An annex in which Abbo rectifies a donation attempted by his uncle Bishop Semforianus of Gap from Abbo's property while the former was his tutor. Abbo states that the original donation had been irregular and hence void, but he fulfills his uncle's intention by making a similar donation to the Church of Gap. Abbo retained usufruct of these donations.[77]

5. A pious donation to the church of St. Jean de Maurienne.[78]

6. A mention of a previous donation to "dulcissimę nostrę Virgilie" of property in the pagus of Gap, Riez, and Sisteron.[79]

7. Directions that Bishop Vualchunus continue after Abbo's death to direct the spiritual and temporal life of the monastery.[80]

8. Donations to Novalesa as in 1 above; a donation to a *"fidelis"* Protadius of confiscated property in the *pagus* of Gap; a bequest to one Tersia of confiscated property in the *pagi* of Die, Gap and Grenoble; and directives that agents of the monastery be permitted to seek out runaway slaves and freedpersons.[81]

Thus, within the body of the testament, very precise information is provided on individual properties, and the various dispositions included in the testament, involved as they are with points of Roman law, family and political alliances in the region etc., could only have been forged with enormous difficulty. As will be evident in the following chapters, only someone with an extremely acute understanding of the structure of agriculture, lordship and kinship in the eighth century could have forged any of the sections of the testament.

This leaves, however, the possibility of simple insertions of place names in the descriptions of *colonicae*. Usually, the place names follow immediately the name of the *pagus*. While the names might be as many as four or five, they are usually fewer. Four suspiciously long and loosely connected such lists occur, three in the area of Novalesa itself[82] and one in the *pagus* of Grenoble.[83] The first two *might* reasonably be seen as the result of Abbo's ex-

---

[76] par. 45–48.

[77] par. 49–50.

[78] par. 51.

[79] par. 52. Tabacco, in "Dalla Novalesa", p. 485 n. 13 and p. 486 n. 16, suggests that Virgilia was possibly a daughter and that she was possibly deceased at the time that the testament was prepared. The first hypothesis is entirely reasonable. The second is doubtful. The text seems to be addressed to Virgilia, confirming that she is to have those properties which Abbo had given her, either next to or (reading *preter* for *propter*) except for those properties which he has given to Novalesa.

[80] par. 53.

[81] par. 54–59.

[82] par. 3: "… hoc est quicquid in ipsa ualle Noualiciis, etiam et in Barro, seu et in Albanato, et ultra Cinisca subtus Crauasca et in Faido, uel cętera loca …" par. 4: "et in Lastadio, Gallionis, Grummo, Camundis, Luxomone, Coruallico, Petracaua, Trebocis;" par. 5: "hoc est in Orbano, Cicimiano, Voroxio, Raudenouiliano."

[83] 23, par. 15: "seu in Arauardo, una cum libertos nostros, Magnebertum una cum germano suo Columbo, Misicasiana, Mesatico, Cambe, Quintiaco, Viennatico."

tensive holding near Susa, although one could suspect that it is in exactly this region that the monastery most wished to press its claims to property in the late tenth and early eleventh centuries. No other documents from Novalesa suggest that these locations were later in dispute, however, and the places themselves are difficult to identify today. The third case, however, is quite different. This list includes precisely those properties Bishop Hugo of Grenoble was disputing with Archbishop Guido of Vienne and which, as the rubric of the cartulary argued, were in the *pagus* of Sermorens: Vinay and Quincieux. Appearing as they do at the end of the enumeration, one suspects that they were added subsequently. Thus one finds within the text certainly one and possibly two interpolations. The first, concerning the region of the monastery itself, may have been added at the time that the document was attached to the Carolingian forgery. The second would have been made when the testament was copied for Hugo of Grenoble.

However, even if this conjecture should prove correct, the validity of using the testament in order to examine the structure of the region in 739 is unaffected: individual properties may have been added, but in its substance and in the myriad details it presents on Abbo's lifetime, the document is certainly genuine, and as such is a precious source for historians.

The Identity of the Testator

We have examined the means by which the testament was preserved, the controversies surrounding its transmission, and the arguments concerning its authenticity. Now we must consider briefly the identity of this Abbo responsible for producing this remarkable document.

Although much can be learned about his family, his social position, and his political alliances from a close reading of his testament, little that is certain can be said of his life. For well over a century historians have argued about his role in Provence before and after 739.[84] All that is absolutely certain is that Abbo, the son of Felix and Rustica, was rector of the region of Maurienne and Susa in 726 when he founded Novalesa on his family estates[85] and that at the time he prepared his testament in 739 he was a loyal and well rewarded follower of Charles Martel.

One is tempted to identify the Abbo of the testament with two other persons carrying this name early in the eighth century. The first is an Abbo in the entourage of Charles Mar-

---

[84] See above, note 21.

[85] Cippola, 7, 9–11. "Ergo una cum consensum pontefecum vel clerum nostrorum Mauriennate et Segucine civitate in quibus nos Deus rectorem esse instituit." On *rectores* see Ingrid Heidrich, "Titulatur und Urkunden der arnulfingischen Hausmeier," *Archiv für Diplomatik* vol. 11/12 (1965–66) pp. 71–279, esp. 98–99.

tel who witnessed a donation of this latter at Trier in 722.[86] The second is the *patricius* Abbo who appears in two documents of St. Victor of Marseille written around 780 but referring to the reign of Charles Martel.[87] If all three persons are identical, then a reasonable image of the rector of Maurienne and Susa could be drawn as follows: Abbo would have been an aristocrat from the Susa region who was a close follower of Charles Martel during the difficult years when Pepin II's bastard son was fighting to gain control of his family and then of the Frankish kingdoms.[88] Later he returned to his home region and there served as *rector* in the later part of the 720s. Probably following the supression of the revolt of Provence in the 730s he would have been made the last *patricius* of Provence. Since, as François Louis Ganshof pointed out, the documents of 780 imply that the *patricius* Abbo had not been dead thirty years, he would probably have died around 751.[89] If Abbo had been born in the last decades of the seventh century, this life span would be quite reasonable: as a young man following Charles Martel, later serving as rector and, finally, governing Provence as its last patricius.

This identification of the testator and the *patricius* was first made by the author of the *Chronicon Novaliciense* in the eleventh century, and most French historians have not doubted its validity.[90]

As with the validity of the testament itself, in Belgium and in Germany, this identity has been largely rejected.[91] Arguments advanced by Rudolf Buchner and F. L. Ganshof can be summarized as follows: First, none of the genuine Carolingian diplomas for Novalesa identify the founder of the monastery as *patricius*. Surely this would have been done had he in fact held such an important office. The second, and in Buchner's mind the most serious objection, is that the likelihood that the two are identical is based largely on the image of Abbo which emerges from the testament. Since he rejected the testament as a mere pancarte, he argued that "the only basis for the identification disappears since the testament is eliminated as a source for the eighth century".[92] Finally, the first identification of the two

---

[86] DMD 11, DM pp. 98–99.

[87] *Gallia Christiana novissima* II Marseille; Valence (Paris: 1899) nos. 41 and 42. For an analysis of these documents see F. L. Ganshof, "Les avatars d'un domaine de l'église de Marseille à la fin du VIIe et au VIIIe siècle," *Studi in onore di Gino Luzzatto* vol. I (Milani 1950) pp. 55–66.

[88] Semmler, "Zur pippinidisch-karolingischen Sukzessionskrise", pp. 1–36.

[89] These documents record a dispute between the bishop of Marseille Maurontus and the agents of Charles concerning the villa Chaudol which had been confiscated during the revolt of Provence under Antenor. A witness of the king had proposed in 780 to prove the thirty year possession of the estate by the king but he failed to establish this proof. Ganshof wisely supposes that the reason is that the estate, confiscated by Antenor, had been returned to the monastery by Abbo. After his death, however, a royal representative Ardingus confiscated the estate as having been part of the rebel patricius' property. Ganshof supposed that it took place ca. 751 or 2. p. 62 note 1.

[90] Ed. Carlo Cipolla, *Monumenta novaliciensia vetustiora* vol. II (Rome: 1901).

[91] Particularly by Ganshof, "Les avatars," and Buchner, *Die Provence*.

[92] Buchner, p. 100.

appears in the *Chronicon*, which presents a wildly inaccurate account of Abbo and of the foundation of Novalesa. Later forged charters referring to Abbo as *patricius* are clearly based on the *Chronicon*.

These objections are not convincing. Most importantly, as we have seen, Buchner's main objection falls since the testament is genuine. Ganshof, who concurred with Buchner's judgement, should have realized the inadequacy of this objection since he elsewhere accepts the validity of the testament.[93] Second, one should not place any value on arguments *ex silentio* based on the Carolingian diplomas. The diploma of Carlomann of 770 and that of Charles the Great of 773 refer to Abbo as founder and patron of the monastery. These references are clearly to the foundation charter and possibly, to the testament as well.[94] Since Abbo did not term himself patricius in either document, one would not expect that confirmations of these documents would give him any further title. Finally, the fact that the author of the *Chronicon* identifies his monastery's founder as *patricius* is not to be rejected because he did not understand what a *patricius* was. In fact, his very confusion suggests that he was reporting a tradition which he did not understand, not that he was inventing one.

The discrediting of the opposing arguments does not, however, demonstrate the validity of the identification. The identification of the Abbo in the diploma of 722 with the founder of Novalesa is certainly arbitrary. Concerning the identity of the Abbo in the testament and the *Abbo Patricius,* one can only conclude that there is no compelling argument on either side. However, even if the identity and personality of the testator remain in shadow, his testament serves as a lens through which to view the Rhône valley in the last decades of the Merovingian Empire. To this text we now turn.

---

[93] He used it later in his "Quelques aspects" published in 1958. Possibly he had realized Buchner's error by this time.

[94] DKar. 52. *BM*² 127 (124) "Ergo dum et Abbo una cum consensu et adiutorium Valcuni episcopi monasterio ... visi sunt edificasse". DKar. 74 *BM*² 156 (153). "... quem Abbo condam visus fuit aedificasse ..."

CHAPTER II
EDITION AND TRANSLATION

The *Testamentum Abbonis* has been edited six times previously, by Carlo Le Cointe, Jean Mabillon, Gian Tommaso Terraneo, Jules Marion, J. M. Pardessus, and most recently by Carlo Cipolla. In addition, the forged diploma of Charles the Great was edited by Engelbert Mühlbacher in the *Monumenta Germaniae historica* edition of the Carolingian diplomas. Concerning the previous editions one should consult Carlo Cipolla's excellent introduction to his edition, pp. 13–18.

The text, written in a clear textura hand of the early twelfth century, presents few paleographic problems. Nevertheless previous editors, including most recently Carlo Cipolla, have made a few minor errors in transcription. Since all previous editions have been based on the unique manuscript, erroneous readings have not been indicated. Only arguable alternate readings proposed by previous editors are noted in the apparatus.

Although the text presents few problems of a paleographic nature, its interpretation is extremely difficult both because of its language and its transmission. The original language was a Latin extremely evolved from the norms of classical grammar, syntax, and orthography.[1] Moreover, the original text was recopied at least twice, once when attached to the Carolingian confirmation and once when entered in the cartulary of Grenoble. Certainly this estimate is the minimum: in all likelihood the cartulary copy is even further removed from the original. Furthermore, at least some of the copyists clearly had great difficulties in reading the text before them, whether it was the original, which would have been written in an eighth-century semi-cursive script, or a later, Carolingian copy.

The result of these difficulties is that the text, through the combined effects of Merovingian usage and scribal error, presents considerable obstacles to interpretation: case endings are often impossible to explain; singular subjects are combined with plural verbs and vice versa; masculine and feminine endings combine to obfuscate the sex of persons mentioned in the testament; certain passages are so corrupt that they defy precise translation; specific terms are so badly garbled in transcription that their meanings remain unclear.

The scribe who copied the text into the cartulary seems to have been aware of these problems, and while he did not systematically correct all syntactical confusions, he did attempt to organize the text, primarily through punctuation and capitalization, in order to provide an intelligible edition. Since this twelfth-century interpretation of the text is the point of departure for any modern reinterpretation, the present edition presents, as closely

---

[1] On the peculiarities of Merovingian Latin, the best English introduction is that provided by J. M. Wallace-Hadrill to his edition and translation of the *Fourth Book of the Chronicle of Fredegar* (London: 1960) pp. xxviii–xxxviii. On the language of Merovingian charters, the most important study is that of Rudolf Falkowski, "Studien zur Sprache der Merowingerdiplome," *Archiv für Diplomatik* vol. 17 (1971) pp. 1–125.

as possible, the characteristics of the cartulary copy. Thus it retains the orthography, punctuation, and capitalization of the manuscript.[2] The only changes are the expansion of all abbreviations, none of which present any difficulties, and the division into paragraphs, a step taken in order to facilitate consultation. Proper names are not capitalized because the determination that a word is a proper name is often itself an interpretation. This editing program has been adopted with the recognition that this method of edition is a variance with the guidelines proposed by the Commission internationale de diplomatique for the publication of charters but is justified by the unique problems posed by the text.[3]

All interpretations of the text have been confined to the translation and the notes. At every point the translation attempts to convey a sense of the text, but often this sense is the result of a judgment based on an informed guess of the meaning of the passage. The translation attempts to convey something of the confusion of the original text in order not to be more precise than the testament itself.

The translation cannot be read or understood without reference to the more detailed commentaries in Chapters III, IV, and V, on the content and context of the testament. Thus justifications for translations of certain technical terms such as *colonica, curtis, seruus,* and *locella* are to be sought there.

The identification of the hundreds of places named in the testament has posed problems to editors across the centuries. Besides his own attempts to verify and improve the earlier suggestions of Cipolla and Marion, the author has been enormously helped by a number of scholars whose assistance he gratefully acknowledges. These include M. André Perret, Directeur honoraire des services d'archives de Savoie, Professor Ernst Hirsch, Professor Giuseppe Sergi, Professor Giuliano Gasca Queirazza, and Mme Moulon of the Archives de France. In spite of the generous assistance of these scholars, many of the identifications remain tentative and others are impossible to determine with any precision. For this reason a map indicating precise locations of properties would be misleading, and for an idea of the extent of Abbo's properties one should consult the more general maps on p. 82–83, which indicate the distribution of his property by *pagus*.

---

[2] In the edition a comma indicates a point not followed by a capital; a period a point followed by a capital; a semi-colon the scribe's!; and a colon a colon.

[3] See the report of R.-H. Bautier, to the Assemblé à l'occasion du Ve Congrès International de Diplomatique (Paris: 12–16 septembre 1977), "Normalisation internationale des methodes de publication des documents latins du moyen âge," pp. 1–37.

In nomine Patris, et filii, et spiritus Sancti.[1a] Karolus imperator, augustus, piissimus, a deo coronatus, magnus, pacificus imperator, romanum gubernans imperium, qui et per misericordiam dei rex francorum et longobardorum. Igitur notum sit omnium fidelium nostrorum magnitudinum presentium scilicet et futurorum, quia uir uenerabilis frodinus[2] abba ex monasterio quod est constructum in honore sanctorum principum apostolorum, loco nuncupato Noualiciis, missa petitione et religiosos monachos, Gislarannum[3] scilicet et agabertum[4]

fol. 38v serenitati nostrę suggessit,/ qualiter abbo quondam uir deo deuotus, per testamentum donationis suę aliquas res ad ipsum sanctum locum Noualiciis delegasset, unde ipsa casa dei et monachi ibidem consistentes, seu pauperes et peregrini euntes et redeuntes maximam consolationem habere uidentur, et ipsum testamentum nostris detulerunt obtutibus ad relegendum. Sed quia sepissime per placita comitum, per diuersos pagos necessitate cogente, ipsum ad relegendum detulerunt; iam ex parte ualde dirutum esse uidebatur. Et ideo quia per se non fuerunt ausi ipsum testamentum renouare, petierunt celsitudini nostrę, ut per nostram iussionem denuo fuisset renouatus; Eo tenore sicut ipse ad hoc relegi melius potuisset. Nos autem considerantes eorum necessitate, et mercedis nostrę augmentum; iussimus per fideles notarios nostros, infra palatium ipsum testamentum denuo renouare: ita ut deinceps pro mercedis

fol. 39r nostrę augmentum, inspecto/ ipso testamento, sicut inibi declaratur, ad ipsam casam dei nostris futurisque temporibus, in augmentis profitiat. Non enim ex

---

[1] Authentic diplomas of Charles the Great have no *invocatio*.

[2] Abbot Frodinus appears in the authentic diploma of Charles the Great for Novalesa of 773 DKar 74 (BM 153) as Frodoenus, in a charter of one "Teutcarius Alamannus" dating from 810 as Frodoinus (Cipolla I, p. 63). According to the *Chronicon novaliciense,* he was the son of one "vir quidam inclitus nomine Magafredus, qui et ipse Francigena extitit (Cipolla, II, 169), and his wife Anza. The necrology of Novalesa celebrated his *depositio* May 10 (Cipolla I, p. 301). In the Novalesa entry in the Reichenau *Verbrüderungsbuch MGH Libri memoriales et necrologia, nova Series* I (Hannover: 1979), 9[B1], he appears as E(for F?)rodoinus.

[3] Gislarannus appears in the Novalesa entry in the Reichenau *Verbrüderungsbuch,* 9[C3]. Although the principle by which names were included in this entry awaits thorough clarification, the position of the name in the third column suggests that the name may have been among the "nomina defunctorum" of this entry.

[4] An Agabertus also appears in the third column of the Novalesa entry in the Reichenau *Verbrüderungsbuch,* 9[C4].

---

[a] Rubric: Hęc carta quę est de monasterio Noulacię dicit quod castrum de Vinniaco et uilla Quintiacum quę est in mandamento Sancti Georgii (in marg.: in pago Salmotiacensi et) in episcopatu Gratianopolitano sunt.

In the name of the Father and of the Son and of the Holy Spirit. Charles, Emperor, Augustus, pious, crowned by God, great, peaceful Emperor, governing the Roman Empire, who is through the mercy of God king of the Franks and of the Lombards. Therefore let it be known by the entirety of all our faithful both in the present and the future, that the venerable man Frodoinus, abbot from the monastery that is constructed in honor of the saintly princes of the apostles at the place called Novalesa, by means of a petition and by the religious monks Gislarannus and Agabertus, communicated to our serenity that the late Abbo a man devoted to God had bequeathed by a testament of donation certain of his properties to this same holy place of Novalesa, so that this house of God and the monks established there and the poor and travelers going and returning might be seen to have the greatest comfort. And they brought this testament to us seeking that it be reread. But, because out of necessity they had carried it very often to comital assemblies thinking of the need for its rereading in diverse pagi, now in part it seemed greatly damaged, and hence because they had not dared to renew this testament by their own authority they asked our highness that it might be renewed through our order, with the same wording as the original in order that it might better continue to be reread for those purposes. We however considering their need and the increase of our graciousness, have ordered this testament to be renewed again by our faithful notaries in the palace. So that from this time forward for the increase of our graciousness, after this testament had been in-

consuetudine anteriorum regum hoc facere decreuimus, sed solummodo propter necessitatem et mercedis augmentum transcribere precipimus hoc modo, et subter plumbum sigillari iussimus.[b]

1. In nomine patris, et filii, et spiritus sancti, sub die tercio nonas maias, anno uigesimo primo gubernante inlustrissimo nostro Karolo regna francorum, in inditione, VIIa[5], feliciter. Ego in dei nomine Abbo filius felici et Rusticę nomine quondam sana mente, atque consilio; cogitans casus humani fragilitatis, testamentum condidi, quem uenerabili hytberto clerico scribendo rogaui, quod testamentum meum si quo casum et iure pretorio, uel quale cuius lege adinuentionis quę quomodo ualere nequiuerit, ac si ab intestato ad uicem[c] codicellorum fol. 39v eum ualere uolo ac iubeo,/ quos quas[d] liberosue esse decreuero, liberi libereue sint omnis, et quęque per hoc testamentum meum dedero, legauero, dare iussero, id ut fiat detur, prestetur fidei heredes mei committo.

2. Ego in dei nomine Abbo, cum me dispensatio diuina de hac luce migrare preceperit, dibitoue natore compleuero,[e] tunc tu sacrosancta ęcclesia, in honore beati Petri apostoli, seu et cęterorum sanctorum Noualiciis monasterii in ualle sigusina, quem ex opere nostro in rem proprietatis nostrę construximus, ubi norma monachorum[f] sub religionis ordine spiritale, et regula sancti benedicti custodiendis deo[g] adiuuante, conlocauimus, ubi apresens[h] uir Abbo preesse uidetur, heres michi es tu, heredem meam te esse uolo ac iubeo, cęteri cęterę ex heredis sint tote;[i]

3. te uero sancta ęcclesia beati petri apostoli superscripti[j] monasterii, in ualle fol. 40r sigusina, tam infra muros[k] ipsius ciuitatis quam/ et in ipso pago ex alode paren-

---

[5] Year 739 dated from Charles Martel's victory at Soissons over the Neustrian opposition in 719 and hence the first year in which he could be said to be "governing the kingdoms of the Franks." The indiction is likewise correct.

---

[b] Erasure of the last five words corrected by first hand.

[c] ad *ui* first hand over erasure.

[d] *liberas* omitted.

[e] Original *precepero* corrected by slightly later hand.

[f] Interlinear but first hand. *norma* possible scribal error for *turma*.

[g] Original *do* corrected by first hand.

[h] Cipolla suggests the original read *uu* (uenerabilis uir).

[i] *Sint tote* for *sinto* (third plural imperative form). See above p. 29 note 65.

[j] *Superscript* corrected to *superscripti* by other hand.

[k] *Murus* corrected, but direction of correction uncertain.

spected, as is declared in it, it might be of greater profit to this house of God both in our time and in the future. We did not decree this to be done out of the custom of previous kings, but only because of necessity and the increase of [our] graciousness did we order it to be transcribed in this manner, and did we order it to be sealed below with lead.

1. In the name of the Father and of the Son and of the Holy Spirit, on the third day of the nones of May (May 5), in the twenty-first year of our most illustrious Charles ruling the kingdoms of the Franks, in the seventh indiction, in good fortune. I, in God's name Abbo, son of the deceased Felix and Rustica, being of sound mind and judgment, pondering the accidents of human fragility, have made this testament which I have asked the venerable cleric Hytbertus to write. Which testament, if by some chance and by praetorian law or by such a law of whatever invention in whatever way, is not able to be valid as if by one intestate in place of codicils, I commit to the faith of my heirs that all those be free whomever I shall have decreed free and that whatever I shall have given bequeathed or ordered to give, that it shall be done.

2. I in God's name Abbo, when divine providence shall have ordered me to depart from this light and when I pay back the debt of nature, then I wish and order you, sacrosanct church in honor of Blessed Peter the apostle and of all the saints of the monastery of Novalesa in the valley of Susa, which we built by our own efforts on our own property, where with the help of God we established the troop of monks under the spiritual order of religion keeping the rule of Saint Benedict, where at present the [venerable] man Abbo is seen to preside, to be my heir, you are my heir. All others be entirely excluded from inheritance.

3. I wish and order that you have, holy Church of the above mentioned monastery of the Apostle Peter, in the valley of Susa, both whatever is within the walls

tum meorum uel undecumque michi iustissime ibidem ex legibus obuenit, hoc est quicquid in ipsa ualle noualiciis, etiam et in barro,[6] seu et in albanato,[7] et ultra cinisca[8] subtus crauasca,[9] et in faido,[10] uel cętera loca quod presente tempore ad ipsum monasterium adiacet, uel aspicere uidetur, cum siluis, pratis, alpibus, aquis aquarumue decursibus, quicquid presente tempore ad ipsum sanctum locum aspicere uidetur, tam de proprio quam de conquisto, seu et de commutationis causa promaciano[11] in ualle maurigenica[12] recepimus, unam cum mancipiis, terris, uineis, siluis, cum omni integritate ut habeas; uolo ac iubeo.

4. Similiter quicquid in balmas,[13] ubi oratorius in honore sancti Verani[14] est constructus uisi sumus habere: et in lastadio[15] gallionis,[16] grummo,[17] camundis,[18] luxomone,[19] coruallico,[20] petracaua,[21] trebocis,[22] uel circa ciuitate, quantumcumque ex proprie/ tate parentum nostrorum, uel conquestum in ipsa loca habere uidemur, te heredem meam habere uolo ac iubeo.

fol. 40v

5. Et quicquid circa civitate segusia, uel in ipsa ualle habere uidemur, hoc est in

---

[6] Bar, Piemonte prov. Torino, cne. Condove.

[7] Alberea or Alberedo, Piemonte prov. Torino, cne. Venaus.

[8] Cenischia River which flows into the Dora Riparia at Susa.

[9] Revoisse on the Dora near Esilles.

[10] Unknown location.

[11] Unknown location in the valley of Maurienne.

[12] Valley of Maurienne, arr. Saint-Jean-de Maurienne, Savoie.

[13] Balma, Piemonte, prov. Torino frazione di S. Giorio d. Susa.

[14] Veranus is the name of a number of local saints, including the bishop of Cavillon ca. 585, Lyons ca. 460, and Vence ca. 465. Bishop Veranus of Vence was the son of Bishop Eucherius of Lyons and Galla, and brother of Bishop Salonius of Geneva. See Karl Friedrich Stroheker, *Der senatorische Adel im spätantiken Gallien* (1948 reprint, Darmstadt: 1970), no. 406; *AASS Juni* IV, 250. Jean Pierre Poly and Eric Bournazel, in *La mutation féodale* Nouvelle Clio 16 (Paris: 1980), p. 320, suppose that the Veranus in the *Testamentum* is the son of Eucherius.

[15] Stagno, Piemonte, province of Torino, cne. Mompantero.

[16] Giaglione, Piemonte, province of Torino.

[17] Grimordo, Piemonte, province of Torino, cne. Giaglione.

[18] Chiomonte, Piemonte, province of Torino.

[19] Lisimonte, Piemonte, province of Torino, cne. Gravere.

[20] Croaglie, Piemonte, province of Torino.

[21] Unknown location.

[22] Trebot, Piemonte, province of Torino, cne. Meana.

of this city and that which is in this pagus from the allod of my parents or from wherever it has come to me in that same place most justly by law, that is whatever is in this valley of Novalesa, and in Bar or in Alberede and beyond Moncenisio below Revoisse and in Faido or in other places which are adjacent at present to this monastery or which seem to belong to it, with the forests, meadows, alpine pasturages, waters and water courses, and whatever at present seems to belong to this holy place which has come either as inherited property or from acquisition, and what we received in the valley of Maurienne at *Promacianum* in exchange, together with the slaves, lands, vineyards and forests in all integrity.

4. Likewise I wish and order you my heir to have whatever we seem to have in Balma where has been constructed an oratory in honor of St. Veranus and in Stagno, in Giaglione, Grimondo, Chiomonte, Lisimonte, Croaglie, *Petracava*, and Trebot, or around the city, as much as we seem to have in these places either from the property of our parents or by acquisition.

5. And I wish and order you my heir to have whatever we seem to have around

orbano,[23] cicimiano,[24] uoroxio,[25] raudenouiliano,[26] tu heres mea habere uolo ac iubeo.

6. Et in ualaucis[27] portione, quem a liberto nostro theudaldo dedimus, uolo ut habeat et ipse et infantes sui, ad heredem meam aspicere debeant, uolo ac iubeo.

7. Similiter cammite superiore,[28] et cammite subteriore:[29] brosiolis[30] una cum ingenuis, rogationis,[31] tannoborgonis,[32] una cum ministrale nostro iohanne, et infantes suos libertato, cum infantes suos critouis,[33] orbana,[34] bicorasco,[35] una cum nepotes uualane, hoc est harioldo et germana sua, quem dunimius habet galisiaca[36] et alpes in cinisio,[37] quem de ęcclesia sancto petro, de ipsa constructa lugdunense[38] commutauimus. Ista omnia superius comprehensa, una cum man-

fol. 41r   cipiis,/ libertis, terris, domibus, ędificiis, uineis, campis, pratis, pascuis, siluis, alpibus, uel omnis adiacentias ad se pertinentes, te herede mea habere uolo ac iubeo.

8. Et cella infra regnum langobardorum qui uocatur tollatecus,[39] quicquid ex alode parentum nostrorum michi ibidem[1] obuenit, una cum mancipiis ibi consistentibus, uel omne iure suo, ut habeas uolo ac iubeo.

9. Etiam et colonica in ualle diubiasca,[40] infra fines langobardorum, ubi dicitur

---

[23] Urbiano, Piemonte, province of Torino, cne. of Mompantero.

[24] Comiana, Piemonte, province of Torino, cne. of Mompantero.

[25] Unknown location near Susa.

[26] Marion suggests the unlikely Avigliana, Piemonte, province of Torino. Cipolla divides the word into Raude and Noviliano but provides no suggested identification for either.

[27] Possibly Valgioie or Balgioie, Piemonte, province of Torino.

[28] Unknown location.

[29] Unknown location.

[30] Bruzolo, Piemonte, province of Torino.

[31] Unknown location near Bruzolo, Piemonte, province of Torino.

[32] Borgone, Piemonte, province of Torino cne. of Bruzolo.

[33] Crotte, Piemonte, province of Torino, cne. of Susa.

[34] Urbiano, see above no. 23.

[35] Possibly village of the cne. of Rubiana, Piemonte, province of Torino.

[36] Possibly Galise in the valley of Yène, Piemonte, province of Torino.

[37] Cenischia, see above 8.

[38] Lyon, départ. Rhône.

[39] Talucco, cne. of S. Pietroval Lemina, Piemonte, province of Torino.

[40] The valley of the Dubbione, Piemonte, province of Torino.

---

[1] Partial erasure.

the city of Susa or in this valley, that is in Urbiano, Comiana, *Voroxium, Raude,* and *Novilianum.*

6. And I wish that our freedman Theudaldus have in Balgioie (?) that share which we gave him and I wish and order that he and his children should belong to my heir.

7. Likewise I wish and order that you my heir have our property in upper and lower Caramagne (?), in Bruzolo together with the free born at *Rotatio, Tannum,* Borgone, together with our servant John and his children, Liberatus with his children, at Crotte, at Urbiano, at Rubiana, together with the grandchildren of Wala, this is Harioldus and his sister, whom Dunimius has, at Galise (?) and the alps in Chiomonte, which we exchanged with the Church of Saint Peter constructed in Lyon. We want you to have all of that included above, together with slaves, freedpersons, lands, houses, buildings, vineyards, fields, meadows, pastures, forests, alpine pasturages, and everything adjacent which pertains to them.

8. And I want and order that you have our property at the cell the granary [or little monastery?] within the kingdom of the Lombards which is called Talucco, whatever came to me there from the allod of our parents together with the slaves dwelling there and with all its own rights.

9. Besides I wish and order that you have the farm in the valley of the Dubbione

bicciatis,[41] quem parentes nostri et nos ibidem habuimus, ut habeas uolo atque precipio.

10. Simile namque modo, et quicquid in ualle maurigennica ex alode parentum nostrorum uel per quodlibet[m] titulo iuste et rationabiliter nobis ibidem obuenit, et legitima subpetit redebere, hoc est in ipsa maurogenna domus quem apud ęc-clesię maurigennica[42] commutauimus cum edeficiis, cortiferis, exauis, ortis,

fol. 41v uineis, campis, seu unglis,[n] una cum/ ęcclesia sancto petro quem parentes nostri ibidem construxerunt, cum omni integritate uel adiacentias ad se pertinentes, immo que ęcclesia sancto Pancrasio[43] proprietatis nostrę, una cum colonica in birisco,[44] cum omnis adiacentiis ad se pertinentes, te herede mea habere uolo.

11. Et in ipsa ualle maurigennica loco nuncupante[o] fontana,[45] quicquid ibidem presente tempore de parentes nostris uisi sumus habere seu et in nanosces,[46] una cum illos ingenuos de amberto[47] et liberto nostro de alsede[48] nomen orbano, et ingenua nostra nomen rigouera de bognosco,[49] uel quicquid in bregis[50] de alode parentum nostrorum quem austrualdus in beneficio habet, te superscripta ęc-clesia sancto petro heres mea habere uolo, ac iubeo.

fol. 42r 12. Pro modo simile quicquid de domna siagria in ipsa ualle mau/rigennica conquesiuimus, misiottano,[51] obliciacis,[52] mago,[53] colonica in albiadis,[54] in

---

[41] Unknown location in the valley of Dubbione.

[42] Saint-Jean-de-Maurienne, Savoie.

[43] *Pignora* of Saint Pancreatus, the Roman martyr, were brought from Rome to Marseille in 590 by Agiulfus, the deacon of Gregory of Tours. See *Liber in Gloria Martyrum,* 82, *MGH SSRM* I, p. 544, and *Historia Francorum* X, 1, *MGH SSRM* I, p. 406. The location is now St. Pancrase, Savoie, Arr. St. Jean de Maurienne, Can. St.-Jean-de-Maurienne.

[44] Possibly Avrieux (Savoie), can. Modane.

[45] There are at least fifteen places named Fontaines in the area. Possibly this one is Fontaines, Savoie, arr. St. Jean de Maurienne, can. St.-Jean-de-Maurienne.

[46] Unknown location.

[47] Villarembert, Savoie, arr. St.-Jean-de-Maurienne, canton St.-Jean-de-Maurienne.

[48] Aussois, Savoie arr. St.-Jean-de-Maurienne, can. Modane.

[49] Possibly Bramans, Savoie, can. Modane.

[50] Brégoz, Savoie, arr. St.-Jean-de-Maurienne, comm. St.-Michel canton St. Michel.

[51] Modane, Savoie, arr. St.-Jean-de-Maurienne, can. Modane.

[52] Unknown location near Modane.

[53] Possibly Les Magnis, Savoie, arr. St.-Jean-de-Maurienne, can. St.-Michel.

[54] Albiez-le-Vieux or Albiez-le-Jeune, Savoie, arr. St.-Jean-de-Mau-rienne, can. St.-Jean-de-Maurienne.

---

[m] Preceding seven words over erasure.

[n] Cipolla suggests emendation to *pratis*.

[o] Cipolla suggests that the third *n* was added by a later hand.

within the borders of the Lombards, at the place called *Bicciatis,* which our parents and we ourselves had.

10. In like manner I want you my heir to have whatever came to us from the allod of our parents or through whatever title just and reasonably and is available to be legitimately ceded in the valley of Maurienne, this is in Maurienne, the house which we exchanged with the church of Maurienne with buildings, farm buildings, assarts, gardens, vineyards, fields or meadows (?) along with the church of Saint Peter which our parents built there, with everything included and everything adjacent which pertains to them; and also the church of Saint Pancrasius belonging to us along with the farm in Aurieux (?) with everything adjacent which pertains to them.

11. And I want and order you, above mentioned church of Saint Peter, my heir, to have in that same valley of Maurienne in the place called Fontaines whatever there at the present time we seem to have from our parents and at *Nanosces,* together with those free persons from Villarmbert and our freedman from Aussois named Orbanus, and our free born woman named Rigovera from Bramans (?), and whatever [came to us] in Brégoz from the allod of our parents which Austrualdus has in benefice.

12. Likewise I want and order you, sacrosanct church, to have whatever I acquired from Lady Siagria in that valley of Maurienne, at Modane, *Obliciacis,*

bausetis,[55] et colonica super bricoscis,[56] et amalicione[57] ubi blancolus[p] uerbicarius manet, et gratauunna,[58] etiam et cętera uocabula[59] cum adiacentiis
earum, te sacrosancta ęcclesia habere uolo ac iubeo.

13. Immoque quicquid in ualle Darentasiense,[60] ex alode parentum nostrorum,
uel quod de siagria ibidem ad nos peruenit, una cum mancipiis, libertis, colonis,
inquilinis, et seruis, te heredem habere uolo, atque precipio.

14. *De gratianopolitano*[61] *pago. SIMILITER*[q] in pago gratianopolitano olonna,[62] quem ad liberta mea nomen sendeberti dedi,[r] uolo ut habeat missoriano,[63]
quem de siagria conquesiui, piniano,[64] et corennum,[65] quem a liberta mea nomen auriliana dedi; ipsas libertas meas cum ipsas res; uolo ut ha/beas ac iubeo.

fol. 42v

15. Seu in arauardo,[66] una cum libertos nostros, magnebertum una cum germano suo columbo, misicasiana,[67] mesatico,[68] cambe,[69] quintiaco,[70] viennatico.[71] Ista omnia supra scripta una cum libertis ac colonis, et seruis, uel
omnes adiacentias suas ad ipsa loca pertinentes in suprascripto pago
gratianopolitano, tu heres mea ut habeas uolo[s] atque discerno.

16. Item quam in pago uiennense[72] maconiano[73] quem de alode parentum

---

[55] Baussent Savoie, arr. St. Jean-de-Maurienne, can. Modane.
[56] Possibly Brigot, Savoie, can. St. Michel-de-Maurienne.
[57] Hermillon, Savoie, arr. and can. St.-Jean-de-Maurienne.
[58] Unknown location near St.-Jean-de-Maurienne.
[59] The translation presumes that the text is correct. One could interpret *et cetera vocabula* as implying that the scribe was unable to read the text from which he was copying at this point, or with Le
Cointe, that the scribe simply omitted here a series of names.
[60] Tarantaise, Savoie, arr. Moutiers-en-Tarantaise.
[61] Grenoble, ch. 1 dép. Isère.
[62] Meylans, Isère, comm. Meylans.
[63] Mizoën, Isère, arr. Grenoble, can. Bourg-d'Oisans.
[64] Biviers, Isère, comm. Biviers.
[65] Corenc, Isère, arr. Grenoble, can. Grenoble.
[66] Allevard, Isère, arr. Grenoble can. Allevard.
[67] Unknown location near Grenoble.
[68] Probably Notre Dame de Mésage Isère, arr. Grenoble, can. Vizille.
[69] Champs, Isère, arr. Grenoble, can. Vizille.
[70] Quincieux, Isère, arr. St.-Marcellin can. Tullins.
[71] Vinay, Isère, arr. St.-Marcellin, can. Vinay.
[72] Viennois, Isère.
[73] Maconin, Isère, can. Chanignieu.

---

[p] Cipolla reads *Blancollus*.
[q] *De Gratianopolitano pago. Similiter* in rubricated capitals.
[r] Over erasure.
[s] *ac* cancelled by first hand.

Les Magnis (?), the farm in Albiez, in Baussent and the farm above Brigot (?) and at Hermillon where our shepherd Blancalus dwells and at *Gratavunna* and the other places with their adjacencies.

13. Moreover I wish and order that you my heir have whatever came to us in the valley of Tarantaise from the allod of our parents or from Siagria along with the slaves, freedpersons, colons, tenants and servants.

14. CONCERNING THE PAGUS OF GRENOBLE Likewise I want and order you to have what I gave to my freedwoman named Sendebertus [I want him/her? to have it] in the pagus of Grenoble at Meglan, at Mizoën what I acquired from Siagria, at Biviers and Corenc what I gave to my freedwoman named Auriliana — these freedpersons with these properties.

15. And I want and set apart you my heir to have in Allevard along with our freedpersons, Magnebertus with his brother Columbus, at *Misicasiana*, at Mésage, at Champs, at Quincieux, at Vinay all the above mentioned together with freed persons and colons and servants and everything adjacent which pertains to them in the above mentioned pagus of Grenoble.

16. Likewise I wish and order that you my heir have in the pagus of Vienne at

meorum nobis obuenit, et quod de siagria conquisiuimus, et colonica in ipso pago viennense,[t] baccoriaco[74] super fluuium carusium,[75] ubi faber noster maiorianus mansit, et filius eius Ramnulfus de blaciaco[76] quem incontra ardulfo per iudicio agnarico[77] patricio euindicauimus. Similiter et in pago uianense,[78] et leudunense,[79] bornaco,[80] basciasco,[81] amblariaco,[82] blaciaco,[83] colo/nica

fol. 43r   seuorio.[84] Ista omnia superscripta, una cum terris, domibus, uineis, campis, pratis, uel cum omne iure earum, ac colonis, seruis, et libertis ad ipsa loca aspicientes, tu heres mea ut habeas[u] atque precipio.

17. Item in pago matascense[85] carnaco,[86] ębasciaco,[87] quem de siagria conquesiuimus, una cum ingenuis, libertis, ac colonis, et seruis, uel omnes adiacentiis ad ipsa loca aspicientes, ut habeas uolo ac iubeo.

18. Similiter et in pago briantino,[88] et aquisiana,[89] et anneuasca,[90] in loca nuncupantes briancione, ualle, una cum libertis ac colonis[v] et seruis annedę,[91] una cum ingenuis, libertis et seruis agracianis,[92] exoratiana,[93] aquisleuas,[94] cum libertis et seruis, uel omnes adiacentias ad se pertinentes, te sacrosancta ęcclesia ut habeas uolo atque precipio.

---

[74] Criau, Isère, can. Chozéau.

[75] The Chéruis or the Bourbre river, Isère, arr. Tour-du-Pin.

[76] Blet, Isère, cne. Porcieu-Amblagnieu.

[77] *Agnaricus patricius* can be identified with the *(Ch)agnericus vir illuster* and *optimus* in the diplomas of Clovis III in 693 (DM 66, LS 23) and Childebert III in 697 (DM 70, LS 27). See Horst Ebling, *Prosopographie der Amtsträger des Merowingerreiches von Chlothar II (613) bis Karl Martel (741)* (Beihefte der Francia 2) (Munich: 1974), XCIX.

[78] Viennois, see 71 above.

[79] Lyonnais, Rhône.

[80] St. Pierre de Bournay, Isère, arr. Vienne, cne. St.-Jean-de-Bournay, can. St.-Jean-de-Bournay.

[81] Baix, Isère can. St. Baudille.

[82] Amblérieu, Isère, arr. Tour-du-Pin, cne. 1a Balme, can. Crémieu.

[83] Balésieux, see above 76.

[84] Saboire, Isère, h. cne. St. Savin.

[85] The Mâconnais, Saône-et-Loire.

[86] Charnay-lès-Mâcon, Saône-et-Loire, arr. and can. Mâcon.

[87] Possibly Passy, Saône-et-Loire, arr. Mâcon, can. St.-Gengoux-le-Royal, or Bassy, cne. St. Gengoux-de-Seissé.

[88] Briançon, ch. 1. dép. Hautes-Alpes.

[89] Valley of the Guisanne, Hautes-Alpes.

[90] Névache, Hautes-Alpes, arr. and can. Briançon.

[91] Unknown location in the pagus of Briançon.

[92] Possibly La Grave, Hautes-Alpes, arr. Briançon.

---

[t] *Viennensis* in margin in first hand.

[u] *uolo* omitted.

[v] Preceding five words over erasure.

Maconin what came to us from the allod of my parents, and what we acquired from Siagria, and the farm in this pagus of Vienne at Criau beyond the river Cheruis, where our smith Maiorianus dwells and his son Ramnulfus from Blet, which we recovered from Ardulfus by the judgement of the *Patricius* Agnaricus. Likewise in the pagus of Vienne, in the Lyonnais, at Bournay, at Baix, at Amblérieu, at Blés, and the farm at Saboire, all the above mentioned together with lands, houses, vineyards, fields, meadows, and with all their own rights and their colons, servants and freedpersons belonging to these places.

17. Likewise I wish and order that you have [our properties] in the pagus of Macon at Charnay, Passy, which we acquired from Siagria, along with the free born persons, the freedpersons and the colons and servants and all the adjacencies belonging to these places.

18. Likewise I wish and order that you, sacrosanct church, have our properties in the pagus of Briançon in the valley of the Guisanne, at Névache, in the places named in the valley of Briançon, along with the freedpersons and colons and slaves and at Anneda together with the free and freedpersons and servants at La Grave (?), at Eysserères (?), at Le Laret (?), with the freedpersons and servants and everything adjacent which pertains to it.

19. Et colonicas infra ipsa ualle briantina, et aquisiana quem de uuidegunde
fol. 43v   conquesiuimus, unde/ bardinus capitolarius est.

20. Similiter et in gerentonnis[95] colonicas de ipsa ratione uuindegundi,[96] quod
ad nos peruenerunt, quem sigualdus libertus noster in benefitio habet; Colonica
quem de muliere gismundo nomen pannutia in ipsa ualle in tercia[97] recepimus,
ubi marius noster uerbecarius in ipsa colonica manet.

21. Similiter curte mea salliaris,[98] alpes, prata, ingenua, uendanum,[99] mullinaricus,[100] uuilla uitole.[101] Ista omnia suprascripta una cum libertis, ac colonis,
seruis uel omnes adiacentias earum ad ipsa loca aspicientes, tu heres mea ut
habeas uolo ac iubeo.

22. Et colonicas in ualle gerentonica,[102] et in ralis,[103] quem ad libertos meos
quem theudoaldo et honorio dedi, ut ipsi et infantes ipsorum habeant, et ad
fol. 44r   heredem meam sacrosancta ęcclesia aspiciant. Ista omnia supe/rius comprehensa, una cum adiunctis adiacentiisque suis, campis, pratis, pascuis, siluis, alpibus,
montibus, riuis, aquarumue decursibus, accisque omnibus, cum omnem iure uel
terminum earum, tu sacrosancta ęcclesia heres mea ut habeas uolo ac iubeo.

23. Similiter libertus nostros in ualle aquisiana,[104] qui ad parentes nostros aspexerunt, seu et in ipso pago brigantino commanere uidentur, unde uitalis
capitularius est ad memorata ęcclesia heredem meam ut aspiciant, et inpen-
sionem faciant, uolo ac iubeo.

24. Emmo quem[w] in pago ebredunense[105] et ualle occense[106] brintico[107] por-

---

[93] Possibly Eysserères, Hautes-Alpes, cne. Gap.
[94] Possibly Le Lauzet or Le Laret, Hautes-Alpes, arr. Briançon, can. Monestier.
[95] Vallouise on the banks of the Gironde, Hautes-Alpes, arr. Briançon, can. Largentière.
[96] *De ipsa ratione Vuindegundi* presumably refers to the Vuidegunda of par. 19. *Ratio* may here
mean testament.
[97] Unknown location near Briançon.
[98] La Salle, Hautes-Alpes, arr. Briançon, can. Monestier, or the pass of the Sellar, cne. Vallouise.
[99] Le Veyer, Hautes-Alpes, arr. Briançon, can. Monestier.
[100] Molines-en-Queyras, Hautes-Alpes, arr. Briançon, can. Aiguilles.
[101] Villevieille, Hautes-Alpes, arr. Briançon, cne. Château-Villevieille, can. Aiguilles.
[102] The Gironde.
[103] Possibly Realon, Hautes-Alpes.
[104] Valley of the Guisanne.
[105] Pagus of Embrun, Hautes-Alpes, ch. 1. arr. Embrun.
[106] Ubayette valley.
[107] Unknown location in the valley of the Ubayette.

---

[w] Cipolla suggested correcting to *emmoque*.

19. And I wish and order you, my heir, that you have the farms within this valley of Briançon and that of the Guisanne which we acquired from Widegunda, from which place Bardinus is the revenue collector.

20. Likewise, in the valley of the Gironde the farms which came to us from the will of Widegunda itself, which our freedman Sigualdus has in benefice; the farm which we received from the wife of Gismundus named Pannutia in this same valley at *Tercia* where dwells our shepherd Marius.

21. Likewise my estate at La Salle, with its alpine pasturages, meadows, freeborn, and at Le Veyer (?), Molines-en-Queyras, and Villevieille. I want you to have all this along with the freedpersons, and colons, servants and all adjacencies belonging to these places.

22. And I want and order you, sacrosanct church my heir, to have the farms in the valley of Gironde and in Realon which I gave to my freedmen Theudoaldus and Honorius, so that they and their children might have them and that they might belong to my heir the sacrosanct church. I wish and order that you sacrosanct church my heir to have all of the above included together with the attachments and adjacencies, fields, meadows, pastures, forests, alpine pasturages, mountains, brooks and water courses and all with all of their rights and boundaries.

23. Likewise I wish and order that our freedpersons in the valley of the Guisanne who belonged to our parents and who are seen to dwell in the pagus of Briançon where Vitalis is revenue collector should belong to the above mentioned church my heir and should make their payments to it.

24. Moreover I wish and order that you have our portions in the pagus of Em-

tiones nostras quem de uualdeberto presbitero et de rigaberga conquisiuimus, et
de proprio alode meo, et quod de parente mea godane ad me peruenit, et in ipsa

fol. 44v   ualle moccense quem de siagria conquisiuimus, una cum alpes, et quem de/
dodone et godane ad nos peruenit, seu et quod domno Vualdeberto episcopo et
de Riguberga ibidem conquisiuimus. Et colonica ubi dicitur albariosco,[108] quem
marcianus seruos noster habet, quem de[x] dodone parente meo in ipso pago ebredunense ad me peruenit. Necnon et colonicas nostras in pago rigomagense[109]
quem baronta libertus noster in benefitium habet, et liberto meo ipsum baron-
tane, una apud solia[110] quem ei dedimus, ut ad te heres meam ipse baronta aspicere debeat, uolo ac iubeo.

25. Item in ipsum pago ebredunense, colonicas in boresio,[111] quem sauina in
benefitio habet. Rodis[112] ubi uerbicarius noster nomen laurentius manet. Colonicas in uelentio,[113] quem per preceptionem dominica de ratione riculfu et
germano suo rodbaldo ad nos peruenit.[114] Omnia et ex omnibus, quicquid in ip-

fol. 45r   sum pago ebredunense,/ seu et in valle moccense, et rigomagense, tam de con-
questo quam de alode parentum nostrorum, nobis in ipsus pagos obuenit aduenit[y] ad integrum, una cum alpes, tibi suprascripta heres meam sacrosancta ęcclesia habere uolo ac iubeo.

26. Simile namque modo in pago uuapencense,[115] corte mea talarno,[116] una
cum libertus nostros sicualdo cum sorores suas, et infantes earum maximo cum
uxore[z] sua et infantes eorum calaico,[117] una cum libertus nostros et allionicos[118]
quem de uuidegunde conquisiuimus, et liberti nostri in ipsum allionicus commanere uidentur. Marius cum germanos suos, et libertus nostros in uenauella,[119]

---

[108] Baratier, Hautes-Alpes, arr. and can. Embrun, or cne. Orcierès.

[109] Pagus in the Ubaye from Jausiers to Lauzet. See Guy Barruol, *Les peuples préromains du sud-est de la Gaule: Etude de géographie historique (Revue archéologique de Narbonnaise,* Suppléments I) (Paris: 1969), pp. 347–357.

[110] Probably Mont-Soleil, Hautes-Alpes, arr. Embrun, can. Chorges, cne. Rousset.

[111] Unknown location near Embrun.

[112] Unknown location near Embrun.

[113] Unknown location near Embrun.

[114] See below, chapter five, p. 141–43.

[115] Pagus of Gap. Hautes-Alpes, ch. 1, arr. and can. Gap.

[116] Tallard, Hautes-Alpes, arr. Gap. can. Tallard.

[117] Possibly Le Caire, Alpes-de-Haute-Provence, arr. Sisteron, can. La Motte-du-Caire.

[118] Unknown location near Sisteron?

[119] Possibly Vaumeilh, Alpes-de-Haute-Provence, arr. Sisteron, can. La Motte-du-Caire.

---

[x] Previous two words in first hand over erasure.

[y] *Aduenit* scribal error?

[z] Over erasure but in first hand.

brun and in the valley of the Ubayette, at *Brinticum,* which we acquired from the priest Waldebertus and from Rigaberga and from my own allod which devolved to me from my kinswoman Goda and whatever we acquired from Siagria in this valley of the Ubayette together with the alps, and what came to us from Dodo and Goda and what we acquired from lord Bishop Waldebertus and from Riguberga here, and the farm at the place called Baratier which our servant Marcianus has which came to me from my kinsman Dodo in this pagus of Embrun and also our farms in the pagus of Ubaye, which our freedman Baronta has in benefice, and what we gave to our freedman Baronta at Mont Soleil (?), that he should belong to you my heir.

25. Likewise I wish and order you, above mentioned heir, sacrosanct church, to have in this same pagus of Embrun the farms in *Boresium* which Savina has in benefice, at *Rodis* where our shepherd named Laurentius dwells, the farms in *Velentium* which came to us through royal precept from the affair of Riculfus and his brother Rodbaldus: all and whatever part of it in this *pagus* of Embrun and in the valley of the Ubayette and in the pagus of Ubaye, which devolved to us not so much by acquisition as from the allod of our parents, together with the alpine pasturages.

26. Similarily I wish and order you, sacrosanct church, that you have in the pagus of Gap my estate at Tallard along with our freedman Sicualdus with his sisters and children, with Maximus and his wife and their children, [our property] at Le Caire (?) together with our freedpersons and at *Allonicum* that which we acquired from Widegunda; and our freedpersons who are seen to dwell in

hidebertum cum uxore sua, et infantes eorum quem de uuidegunde ad nos peruenerunt. Kalares[120] quem de ipsa uuidegunde conquisiuimus, matarellos libertus noster manet. In colonica dominicale/ et extra sunt terras et uineas dominicales.[aa] Ista omnia supra scripta, una cum libertis ac colonis et seruis, una cum adiunctis adiacentiisque suis, ad ipsa loca pertinentes, te sacrosancta ęcclesia ut habeas uolo ac iubeo.

fol. 45v

27. Et dono liberto meo ad ipsa ęcclesia nomen amalberto, qui habet uxore filia ipsius mattalello,[bb] quem ego manumisi, et ipsum dua mancipia dedi ad casa uuapencense,[121] his nominibus rusticiu et lupolina. Itemque et in ipsum pago uuapenicense altana,[122] quem de alode parentum meorum habeo, curenno,[123] galisco,[124] ancilla,[125] quem genitor meus de persa conquisiuit, et illas terras ibidem in campania, cum illa alpe cassauda,[126] quem de lauarnosco ibidem habemus, ipsas terras usque ad summa mancipia quem siagria conquisiuimus. Ista omnia suprascripta, una cum/ campis, pratis, siluis pascuis, alpibus adiacentibusque suis ad ipsa loca pertinentis, tu sacrosancta ęcclesia habeas uolo ac iubeo.

fol. 46r

28. Simile namque modo, in ipso pago uuapenicense corte mea opaga[127] cum omnis appenditiis suas ad se pertinentes, quem alode parentum meorum habeo, apud colonica quem de uenatore auunculus meus domnos semforianus episcopus conquisiui, tu heres mea ut habeas uolo ac iubeo.

29. Colonica subtus ripas[128] quem ad libertum meum nomen bertarii dedimus, infantes sui habeant uolo ac iubeo, et ipsi ad herede mea aspicere debeant.

30. Bonis[129] crauiosco[130] tu heres mea sacrosancta ecclesia sancti petri monasterii noualicius, ut habeas uolo ac iubeo.

---

[120] La Motte-du-Caire, Alpes-de-Haute-Provence, arr. Sisteron, can. La Motte-du-Caire.
[121] The text appears corrupt at this point.
[121] Gap, Hautes-Alpes, Ch. 1 arr. and can. Gap.
[122] Autannes, Drôme, arr. Nyon, cne. Ancelle.
[123] Curnier, Drôme, arr. and can. Nyons.
[124] Unknown location.
[125] Ancelle, Hautes-Alpes, arr. Gap, can. Saint-Bonnet.
[126] Montagne des Casses de Faudon, Hautes-Alpes, arr. Gap, can. Saint-Bonnet-en-Champsaur.
[127] Upaix, Hautes-Alpes, arr. Gap, can. Laragne.
[128] Souribes, Alpes-de-Haute-Provence, arr. Sisteron, can. Rives.
[129] Cipolla and Lancelot took Bonis as a place name and suggested as identification le plan de Boung, rather than understanding it as property at Chardavon.
[130] Possibly Chardavon.

[aa] The text appears corrupt at this point.
[bb] *Mattarello* corrected by first hand.

this Aquielles (?): Marius with his brothers, and our freedman in Vaumeilh (?), Hildebertus with his wife and their children which came to us from Widegunda, and at La-Motte-du-Caire what we acquired from this same Widegunda where our freedman Matarellos dwells. The demesne lands and vineyards are both within and outside the demesne farm. I wish and order you to have all of the above, together with freedmen and colons and servants and with its attachments and adjacencies pertaining to these properties.

27. And I give to this church my freedman Amalbertus by name who has as wife the daughter of the same Mattalellus whom I freed, and two slaves whom I gave to them for the house at Gap, by name Rusticius and Luoplina. Likewise I wish and order you, sacrosanct church, to have in this same pagus of Gap at Autannes that which I have from the allod of my parents at Crurnier, *Galiscum,* at Ancelle which my father acquired from Persa and those lands in that same plain with the alpine pasturage Casses de Faudon which we have from Lavornoscus there, those lands down to the last slaves which we acquired from Siagria: all of the above mentioned, along with fields, meadows, forests pastures, alpine pasturages and adjacencies thereunto pertaining.

28. In like manner, I wish and order you, my heir, that you have in this same pagus of Gap my estate at Upaix with its appendages thereunto pertaining which I have from the allod of my parents next to the farm which my uncle lord Semforianus bishop acquired from Venator.

29. Concerning the farm at Souribes [or, on this side of the river] which we gave to my freedman named Bertarius, I wish and order that his children have it and that they must belong to my heir.

30. I want and order you, my heir sacrosanct church of the monastery of St. Peter at Novalesa, that you have my property at Chardavon (?).

31. Similiter corte mea ualerignaca[131] una cum libertum meum sauino cum
fol. 46v filius suos, et filiis liberti mei/ siseberga magnibertum cum germanus suos et
filius suos, uel alius libertus nostros qui ad ipsa curte aspiciunt, habere uolo ac
iubeo.

32. Roma[132] una cum adpendiciis earum et alpes preter quem ad libertus meos
infantes aldefredo et godoberti in ipsa roma dedimus, uolo ut habeant, et ipsi ad
heredem meam aspiciant. Laquatico[133] una cum appenditiis suas,[cc] ad ipsa loca
pertinentes, et quod a liberta mea dumnulina quem commutaui;[dd] Dedi in ipsum
laquatico uolo ut habeat, et ad heredem meam sacrosancta ęcclesia aspiciat. Et
terras in esturbatina[134] quem de boneualo conquisiui, et ad suprascripta liberta
mea nomen sendeberti dedi, uolo ut habeat et ad heredem meam aspiciat. Colonicas in taraone[135] quem de ricuberga conquisiuimus, et terras in crariis,[136] et
fol. 47r libertus nostros maroaldo et uxore sua, uel fi/liis eorum, quem genitrix mea
Rustica de pago geneuense[137] fecit uenire, et super ipsa terra ipsus mansurus
fecit. Terra et mancipia in seuelis[138] quem de auolo presbitero et de freberga
femina auunculos noster domnus senforianus conquisiuit. Et libertos nostros in
artonosco[139] filius uictore, et uere, iohannis iustebertus, paulos, et uerissimus,
iustina, et bertildes, ipsa terra et mancipia in seuelis in benefitio habent, tu heres
mea sacrosancta ęcclesia sancti Petri noualitius monasterii, ut habeas uolo ac
iubeo.

33. Capannas[140] quem ad liberta mea nomen superscripte berteldi, dedi, uolo ut
habeat, et ad heredem mea aspiciat. Vobridio[141] quem de mauro conquisiui, et
ad liberta mea superscripte nomen iustini dedi, quem dadinus habet, uolo ut
fol. 47v habeat, et ad heredem meam/ aspiciat. Colonica utronno[142] ex alode parentum

---

[131] Valernes, Alpes-de-Haute-Provence can. La Motte.
[132] Romette, Alpes-de-Haute-Provence, cne. Gap.
[133] Eygalayes? Drôme, arr. Nyons, can. Séderon, or Eyguians, Hautes Alpes, can. Larague.
[134] Possibly Durbon Hautes-Alpes, arr. Gap. cne. St.-Julien-en-Beauchêne can. Aspres-sur-Buëch.
[135] Saint-Jean, Alpes-de-Haute-Provence, cne. Volonne.
[136] Creyers, Drôme, arr. Die can. Châtillon-en-Diois, cne. Treschenu-Creyers.
[137] Le Génevois, in part the canton of Swiss Geneva, in part Haute-Savoie.
[138] Savel, Drôme, can. Roman et Sauel.
[139] Possibly Laragne. Hautes-Alpes, arr. Gap, can. Laragne.
[140] Unknown location.
[141] Ubrieux, Drôme, arr. Nyons, cne. Buis-les-Baronnies.
[142] Possibly Vitrolles. Hautes-Alpes, arr. Gap, can. Barcellonnette.

[cc] Final *s* over erasure.
[dd] Cipolla reads *au*.

31. Likewise I want and order you to have my estate at Valernes with my freedman Savinus and his sons and the sons of my freedwoman Siseberga, Magnibertus with his brothers and his sons and our other freedmen who belong to this estate.

32. I wish and order that you my heir sacrosanct church of St. Peter of the monastery at Novalesa that you have: at Romette my property together with its appendices and alpine pasturages except that which we gave to our freedman and I wish that his children Aldefredus and Godobertus have it and that they belong to my heir; at Eygalayes (?) my property together with its appendices pertaining to this property and which I gave my freedwoman Dumnulina whom I freed in this same Eygalayes (?), and I wish that she have it and that she belong to my heir the sacrosanct church; and the lands in Durbon (?) which I acquired from Bonevaldus and which I gave to my above mentioned freedwoman named Sendibertus, and which I wish that she have and that she belong to my heir; and the farms at Saint-Jean which we acquired from Ricuberga and the lands in Creyers; and our freedman Maroaldus and his wife and their sons whom my mother Rustica ordered to come from the pagus of Geneva and whom she ordered to dwell on this same land; the lands and slaves in Savel which my uncle Lord Semforianus acquired from the priest Avolus and the woman Freberga; and our freedpersons in Laragnel (?) the son of Victor and Vera, John, Iustebertus, Paul and Verissimus, Iustina and Bertildes, who have this land and slaves in Savel in benefice.

33. I wish and order that you my heir might have: At *Capannae* that which I gave to my freedwoman the above mentioned Berteldis, I wish that she have it and that she belong to my heir; At Ubrieux what I acquired from Maurus and gave to my above mentioned freedman named Iustinus, which Dadinus has, I

meorum glasia,[143] pentus[144] bullone,[145] muccunaua[146] bladonis,[147] tu heres mea ut habeas uolo ac iubeo.

34. Similiter et res illas maurouila,[148] rodanone,[149] una cum adiacentias earum, uel quicquid de parentes nostros dodone, et godane nobis ibidem obuenit, et res illas quem de gondoberto conquisiuimus, quem marabertus in benefitio habet, et illas res quem de escussario conquisiuimus, una cum mancipiis, terris, uel omnes adiacentias ad ipsa loca aspicientes. Ista omnia suprascripta te sacrosancta ęcclesia domni petri heredem meam habere uolo atque precipio.

35. In cronno[150] luciano,[151] ex alode parentum meorum, et in latiomaus[152] ibi mora ancilla nostra manet, quod de genitrice nostra Rustica michi obuenit. Col-

fol. 48r onicas in gradosa[153] quem ministe/rialis noster baio in benefitio habuit, tu heres meam ut habeas uolo ac iubeo.

36. Quonaone[154] in pago uasense,[155] una cum ingenuis, quem de uuidegunde conquisiuimus. Doliana[156] in pago uendascino,[157] quem de ipsa uuidegunde ad nos peruenit, et superscripti liberti mei, iustini, et dadino dedimus, uolo ut habeant, et ad heredem meam sacrosancta ęcclesia aspiciant. In pago siges-terico,[158] uineas et terras in planciano,[159] quem de parente nostro uuandalberto abbate conquisiuimus. Et in massilia[160] res nostras proprias casas, et ortiles, quem de auunculo meo dodone michi obuenit, et de auia nostra dodina. Simili-ter ad pero,[161] casas et ortiles, qui michi de parente mea godane obuenit, et cam-

---

[143] Glaise, Hautes-Alpes, arr. Gap, comm. and can. Veynes.
[144] Unknown location, possibly to be read with Bullone as one location.
[145] Ballons, Drôme, arr. Nyons, can. Séderon.
[146] Possibly in the valley of the Ubaye.
[147] Possibly on the River Bleone.
[148] Méreuil, Hautes-Alpes, arr. Gap, can. Serres.
[149] Rosans, Hautes-Alpes, arr. Gap, can. Rosans.
[150] Read by Marion as one location, Cronnum Locianae [sic]; Cipolla suggests that the locations are distinct although punctuation favors Marion's estimation.
[151] Unknown location near Gap?
[152] Laye? Hautes-Alpes, arr. Gap. can. Saint-Bonnet-en-Champsaur.
[153] Possible Gresse, Drôme, arr. Nyons, cne. Mévouillon, can. Séderon.
[154] Possibly Cairanne, Vaucluse, arr. Orange, can. Vaison.
[155] Vaison, Vaucluse, arr. Orange, can. Vaison.
[156] Daulan or Dolan? Vaucluse, comm. Avignon.
[157] The Venaissin, Vaucluse and Alpes-de-Haute-Provence.
[158] Sisteron, Alpes-de-haute-Provence ch. l. arr. Sisteron.
[159] Plaisians, Drôme, arr. Nyons, can. Buis.
[160] Marseille, ch. 1. dép. Bouches-du-Rhône.
[161] Unknown location near Marseille.

wish that he have it and that she belong to my heir; the farm at Vitrolles (?) from the allod of my parents in Glaise, in *Pentus,* in Ballons, in *Muccunava,* in *Bladonis.*

34. Likewise I wish and order that you, sacrosanct church of the lord Peter my heir, have those things at Méreuil, at Rosans together with the adjacencies and whatever there devolved to us from our kin Dodo and Goda and those things which we acquired from Gondobertus which Marabertus has in benefice, and those things which we acquired from Escussarius, together with slaves, lands and all adjacencies belonging to these properties.

35. I wish and order that you my heir have those things in *Cronnum,* at *Lucianum* from the allod of my parents and in Layel (?) where our servant girl Mora dwells which came to me from my mother Rustica; the farms in Gresse (?) which our ministerialis Baio had in benefice.

36. I wish and order that you, my heir have: those things at Cairanne (?) in the pagus of Vaison together with the freeborn persons which we acquired from Widegunda; at Daulan (?) in the pagus of Vendasque what devolved to us from this same Widegunda, and which I gave to my above mentioned freemen, Iustinus and Dadino – I wish that they might have them and that they might belong to my heir the sacrosanct church; in the pagus of Sisteron, the vineyards and lands in Plaisians which we acquired from our kinsman Abbot Wandalbertus; and in Marseille our own properties, houses and gardens which devolved to me

pos et uineas infra ciuitate, et portione nostra in centronis,[162] et ad fontem liso-
fol. 48v   la[163] terras et pascuis, in pago arlatino.[164] Anglarias[165]/ et uiuario[166] portione
nostra, et illa alia quem auunculo meo dodone michi obuenit, tu heres mea
habeas, uolo ac iubeo.

37. Cronia[167] in pago tolonense,[168] una cum libertis ac colonis, et seruis, terris,
uineis, oliuetis, seu et adiacentias ad se aspicientis, te herede mea sacrosancta ęcclesia sancti petri monasterie noualicis, habere uolo, atque discerno.

38. In pago regense[169] uuardacelis,[170] illo proprio nostro, et illa portione quem
de Godane conquisiuimus, una cum colonica in cumbolis,[171] et in pratalioni[172]
qui ad uuardacęlis aspicit, ubi siricarius noster peter mansit, tu heres mea ut
habeas uolo ac iubeo.

39. Salines in uiu[173] in pago arelatense, quem de godane parente nostra ad nos
peruenerunt, et illa portione siagrię, quem de ipsa conquisiuimus, una cum
fol. 49r   arias[ee] et campos, uineis et oliuetis, mancipiis pascuis,/ ibidem et in campo,[174] et
illas salines in alterneto,[175] cattorosco,[176] et in leonio,[177] tam nostra portione
quam et quod de auunculo nostro dodone ibidem conquisiuimus. In pago
diense[178] cassies[179] sibi teptis[180] et portione nostra in bosedone,[181] quem de siag-

---

[162] St.-Tronc, Bouches-du-Rhône, cne. Marseille, village St.-Loup.
[163] Font-Douille, Bouches-du-Rhône, arr. Aix, comm. Pennes, can. Satillieu.
[164] Arles, Bouches-du-Rhône, ch. 1. arr. Arles.
[165] Possibly Eyguières, Bouches-du-Rhône, cnes. Senas and Lamanon.
[166] Unknown location near Arles.
[167] Unknown location near Toulon.
[168] The Toulonnais, Var.
[169] Pagus of Riez, Alpes-de-Haute-Provence, arr. Digne, can. Riez.
[170] Varages, Var. arr. Brignolles, can. Barjols.
[171] Unknown location near Riez.
[172] Unknown location.
[173] Possibly Viougue. Bouches-du-Rhône, cne. Salon.
[174] Unknown location near Arles.
[175] Unknown location near Arles.
[176] Possibly Cadarache, Bouches-du-Rhône.
[177] Possibly Ligagnau. A marsh on the Plan du Bourg, Bouches-du-Rhône, cne. Arles.
[178] The Diois, region of Die, Drôme, ch. 1. arr. Die.
[179] Cassières, Isère, arr. Grenoble, can. Clelles.
[180] Du Cange suggested that *teptis* might be a synonym for sectio, pars, or portio and derived it from
τέμνειν. However, his only example of its use is this occurrence in the *Testamentum. Glossarium
mediae et infinae latinitatis* vol. 8 (Graz: 1954), p. 5. An alternative is to emend *sibi* to *siue* and to
understand Teptis as a place name.
[181] Bezaudun, Drôme, arr. Die, can. Bourdeaux.

[ee] Second over erasure but in first hand.

from my uncle Dodo and from our grandmother Dodina. Likewise at *Perum,* the houses and gardens which devolved to me from my relative Goda, and the fields and vineyards within the city, and our share in St.-Tronc and at the Font-Douille the lands and pastures; and in the pagus of Arles at Eyquières (?) and at *Viuarium* our portion and that which devolved to me from my uncle Dodo.

37. I wish and set aside that you my heir sacrosanct church of the monastery of Saint Peter have (my property) at *Cronia* in the pagus of Toulon together with the freedpersons and colons, and servants, lands, vineyards, olive groves, and the adjacencies belonging to it.

38. I wish and order that you, my heir, might have my property in the pagus of Riez at Varages, both that of our own [allod] and that portion which we acquired from Goda, together with the farms in *Cumbulae* and in *Pratalio* which belong to Varages where our silkworker Peter dwells.

39. I wish and order that you have the salt works in Viouguel (?) in the pagus of Arles which came to us from our kinswoman Goda and that portion of Siagria which we acquired from her together with the unworked fields and fruitful fields, [vineyards, and olive groves, slaves, pastures there and in the field] or in *Campo* and those salt works in *Alternetum,* in Cadarache (?), and in Ligagnau, both our portion and that which we acquired there from our uncle Dodo, in the

ria conquisiuimus, una cum libertis et seruis, uel adpendices suas, et libertum nostro unebertum, et filius suos, quem ex alode de genitore meo habeo, ut habeas uolo ac iubeo.

40. In ambillis[182] ubi gauioaldus seruos noster manet, una cum cultura, quem de domna siagria ad nos peruenit, quem ipse unebertus in benefitio habet, et illa colonica de ratione parenti mei godane, super dederauso in pago diense ubi orbicianus seruos manet, ubi dicitur riaciosco[183] te heredem meam sacrosancta ęcclesia habere uolo ac iubeo.

41. Colonicas in pago attense,[184] in uariates,[185] et colonicas in pago cauel-

fol. 49v lico,[186] attanisco,[187] quossis,[188] pecciano[189]/ torrido[190] qui mihi ex alode genitrici mei Rusticę et auunculo meo dodone obuenit. Ista omnia superscripta, una cum adiunctis adiacentibus suis ad ipsa loca aspicientis, te sacrosancta ęcclesia beati Petri apostoli noualicis monasterii, te heredem meam habere uolo atque precipio.

42. Colonicas in pago diense,[191] ubi dicitur macitha,[192] una cum salines ad uerdone,[193] qui ad lauariosco[194] corte nostra aspexerunt, quam de domna siagria conquisiuimus, te heredem meam habere uolo ac iubeo.

43. Casalis in tenegaudia[195] una cum terris, et pascos in ipso monte, quem de ualeriano genitor meus conquisiuit, te heredem meam sacrosancta ęcclesia domni petri monasterii habere uolo ac iubeo.

44. Et placuit michi in hanc pagina testamentis mei adnecti de alode paren-

fol. 50r torum meorum auiis meis maurino et dodinę quem apud con/subrina mea honorata filia eptolenę amitę mei, pro pectionis titulum inter nos diuisimus, noscitur conuenisset, ut ipsa omnem portionem suam de ipsa facultate presentaliter recipit, et de proprietate nostre quod pro falcidia se nos ipsa uel heredis sui super-

[182] Ambel, Hautes-Alpes, arr. Gap, can. St.-Firmin-en-Valgoldemard.
[183] Roissard, Isère, arr. Grenoble, can. Monesteir-de-Clermont.
[184] Apt, Vaucluse, ch. lieu arr. Apt.
[185] Unknown location near Apt.
[186] Cavaillon, Vaucluse, arr. Avignon, can. Cavaillon.
[187] Marion suggests Althen-des-Paluds, Vaucluse, arr. and can. Carpentras or Lagnes, Vaucluse, arr. Avignon, can. L'Isle. An alternate might be Apt.
[188] Unknown location near Cavaillon.
[189] Unknown location near Cavaillon.
[190] Possibly Les Tourretts, Vaucluse, cne. Apt.
[191] The Diois, see above note 203.
[192] Massette, Isère, cne. St. Guillaume.
[193] The Verdon river, déps. Alpes-de-Haute-Provence, Bouches-du-Rhône.
[194] Lavars, Isère, arr. Grenoble, can. Mens.
[195] Le Than, Isère, cne. Mens.

pagus of Die, at Cassières or at *Teptis* (?) and our share at Bezaudun which we acquired from Siagria, together with the freedpersons and servants and its appendices and our freedman Unebertus and his son(s)? which I have from the allod of my father.

40. I wish and order that you, sacrosanct church my heir, have my property at Ambel where our servant Gavioaldus dwells together with the cultivated lands which devolved to us from Lady Siagria which this Unebertus has in benefice, and that farm from the will of my kinswoman Goda beyond the River Drac in the pagus of Die where our slave Orbicianus dwells, at the place called Roissard.

41. I wish and order you, sacrosanct church of the blessed Apostle Peter of the monastery of Novalesa, have the farms in the pagus of Apt, at *Variates* and the farms in the pagus of Cavillion, at *Attaniscum, Quossis, Peccianum,* Les Tourettes, which came to me from the allod of my mother Rustica and my uncle Dodo: all of this above mentioned together with the appendices adjacent to them belonging to these places.

42. I wish and order that you my heir have those farms in the pagus of Die at the place called Massette together with the salt works at the Verdon which belong to our estate at Lavars which we acquired from Lady Siagria.

43. I wish and order that you my heir, sacrosanct church of the monastery of Lord Peter, to have the cottages in Le Than together with the lands and pastures in this mountain which my father acquired from Valerianus.

44. And it has pleased me to attach in this page of my testament concerning the allod of my kin of my grandparents Maurinus and Dodina, which was in the hands of my cousin Honorata daughter of my aunt Eptolena, which we divided between us according to a pact. It is known that it has been agreed that she herself immediately receive her entire portion of the aforementioned property, and

stites fuerunt, estare aut per lege recipere potuissent eis presentaliter; de proprietatis portione nostrę loca dominata,[ff] quem in pactionis nostrę continetur; et
scripte in falcidia reputata dimisimus, ut nullum quam tempore in postmodo
ipsa nec heredes sui contra hanc testamento meo nec proiesta nostra ambulare
nec refragare debeant. Quod si fecerint; pęna quod in pectionis[gg] nostrę per
commune consensum continet incurrant; et quod repitent, euendicare non
ualeaNT.[hh]

45. Et uolo ut omnis liberti nostri, quos quas parentes nostri fecerunt liberos, et
fol. 50v   nos/ postea fecimus, ut ad ipsam heredem meam[ii] ęcclesiam sancto petro aspiciant, et obsequium et impensionem sicut ad parentes nostros et nobis iuxta
legis ordine debent impendere.[196] Ita et in antia ad ipsa herede meam sancto
petro noualicis monasterii constructa, facere debeant. Quod si contumacis, aut
ingrati ad heredem meam suprascripta ęcclesia steterint, et reuellare uoluerint,
tunc liceat agentes herede meam eos cum pietatis ordine cohercere. Vt ipsi impensionem faciant, sicut ad parentes nostros et nos fecerunt. Quod si ingrati et
rebelli prestiterint, tunc quod lex de ingratis et contumacis, libertis continet, cum
iudice interpellatione et distractione[jj] ad herede mea exsoluant, et ad ipsa reuer-
tant, uolo ac iubeo.[197]

46. Et dono[kk] superscripto pago gratianopolitano liberta mea sanctitildę, qui
fol. 51r   manet in pino,[198] cum filius suos sicufre/do, et sigirico, sicumare et germanos
eorum helene, et sigilinę, et in ipsum pago gratiapolitano donamus liberto nostro nomen gondoberto eunucu et germanas suas cum omni rem quem uuidegun-
das ad parentes suos in pagnanum[199] per cessione dedit, uolo ut habeant, et ad
herede mea aspiciant.
47. Donamus liberta nostra droctesenda cum filius suos, et habet ipsa liberta

---

[196] See below pp. 95–96.
[197] Cod. lib. VI, vii, 2, 3. De libertis et eorum liberis.
[198] La-Tour-du-Pin, Isère, ch. 1. arr. La-Tour-du-Pin.
[199] Unknown location near Grenoble.

[ff] Cipolla suggests *denominata.*
[gg] The *e* and the final *i* are in first hand over erasures.
[hh] NT capitas in Ms.
[ii] *Heredem meam* in first hand over erasure.
[jj] Cipolla reads *distructione,* Le Cointe emends to *districtione.*
[kk] *In* omitted.

of my property, what according to the [*lex*] *Falcidia* she herself or whatever survivors there were of her could have received by law. That is, the places named from my portion of the property which is contained in the pact and is calculated in writing according to the [*lex*] *Falcidia,* we give immediately to them so that at no time afterwards she herself or her heirs should circumvent or resist this my testament or our designs. If they should do it let them incur the penalty which is contained in our agreement by mutual consent and what they seek let them not be able to achieve.

45. And I wish that all of our freedpersons, all those whom our parents made free and those we made [free] afterwards should belong to my heir the church of Saint Peter and they should pay obedience and duties just as to our parents and to us in conformity with the order of the law. Thus as before they ought to do for this my heir the church of Saint Peter constructed for the monastery at Novalesa. If they should persist as insolent or ungrateful to my heir the above mentioned church, and if they should wish to revolt, then let it be permitted to the agents of my heir to restrain them by the rule of duty, so that they might make these payments an they had made them to our parents and to us. But if they should still persist as ungrateful and rebellious then as the law of ungrateful and contumacious freedmen stipulates, I wish and order that with the intervention and coërcion of a judge let them pay my heir and let them revert to my heir in servitude.

46. And I give in the above mentioned pagus of Grenoble my freedwoman Sanctitilda who dwells in La-Tour-du-Pin with her sons Sicufredus, and Sigiricus and Sicumarus and their sisters Helena and Sigilina, in this pagus of Grenoble we give to our freedman named Gondobertus the eunuch and his brothers with all the things which Widegundas gave to his [our?] parents in *Paganum* by formal transferral of title – I wish that they have them and that they belong to my heir.

47. We give to our freedwoman Droctosenda with her sons, who has a freeborn

nostra homo ingenuus, nomen radbertus, dedimus celseberto; Colonica in glisione[200] prope de arcia,[201] uolo ut habeat, et ad herede mea aspiciat.

48. Colonicas, terras et uineas dominicales, quem iocos lerator[ll] noster in cessione, et opilonicus usque nunc in benefitium[mm] habuit, quem de sicuberga[nn] conquisiuimus, uolo ut ipse per testamento nostrum libertus fiat, et ipsas colonicas sub nomen libertinitatis habeat, et ad heredem meam sicut liberti nostri

fol. 51v   aspiciunt; Ita et ipse sic facere debeat. Et si ipse de ipso mo/nasterio sicut libertus se abstrahere uoluerit, in pristinu seruitio reuertatur, et ipsas colonicas, et ipsi monachi ad parte herede meam sancti petri monasterii respiciant.

49. Et illud michi in hunc testamento meum addere placut,[oo] ut dum et domnos patrunus[pp] meus semforianus condam episcopatum uuapencense in suam habuit gubernatione, et deuotione suę, ut medietate de rogationes[202] portionis ipsius, in ualle segucia, ad ipsa ęcclesia per sua esturmenta delegare uoluit, et diebus uitę suę tutillam meam in suam habuit recepta potestate, et apud nos nullam deduxit ratione, et dum per lege nulla exinde potuit delegare. Et facultates nostras indiuisas remanserunt, ipse carta donationis de medietate locello nostro commune de rogationes in ualle sigusina ad iam dicta ęcclesia sanctę marię uuapensense

fol. 52r   quod scripserat. Dum et lex hoc/ prohibit,[qq] et postea ipse de ipso onos[rr] episcopato a malis hominibus eiectus fuit, et ipsa portio de rogationis ad ipsa ęcclesia uuapencense numquam fuit tradita, nec recepta. Ideoque nos tam pro animę nostrę remedio, quam et pro ipsius suprascriptus patruum nostrum communi ratione domno senforiano, donamus ad ipsa ęcclesia sancte marię uuapencense locella nostra in pago regense, nuncupantes[ss] braccio,[203] una cum uoconcio,[204] quem de parente nostra godane ad nos peruenit, una cum libertis ac colanis, et seruis, domibus, ędifitiis, terris, uineis, campis, pratis, pascuis, siluis.

---

[200] Glysin, Isère, cne. Pinsot.

[201] Arces, Isère, arr. and can. Grenoble, cne. St.-Ismier.

[202] Unknown location near Susa.

[203] Bras-d'Asse, Alpes-de-Haute-Provence, arr. Digne, can. Mezel.

[204] Unknown location near Digne.

[ll] Cipolla proposes emendation *leuator*. Prof. Franz Staab has proposed Lyrator, harpist or musician, a suggestion which is particularly appealing given the individual's name, Iocos.

[mm] First *benefitio,* then corrected by first hand.

[nn] Cipolla suggests emendation *Ricuberga*.

[oo] Cipolla emends to *placuit*.

[pp] Read *patruus*.

[qq] Cipolla emends to *nuncupantes*.

[rr] Space in MS after *onos*.

[ss] Cipolla reads *nuncupates*.

man named Radbertus as husband and to Celsebertus, the farm in Glysin near Arces — I wish that she (?) have it and that she (?) belong to my heir.

48. Concerning those farms, lands and vineyards in demesne which Iocos our harpist held by formal transfer of title and which Opilonicus had until now in benefice, which we acquired from Sicuberga, I wish that by this our testament he might be a freedman and that he have these farms under the condition of a freedman and that as our freedmen belong to my heirs thus should he do. And if he should wish to remove himself from this monastery as a freedman let him fall back into his original servitude and let these farms and these monks [?] belong to the share of my heir the monastery of Saint Peter [and to these monks?].

49. And it has pleased me to add in this my testament, that when my deceased Lord Uncle Semforianus had the bishopric of Gap in his governance, out of his devotion he wished to grant by written document one half of the share of *Rogationes* in the valley of Susa to this same church. During his life he had received my wardship in his power. However, since he had not drawn up a reckoning of our respective accounts and hence by law was not able to delegate anything, and our properties remained undivided, this charter of donation of the half of our common little property of *Rogationes* in the valley of Susa to the above mentioned church of Saint Mary of Gap, which he wrote [was invalid,] since law prohibited it and afterwards he was expelled from his episcopal charge by evil men. Thus this share of *Rogationes* was never transferred to this church of Gap nor was it received [by it]. Hence, we, as much for the salvation of our soul as for the common cause of our above mentioned uncle Lord Senforianus give to this church of Saint Mary of Gap the little place in the pagus of Riez called Bras d'Asse together with *Voconcium* which devolved to us from our kinswoman Goda, along with the freedpersons and colons and servants, houses,

Omnia et ex omnibus quicquid infra ipsum pago regense, ad ipsum bractio, et uocontio aspicere uidetur, preter quod superius scriptum est, quod dum heredem meam ęcclesia sancti petri dedi, ut tam pro animę nostrę remedie ut di-

fol. 52v ximus, quam et pro deuotione patruum/ nostrorum domno senforiano in luminaribus ipsius ęcclesię, et pro substantia pauperorum, perhennis temporibus profitiat, in augmentis; uolo ac iubeo.

50. Emmoquę donamus ad ipsa ęcclesia sanctę marię uuapencense locella nostra in ipso pago uuapencense, nucupante ruarmo,[205] ambillis in taraone,[206] una cum libertis ad ipsa loca aspicientes. In pago cauellico memiana,[207] quem domnos et auuos noster Marro[208] condam de domno crammelino[209] episcopo conquisiuit. De ista omnia suprascripta, dum adhuc uixero usum et fructum michi reseruo; post obitum quidem meum, quandoquidem deus uoluerit, agentes ęcclesię sanctę marię uuapencense, ipsa loca recipiant, et habeant, uolo ac iubeo.

51. Simile modo donamus ad ęcclesia sancti iohannis baptistę maurogenna in luminaribus ipsius sancti loce, et pro animę nostrę remedio, loca nucupantis in

fol. 53r pago gratianopolitano crispiaco,[210] quem de siagria conquisiuimus./Abrici[211] colonica in pago uiennense, quem de ipsa siagria ad nos peruenit, macciano,[212] quem de alode parentum[tt] habeo, et in commutationis causę ad ipsa casa maurogennica pro colonicas in uenauis,[213] in ualle segusina dedimus. Vircarias in malenciano,[214] quem ad filio bertelino seruo sancti iohanni pro ingenuitatis dedimus. Ipsa uero loca, una cum colonis, ac colanis, seruis, libertis in ipsa loca commanentes, cum omnes adiacentias ad se pertinentes, in luminaribus ipsius ęcclesię sancto iohanne maurogennica, et pro substantia pauperorum uolo ut habeat, et proficiat in augmentis.

---

[205] Unknown location near Gap.

[206] Ambel-en-Trièves, Isère, arr. Grenoble, Can. Corps.

[207] St. Antoine-de-Ménémènès, Vaucluse, cne. Isle-sur-Sorgue.

[208] Cipolla supposes without reason that the name should read *Mauro* and refer to Abbo's maternal grandfather.

[209] Possibly Bishop Chramnelenus of Embrun deposed in 677 by Theuderic III. See below, Chapter IV, pp. 103–104.

[210] Charpieux. Isère, arr. Grenoble, cne. St.-Pierre-d'Allevard, can. Allevard.

[211] Les Abrets, Isère, can. Pont-de-Beauvoisin.

[212] Massieu, Isère.

[213] Venaux, Piemonte, prov. Torino.

[214] Unknown location near St.-Jean de-Maurienne.

[tt] Cipolla suggests addition of *meorum*.

buildings, lands vineyards, fields, meadows, pastures, forests and all of whatever is seen to depend in this pagus of Riez at this Bras d'Asse and *Voconcium,* except that which was written above, which I gave to my heir the church of Saint Peter, both for the salvation of our soul, as we have said, and for the devotion of our uncle Lord Semforianus, for the lighting of the Church and for the fund of the poor, so that it might be profitable in increase throughout time. This I wish and order.

50. Moreover we give to this church of Saint Mary at Gap our little places in this pagus of Gap called *Ruarmum,* and Ambel-en-Trèves together with the freedpersons belonging to these places, and in the pagus of Cavaillon at St. Antoine-de-Ménémènès that which our late lord and grandfather Marro acquired from Lord Bishop Crammelinus. I reserve for myself the usufruct of all this above mentioned as long as I live, and after my death, whenever God wills that to be, I wish and order that the agents of the Church of Saint Mary of Gap receive and have these places.

51. In like manner we give to the church of Saint John the Baptist at Maurienne for the lighting of this holy place and for the salvation of our soul the places in the pagus of Grenoble called Charpieux which we acquired from Siagria, the farm of les Abrets in the pagus of Vienne, which devolved from this same Siagria to us, at Massieu which I have from the allod of my parents and which we gave in exchange to this house of Maurienne for farms in Venaux in the valley of Susa. I give to the same church of Saint John the sheep folds in *Malencianum* which we gave to the son of Bertelinus servant of Saint John for his charter of emancipation. I wish that this church have and profit from the increase of this place along with the colons, tenants, servants and freedpersons continuously living in this place, with all adjacencies thereunto pertaining, for the lighting of this church of Saint John of Maurienne and for the fund of the poor.

52. Donauimus dulcissime nostrę uirgilie, loca nucupantis in ipso pago uuapencense laciomaus,[215] et licentiaco,[216uu] cassaniola,[217] ciconiola,[218] quem de domno uualdeberto episcopo,[219] et de domna siagria, et uuidegundę, et deo

fol. 53v   sacrata ricuberta femina in ipsa loca conquisiuimus. Similiter et/ in pago segisterico lauariosco,[220] una cum omnis adiacentias suas, quanto infra ipso pago sigisterico ad ipsa corte aspicere uidentur, quem de domna siagria ad nos peruenit. Etiam et in pago regense cinicino,[221] quem de domno uualdeberto ad nos peruenit in ipsa uero loca, una cum ingenuis, libertis, ac colanis et seruis, terris, domibus, edificiis, mancipiis, campis, pratis, pascuis, siluis, uineis, cum omnis adiacentias earum ad se pertinentes, ut habeas uolo, propter quod in ipsos pagos sigisterico, regense, et uuapencense, ad heredem meam ęcclesia sancto petro monasterii noualicis dedimus ut habeat, uolo ac iubeo.

53. Et placuit michi in hunc testamentum meum plenissima uoluntatem scribere, dum et domnos et in christo pater noster uualchuni episcopus,[222] ab initio

fol. 54r   incoationis opere/ fundamentum ęcclesię sancto petro monasterię noualicis, heredem meam posuit, et usque ad culminis consumationis fabrica perduxit: et in omne opere ędifitiorum adiutor et gubernator stetit. Vt dum ipse aduixerit, sub suo nomine et gubernatione, et nostra commune ipse monasterius sancto petro heredem meam cum omnibus rebus ad ipsum delegandis consistere ualeat. Et quod humanum est quando abbas de ipso monasterio de hac[vv] lucem migrauerit, tunc abbate quem ipse domnos uualchuni episcopus in ipso monasterio elegere uoluerit, ibidem mittat; et ipse abba uel sui monachi taliter agant, dum et

---

[215] Laye, see above, no. 152.

[216] Unknown location near Gap.

[217] Possibly St.-Jean-de-Chassagne. Hautes-Alpes, comm. Gap.

[218] Sigoyer, Hautes-Alpes, arr. Gap can. Tallard.

[219] Possibly the same as the Waldebertus abbas who appears elsewhere in the testament. The different title may result from the variety of documents used to compile the list of properties in the testament. Acquisitions from Waldebertus prior to his elevation to the episcopacy (of Arles?) would thus have been copied into the testament with his title at the time he sold or transferred the property to Abbo.

[220] Lavars, see above, note 194.

[221] Possibly Senez, Alpes-de-Haute-Provence, arr. Castellane, can. Senez.

[222] Walchunus' see has been variously located as Embrun, St.-Jean-de-Maurienne, Torino, and even Ivrea. See Cipolla, I, pp. 7–8 note 1. Cipolla opted for Embrun, a suggestion which seems all the more reasonable in light of the close connections between the family of Abbo and other bishops of Embrun. See below, chapter IV, pp. 103–104.

[uu] Corrected by later hand to *Lecentiaco*.

[vv] *hoc* corrected in first hand to hac.

52. We have given to our very dear Virgilia: the places in this pagus of Gap called Laye and *Licentiacum,* St.-Jean-de-Chassagne (?), Sigoyer, which we acquired from Lord Bishop Waldebertus and from Lady Siagria and Widegunda and the woman consecrated to God Ricuberta; likewise in the pagus of Sisteron at Lavars together with all its adjacencies, as much as is seen to belong to this estate within this pagus of Sisteron, which devolved to us from Lady Siagria; moreover, in the pagus of Riez at Senez (?), that which devolved to us from Lord Waldebertus. I wish and order that you should have [these properties] in these places, together with the free born persons, freedmen and colons and servants, lands, houses, buildings, slaves, fields, meadows, pastures, forests, and vineyards with everything adjacent which pertains to them except [reading *preter*] those things in these pagi of Sisteron, Riez and Gap which we gave to my heir the church of Saint Peter of the monastery of Novalesa.

53. And it has pleased me in this my testament to write my most complete desire: since our lord and father in Christ Bishop Walchunus undertook from the beginning the hardly begun foundations of the Church of Saint Peter of the monastery of Novalesa my heir, and guided the construction to its final consumation, and stood as helper and director in all the work of construction, then as long as he shall live let this monastery of Saint Peter my heir with all properties made over to it remain under his own name and our common governance. And, as is human, when the abbot of this monastery departs from this light, then let this Lord Bishop Walchunus place here as abbot whom he wishes to choose and let this abbot and his monks conduct themselves, as long as this lord Walchunus

ipse domnos uualchuni aduixerit, qualiter ipse eos spiritualiter monere uoluerit, et licentia non habeat de ipsis rebus aliud faciendi, nisi quod ipse suprascriptos

fol. 54v   domnos uualchuni episcopus pro commune utili/tatem ipsius monasterii eis iusserit. Et ita michi placuit addendo, ut omnis facultas mea quem per hunc testamentum meum uel epistolas ad ipso monasterio delegaui, dum et ego et ipse domnos uualchuni aduixerimus, sicut iam dictum est sub suo nomine et nostrum diebus uitę suę ad profectum iam dicti monasterii consistere ualeat. Et si michi superestis fuerit, diebus uitę suę in sua permaneat potestate. Et si quislibet quod esse non debet de monachis ipsius monasterii contumax aut corruptor fabulis insidiarum contra iam dictum domno uualchuni episcopo estiterit aut rebellare uoluerit, licentia habeat eos iuxta qualitatis opere suę cohercere, et sententia iuxta canonica regula sancti benedicti institutionis iudicare. Et si noluerit se in

fol. 55r   sua castigatione corrigere, et rebellis extiterit,/ licentia habeat eum de ipsum monasterio in sua contumatia eicere.

54. Dono ad suprascripta heredem meam sacrosancta ęcclesię sancti petri monasterii noualicis, terras et uineas, una cum mancipiis in matanatis,[223] quem de alode parentum meorum habeo, quem beroleos in benefitio habuit, uolo ut habeas ac iubeo.

55. Dono fidele meo protadio[224] res illas in pago uuapencense, ubi dicitur semprugnanum[225] cum adpendices suas, quem de agloaldo conquesiuimus, et illa portione quem de maurengo clerico pro sua infidelitate quod nobis mentiuit, et per uerbo dominico conquisiuimus, dum et ipse nobis mentitus fuit, ipsas res palatius nobis cessit uolo ut habeat.[226]

56. Donamus tersię filię honorię liberti nostrę, quem teudaldos de seguciu huxorem habuit, res illas quę fuerunt riculfum filium rodulfum condam, quem pro

fol. 55v   preceptione domno theoderico/ rege,[227] et illuster, uero[ww] domno Karolo,[228] in

---

[223] Region of Matésine, Isère.

[224] The name Protadius appears in the region of the Jura connected with the family of Waldelenus and Chramnelenus (see below, Chapter IV, 179–180) in the persons of the Mayor Protadius (died 604/05) and Bishop Protadius of Besançon in 614. Gérard Moyse, "La Bourgogne septentrionale et particulièrement le diocèse Besançon de la fin du monde antique au seuil de l'âge carolingien (Ve–VIIIe siècles) in *Von der Spätantike zum frühen Mittelalter: Aktuelle Probleme in historischer Sicht,* ed. Joachim Werner and Eugen Ewig *Vorträge und Forschungen* vol. 25 (Sigmaringen: 1979), pp. 476 and 480.

[225] Possibly Savournon, Hautes-Alpes, arr. Gap can. Serres.

[226] On this passage see below, Chapter V, p. 130.

[227] Theuderic IV (721–737).

[228] Charles Martel.

[ww] read *uiro.*

shall live accordingly as he wishes to admonish them spiritually and let him not presume to do with these properties anything except what this above mentioned lord bishop Walchunus orders him to do for the common utility of this monastery. And it has pleased me to add that all my property which I have delegated to this monastery by this my testament or by letters, so long as I and this Lord Walchunus shall live, as has been said, let it remain under his and our responsibility in the days of his life to the improvement of this above mentioned monastery, and if he should survive me, let it remain in his power all the days of his life. And if any (which should not be) of the monks of this monastery should be stubborn or a seducer by lies of trickery against the above named Lord Bishop Walchunus, or should wish to revolt let him have the permission to correct them according to the nature of their action, and to judge them according to the canonical rule of the institute of Saint Benedict. And if he does not wish to improve himself in his correction and should remain in revolt, let him have the permission to eject him in his stubbornness from this monastery.

54. I give to the above mentioned heir the sacrosanct church of Saint Peter of the monastery of Novalesa the lands and vineyards together with the slaves in the Matésine which I have from the allod of my parents which Beroleos had in benefice – I wish and order that you have them.

55. I give to my *fidelis* Protadius those things in the pagus of Gap at the place called Savournon (?) with its appendices which we acquired from Agloaldus, and that portion which we acquired through royal judgment from the cleric Marengus for his infidelity because he lied to us and since he had lied to us the palace ceded these properties to us – I wish that he have them.

56. We give to Tersia daughter of our freedwoman Honoria whom Theudaldus from Segucius had as wife those properties which were of Riculfus son of the deceased Rodulfus which by order of the lord King Theuderic and the illustrious

pago diense, uuapencense, et gratianopolitano conquesiuimus; preter colonicas in pago ebredunense, in uelencio,[229] quem ad monasterio sancto petro herede meam delegauimus, dum et ipse riculfus apud gente sarraceorum ad infidelitatem regni francorum sibi sociauit, et multa mala cum ipsa gentem pagana fecit, uolo ut ipsa tersia ipsas suprascriptas facultatis habere debeat, et uolo ut liberti nostri filii uualane cum illas res quem ipsius uualane dedimus, ad herede meam ęcclesia sancto petro aspiciant.

57. Dono liberta mea ad herede meam ęcclesia sancto petro nomen fredeberga uxore tasculfum, cum nepotes ipsius fredbergę in etone[230] aut in pareliano[231] manere uidentur, ut liberti cam[xx] eorum res ad ipsa ęcclesia aspiciant; uolo ac iubeo.

fol. 56r　58. Et notamini in hanc pagina testamentis/ mei addendum placuit, dum et prouintias iustas[yy] ad gentes serracenorum dissolatas et distructas sunt, et tam liberti nostri, quam et serui et ancillas, utriusque generis, per plura loca uicinorum per necessitate dispersas fuerunt, uolo ut ubicumque adgentes heredem meam monasterii sancto petro noualicis constructum, eos inuenire potuerint, ut licentia habeant in eorum absque cuiuslibet contradictione reuocare dominatione. Et sicut ad parentes nostros et ad nos aspexerunt, ita et ad herede meam ęcclesia sancto petro monasterie noualicis aspicere debeant; uolo ac iubeo.

59. Et uolo ut gislarannus libertus noster et uxor sua, quem de domna siagria ad nos peruenerunt, unam cum colonicas illas quem eis in comario[232] in pago gratianopolitano dedimus, ut ipsas habeant, et ad herede meam monasterio sancto petro noualicis aspicere debeant.

fol. 56v　60. Et illa quę non/ sunt nominata et ad nostro iure pertinet et alicubi non delegauimus, uolo ut ad herede meam perueniant.

61. Et si qua karaxatura, aut litteratura in hanc paginam testamentis mei, reperteque[zz] fuerint; nos eas fieri rogauimus.

62. Dum et non semel sed sepius eum requisiuimus, et humiliter preco[aaa] dom-

---

[229] Unknown location near Embrun.
[230] Aiton, Savoie, arr. Saint Jean-de-Maurienne, can. Aigue-belle.
[231] Unknown location, probably near Aiton.
[232] Saint-Georges-de-Commiers, Isère, arr. Grenoble, can. Goncelin.

[xx] Cipolla emends to *liberti cum*.
[yy] Read *istas*.
[zz] Initial *r* corrected from *t* by first hand.
[aaa] Blank space follows *preco*.

man lord Charles Martel we acquired in the pagus of Die, Gap and Grenoble, except for those farms in the pagus of Embrun, at *Velencium* which we granted to our heir the monastery of Saint Peter, since this Riculfus associated himself with the people of the Saracens to infidelity against the Kingdom of the Franks and did many evil things with this pagan people. I wish that Tersia should have control over these above mentioned things. And I wish that our freedmen, the sons of Wala, might belong to my heir the church of Saint Peter with those things which I gave to this same Wala.

57. I give my freedwoman named Fredeberga wife of Tasculfus, to my heir the Church of Saint Peter with the grandchildren of this Fredeberga who are seen to dwell in Aiton or in *Parelianum*. I wish and order that these freedpersons with all their property belong to this church.

58. And it has pleased me that it should be added in this page of my testament that since these provinces were desolated and destroyed by the people of the Saracens both our freedpersons and our male and female servants were dispersed by necessity through many neighboring places, I wish that wherever the agents of my heir the monastery of Saint Peter constructed at Novalesa are able to find them, they have the permission without any contradiction to recall them to subjugation just as they belonged to our parents and to us. I wish and order that they ought to belong to my heir the Church of Saint Peter of the Monastery of Novalesa.

59. And I wish that Gislarannus our freedman and his wife, who came to us from Lady Siagria together with those farms which we gave them in St.-Georges-de-Commièrs in the pagus of Grenoble, have them, and they ought to belong to my heir the monastery of Saint Peter in Novalesa.

60. And those things which are not named and which pertain to our rights and which we have not delegated to another, I wish that they should go to my heir.

61. And if any correction or writing should be found in the page of this my testament, we had requested that they be there.

62. And we have asked not once but repeatedly and we humbly pray the lord

nis principibus, uel omnium potestatibus,[bbb] et episcopis, per patre et filio, et spiritu sancto, qui potestatem dominandi regendi habeatis, ut hunc uoluntatis nostrę, quem per hunc testamentum meum ad heredem meam ęcclesia sancto petro monasterio pro substantia monachorum et pauperorum delegaui, ut in nullo permittatis conuellere nec irrumpere, ut ad augmentis mercedis uestrę commune pertineat.

fol. 57r   63. Et si quis sperat hoc temerario contra hanc uoluntatem meam quem/ promptissimam deuotionem conscribere rogaui insidiator extiterit, et sese[ccc] noluerit; iram cęlestem incurrat, et ad communionem omnium ęcclesiarum excommunicatus appareat, et insuper inferat ad ipsum sanctum locum heredem meam sociantem fisco auri libras quinquaginta, et quod repetit et uindicare non ualeat, stipulatione pro omni firmitate subnixa.

64. Ego Abbo hunc testamentum a me factum, subscripsi (…conscripsit).[ddd]
Rusticius[eee] uel[fff] clarissimus, subscripsi.
Magnabertus uir clarissimus, subscripsi
Vuidbertus uir clarissimus, subscripsi.
Semphorianus uir clarissimus, subscripsi.
Vitalis uir clarissimus, subscripsi.

[bbb] Blank space follows *potestatibus*.
[ccc] *reformare* omitted.
[ddd] *conscripsit* is the probable meaning of the poorly-transcribed tironian notes following *subscripsi*.
[eee] Second *i* added by first hand.
[fff] Read *uir*.

princes and all the powers and bishops through the Father and the Son and the Holy Spirit, you who have the power of ordering and ruling, that this which we have granted by our will through this my testament to my heir the Church of the Monastery of Saint Peter for the sustenance of the monks and of paupers, that you permit it in no way to be overthrown or attacked since it pertains to the increase of your common reward.

63. And if anyone rashly hopes to stand as a plotter in opposition to this will of mine which I, with most ready devotion, asked to be written and he does not wish to reform himself, let him incur celestial wrath and let him appear to the community of all the church as an excommunicate, and in addition let him bring this holy place my heir sharing with the fisc, fifty pounds of gold and let him not be able to seek back and claim ownership of it, the stipulation has been added with all confirmation.

64. § I Abbo have signed this testament made by me.

I the most distinguished man Rusticius have signed.

I the most distinguished man Magnabertus have signed.

I the most distinguished man Widbertus have signed.

I the most distinguished man Semphorianus have signed.

I the most distinguished man Vitalis have signed.

CHAPTER III

LAND AND LORDSHIP

Abbo's testament was not designed to provide either a description of his properties or to serve as an economic or fiscal record. It was prepared to indicate what property and rights he was transferring to his heirs. Hence it does not provide exact boundaries of his lands, descriptions of estates, lists of slaves and freedpersons, or the like. Still less does it attempt to describe the exact nature of the obligations that his dependents owed him and would owe his heirs. Both of these sorts of information would have been available to his heirs from other sorts of records, such as *poletica* (polyptychs) or *descriptiones*, all of course now lost.[1] Nevertheless, it is possible to see through the stipulations of the testament the structure of landholding and agriculture, of power and patronage, as they existed in the Rhône valley in the early eighth century.[2] Through the provisions of the testament one glimpses some aspects of the land and the people of the region, held together through a complex system of economic and legal relationships which formed the basis of local authority and wealth for property owners such as Abbo.

In general the relationship binding Abbo to others is one of property: land, but also the means to work the land such as improvements, structures, rights, and persons. From the perspective of the testament, Abbo's superiors are those who will guarantee his property rights and those of his heirs; his equals, both family and associates, are those from whom he has acquired his property; his inferiors are those who manage and work his land. In subsequent chapters we will examine the relationship between the *potestates* of the region and the wider world of eighth century Francia as well as the elaborate network of kinship

---

[1] On the sorts of records which would have been kept, see Walter Goffart, "From Roman Taxation", especially pp. 375–393. See also F. L. Ganshof, "Les avatars pp. 55–66. To judge from the documents employed at Marseille around the same time discussed by Ganshof, such records might have included a *descriptio* of Abbo's properties (p. 61, n.3) and a *poleticum* or polyptych (p. 65) describing in greater detail Abbo's estates or *cortes*. One must regret that the most recent significant examinations of the transition from late Roman to medieval forms of estate management seem to have been written without much contact among scholars in various areas of the field. Thus, for example, John Percival, in his "Seigneurial aspects of Late Roman estate management", *The English Historical Review*, vol. 332 (1969), pp. 449–473, emphasizes the continuity between late Roman and medieval structures of the demesne and of labor services in apparent ignorance of the important article by Adriaan Verhulst, "La Genèse". Walter Goffart, in "From Roman Taxation", in turn ignores Percival's work. Verhulst and Goffart both fail to take notice of David Herlihy's "The History of Rural Seigneury in Italy, 751–1200", *Agricultural History*, 33, 2 (1959), pp. 58–71.

[2] The most detailed previous examination of these questions based on the testament is that of E. Duprat, in "La Provence dans le haut moyen âge", *Encyclopédie des Bouches-du-Rhône*, vol. II (Marseille: 1923) pp. 261–272.

which secured Abbo's place in this world.[3] The present chapter will examine his land and those who worked it in order to understand the structure of the economy and society of rural Provence.

Land

As has been shown, Abbo's property extended from the Mâconnais in the north to the Mediterranean and from the Rhône to the valley of the Dora Riparia in what is today the Italian Piemonte (see maps pp. 82–83). His holdings included both urban and rural land widely scattered throughout this vast region but in general following the valleys of Dora Riparia, the Isère, the Drac, and the Durance. At Susa, the ancient Roman *castellum* guarding the confluence of the Dora Riparia and the Cenischia under the shadow of Mount Mabin (3378 meters), Abbo's father had the center of his estates and here Abbo had inherited property *infra muros*, within the walls of this city.[4] Far to the south in the city of Marseille Abbo's maternal family had its property, and in this very different, Mediterranean port Abbo owned houses and gardens.[5] Most of his property, however, was made up of farms and estates in the valleys or the present-day départements of Hautes-Alpes, Savoie, Isère, the Alpes-maritimes, and the Alpes-de-Haute-Provence.

The enumerations of the constituent elements of these lands are formulaic as was the case in any legal document from the early Middle Ages. However, the specific formulae used vary by the region, indicating that while standard they are not completely without relationship to the realities of local agriculture and production and thus provide a fair idea of the possible sorts of economic activity present on different lands of the region in the eighth century.

In the mountains, the appurtenances listed include forests, meadows, alpine pasturages, mountains, waters, vineyards, fields, pastures, and gardens.[6] The primary economic activities were, as would be expected, production of forest products and the pasturing of sheep, for which the alpine meadows, fields and pastures play so important a part in the region to the present day. The testament mentions three shepherds: one in the valley of Briançon,[7] one near Embrun,[8] and one at Hermillon near St.-Jean-de-Maurienne.[9] In the protected valleys below could be found the gardens which provided the means of support-

---

[3] par. 62. See below chapters IV and V for the meaning of the word *potestates*.

[4] par. 3.

[5] par. 36.

[6] par. 3, 7, 10, 22.

[7] par. 20.

[8] par. 25.

[9] par. 12.

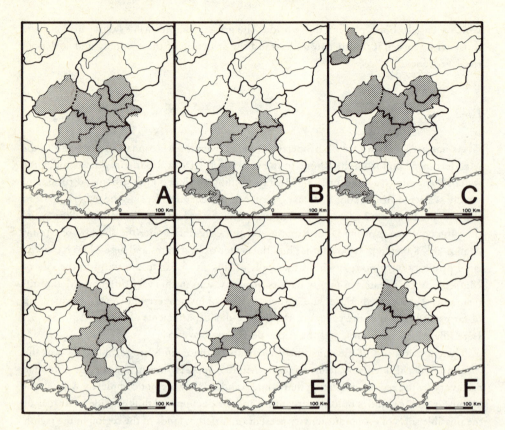

ing those engaged in animal husbandry and forestry. Vineyards are mentioned in the valley of St.-Jean-de-Maurienne on the Arc and near Sisteron, locations whose lower elevations and protected positions made possible some cultivation of grapes and the production of wine.

Below the Durance the appurtenances change form and indicate a different, more Mediterranean form of agriculture. Here, in the areas of Toulon, Marseille and Arles, Abbo lists "lands, gardens, vineyards and olive groves".[10] In addition, he includes salt works near Arles[11] and on the Verdon.[12] These typically Mediterranean producs, wine, olives, and salt, along with a certain amount of pasturing in the Camargue,[13] characterized the agriculture and from which Abbo and others like him drew their wealth in the South.

---

[10] par. 36.
[11] par. 39.
[12] par. 39. On Merovingian saltworks see Rouche, *L'Aquitaine,* pp. 204–206.
[13] par. 39.

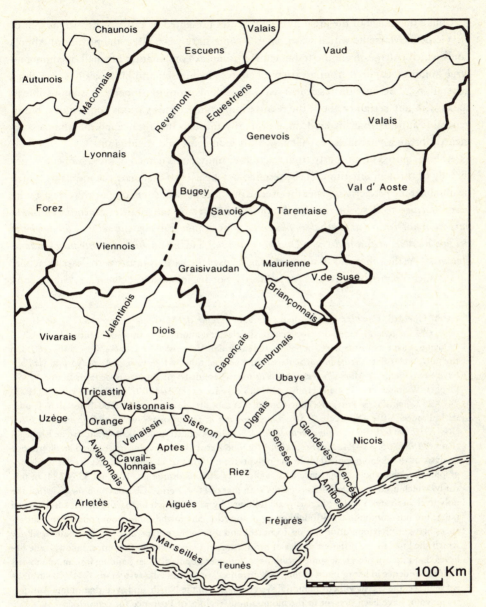

Major sources of Abbo's property by <u>Pagus</u>:

A Father's family   D Rigaberta and Waldebertus
B Mother's family   E Widegunda
C Siagria   F Confiscated from Rebels

Unlike the image of the great monastic estates presented by polyptychs such as that of St. Victor of Marseille which was prepared some sixty years later, the picture of Abbo's lands which emerges from the testament is a complex combination of small, medium and large holdings acquired from a variety of sources by himself and his ancestors over three generations.[14] Because the testament never gives dimensions of property, it is impossible to speak with any certainty about the relative importance of his various acquisitions, but in general it appears that his land came primarily through inheritance, an inheritance augmented through purchases, exchanges, court judgments and royal grants.

Abbo acquired his property from thirty-four individuals named in the testament, either directly or through inheritance. The terminology he uses to designate the means by which he obtained the property is generally precise but does present some obscurities. He uses the verb *obvenire* to describe the devolution of property by inheritance: *quicquid ex alode parentum nostrorum michi ibidem obuenit*[15] for example, but also *qui mihi ex alode genitrici mei Rusticę, et auunculo meo Dodone obuenit*[16] and *qui michi de parente mea Godane obuenit.*[17] At the other end of the spectrum, he uses the verb *conquirere* to describe acquisitions such as purchases which were clearly not by inheritance: *quem de Siagria con-*

---

[14] ed. B. Guérard, *Cartulaire de l'Abbaye de Saint-Victor de Marseille* (Paris: 1857), vol. II, pp. 633–654. In general on the development of the classic manorial structure see François L. Ganshof, "Quelques aspects principaux," pp. 73–101; Adriaan Verhulst, "La Genése," pp. 135–160. On the polyptych of St. Victor in particular see the new edition by J. F. Breggi, *Le polyptique de l'abbaye Saint-Victor de Marseille, essai de réédition,* Thèse de Droit Université de Paris (Paris: 1975); Stephen Weinberger, "Peasant Households in Provence ca. 800–1100," *Speculum* vol. 48 (1973) 247–257. Jean-Pierre Poly, "Régime domanial et rapports de production 'féodalistes' dans le midi de la France (VIIIe–Xe siècles)" *Structures féodales et féodalisme dans l'occident méditerranéen (Xe–XIIIe siècles): Bilan et perspectives de recherches,* Collection de l'Ecole française de Rome 44 (Rome: 1980) pp. 57–84. Most recently, Monique Zerner-Chardavoine has offered an alternative analysis of the demographic data in the polyptych, in "Enfants et jeunes au IXe siècle: La démographie du polyptyque de Marseille 813–814," *Provence historique* no. 126, pp. 355–384. In this study, which disagrees at numerous points with that of Poly, Zerner-Chardavoine suggests that the polyptych indicates a series of crisis years followed by years of high births and infant survivals, an image not uncommon in traditional European societies. She further points out considerable differences between the population in this document and that in the polyptych of St. Germain-des-Prés, which she links to the different modes of production in Francia and in Provence. Likewise she believes that one can detect, at some locations, a "pioneer population" expanding into mountainous regions; evidence in her opinion of the "pulverization" of the old villa system (p. 373). However, as we shall see, the classic villa or manorial system known in the North, and even that of late Antiquity, may not have been present in the mountainous regions of Provence for centuries.

[15] par. 8. For a similar examination of the vocabulary of testaments see Josef Fleckenstein, "Fulrad von Saint-Denis und der fränkische Angriff in den süddeutschen Raum," *Studien und Vorarbeiten zur Geschichte des großfränkischen und frühdeutschen Adels,* ed. G. Tellenbach (Freiburg i. Br.: 1957) pp. 9–39, esp. 15–17.

[16] par. 41.

[17] par. 36.

quesiui,[18] *quem de Vuidegunde conquesiuimus*,[19] *quem de Vualdeberto presbitero et de Rigaberga conquisiuimus*,[20] etc. The term *peruenire* is much less precise. At times the term is used to describe what were apparently inheritances: *quem de Dodone parente meo ... ad me peruenit.*,[21] *quod de proprio alode meo et quod de parente mea Godane ad me peruenit*,[22] etc. At other times, *peruenire* clearly does not mean to devolve through inheritance: *quem per preceptionem dominica ... ad nos peruenit.*[23] Often it seems to imply the same as *conquirere* since it is used of property acquired by persons not elsewhere stated unambiguously to have left Abbo property in inheritance: *quem de Vuidegunda ad nos peruenerunt Kalares quem de ipsa Vuidegunde conquisiuimus*[24]; *quicquid in ualle ... ex alode parentum nostrorum uel quod de Siagria ibidem ad nos peruenit*,[25] *quem de domno Vualdeberto ad nos peruenit.*[26] In general, we take those instances in which he uses the term *peruenire* when describing the devolution of property from someone not explicitly designated as kin to be synonymous with *conquirere,* and when speaking of devolution from kin as *possibly* inheritance, although as we shall see, Abbo also purchased *(conquisiuit)* property from relatives.

Only rarely do other terms for acquisition appear. Other than *cessio* and *commutare* discussed below, one finds *evindicare* in the sense of "win back through judgment",[27] *habere* which, in the context of Abbo's own property is unclear,[28] and *recipere.*[29]

Apparently allodial property was clearly distinguished from property purchased or otherwise acquired even in past generations. This allodial land was that which passed from generation to generation from parent to child as distinct from that inherited from more distant relatives or that purchased by parents and bequeathed to children. Abbo's allodial inheritance came in general from two regions: the region around Susa, Gap, Grenoble, and Briançon where his father's family was mostly richly endowed with land, and the region of Arles, Marseille and the valley of the Durance where his maternal family's wealth lay. These lands, augmented by property acquired in the previous generations by his grandfathers, uncles and father certainly made up the bulk of his estate and were the foundation of his wealth. Abbo's father had increased his holdings in the *pagus* of Gap near Nyons, St.

---

[18] par. 14.
[19] par. 19.
[20] par. 24.
[21] par. 24.
[22] par. 24.
[23] par. 25.
[24] par. 26.
[25] par. 13.
[26] par. 52.
[27] par. 16.
[28] par. 27.
[29] par. 20.

Fermin and St. Bonnet through acquisitions from a woman named Persa and from a certain Valerianus.[30] Abbo himself had purchased or otherwise acquired property from at least fourteen persons including relatives and more distant connections. In general these acquisitions were intended to increase his holdings in those areas in which he had significant inheritances and included purchases of parts of inheritances he had shared with other relatives. Most of these acquisitions were near Grenoble, Die, Gap, Briançon and Nyons.

The same strategy of uniting and increasing holdings in specific areas was pursued through exchanges. These exchanges, involving property on Mont Cenis and in the valley of Maurienne, were with the churches of Lyon and Maurienne.[31]

Some property was also acquired by *cessio*,[32] which could mean simply by gift, but also a bride gift or possibly forfeiture in payment of a debt. The sense is not clear from the context.[33] Finally, Abbo received property in the area of Gap in the *pagi* of Die, Gap and Grenoble which had been confiscated by royal judgment from participants in the revolt of Provence and awarded to him, probably for his role in crushing the resistance to Charles Martel in the area.[34]

The units of property of which Abbo speaks are normally identified by a place name in the locative case and then termed *locus, colonica, portio, terra, res, casa, campum, casalis, lucellum/locello, curtis/cortis, vinea cultura,* or *(h)ortilis*. Nowhere do the words *villa* or *mansus* appear in the text. Ganshof saw the named places as *villae* and some at least of the *colonicae* as *mansi*.[35] *Portiones* he understood as fractions of a former estate.[36] The term *locus* he regarded as often synonymous with *villa*.[37] However, as Ganshof and, after him, Verhulst were careful to point out, the "classic" form of manorial organization which developed from the seventh century in the Parisian region appeared only with considerable differences in more distant areas.[38] Hence the terminology of the testament must be examined on its own terms and not in relationship with some ideal form of pre-Carolingian agricultural structure.

Many of the places named in the testament exist today as villages. Thus one might be tempted to see them, as did Ganshof, as vills.[39] However, if by vill one understands estates, either bipartite or not, then one risks forcing the evidence. In none of the locations named

---

[30] par. 27, 43.

[31] par. 7, 10.

[32] par. 46, 48.

[33] *Cessio* as bride gift: *Formulae Andecavenses, MGH Leges* V, *Formulae,* 1, c, p. 5; no. 40, p. 17; as gift, *Formulae Arvenenses,* no. 6 p. 3.

[34] par. 25, 56.

[35] Ganshof, "Quelques aspects," p. 86.

[36] *Ibid.,* p. 89. Also Rouche, *L'Aquitaine,* p. 210.

[37] *Ibid.,* p. 77.

[38] *Ibid.,* pp. 82–83; Verhulst, "La Genèse," 138 and *passim*.

[39] Ganshof, "Quelques aspects," pp. 77–78.

does Abbo's text suggest that the location forms, even in theory, a unit of production. He does not bequeath these named locations or portions of them – he bequeaths property *at* or near these named locations. The difference is important. While they were quite likely villages or hamlets they were not, at least in the early eighth century, units of seignorial organization as was the case in Francia or as would be the case elsewhere in the later Carolingian period. Lordship and ownership of these places were quite widely divided and there is no reason to suppose that this division was recent.

As a synonym for these named places, the testament speaks of *loca*, a term which does not have a technical meaning in the text.

If, with the exception of five places discussed below, the named locations in the text provide only a geographical reference and were not units of exploitation, the most commonly mentioned unit was the *colonica*.[40] Most of the properties in the testament are so designated, usually by the name of the valley or the name of the place in which they are situated, as for example, "the *colonicae* in the valley of Gironde and at Rollières"[41] and "the *colonica* at the place known as Baratier."[42] These *colonicae* must not be translated too hastily as *mansi*: the specific meanings that *mansus* tends to have in the "classic" manorial system and the various interpretations that scholars have attached to it threaten to obscure the true nature of these Provençal units.[43] Studies of the uses of the terms *colonicae* and *mansus* in other regions, particularly those of Karl Bosl for East Francia[44] and of Wilhelm Störmer for Bavaria, indicate that the terms have quite distinct meanings in the eighth century. In these regions, *mansus* is used normally to designate agricultural units of royal or ducal property. In Bavaria *colonicae* is in contrast the term most frequently used

---

[40] On *colonica* see Ganshof, "Quelques aspects," p. 87 note 40; Poly, "Régime domanial", p. 62, and especially notes 14 and 16. Rouche, *L'Aquitaine*, pp. 210–211. Archibald R. Lewis, in *The Development of Southern French and Catalan Society, 718–1050* (Austin: 1965) p. 15 cites the testament to demonstrate that "In Provence, around Marseille, the villa, made up of *colonicae*, seems to have prevailed, while as far north as Dauphiny, Abbo's will shows the same pattern of land used in the Rhone Valley." In fact, with the exception of the five estates discussed below, which are termed *curtes* and seem to have been exceptionally large units, the testament indicates rather the lack of villa organization in the region.

[41] par. 22.

[42] par. 24.

[43] Poly points out, in "Le régime," p. 62, that the term *mansus* appears in the area only in the latter half of the ninth century and questions whether the two terms in the earlier period may have referred to different units of agrarian production. However, he does equate the term *colonica* with the units of exploitation mentioned in Visigothic law: *MGH Leges* I, 1 *Lex Visigothorum* X, 1, 14, pp. 387–88 and X, 1, 19, pp. 390–91. Walter Goffart, however, wisely cautions against accepting the classic definitions of *mansus* (and, by implication of *colonica*) as the "land of one family." "From Roman Taxation," pp. 165–167.

[44] Karl Bosl, *Franken um 800*, pp. 50–61.

[45] Wilhelm Störmer, *Früher Adel*, vol. I, p. 134.

to designate units donated by nobles.[46] In Burgundy, however, as Walter Schlesinger has pointed out,[47] *colonica* appears in the *Lex Burgundionum* to designate fiscal land as well as former private estates. In the testament, these *colonica* appear as physical units of exploitation including a combination of the dwelling, outbuildings, lands and rights to the use of waters, woods, pastures and so forth which constituted the unit. Often they were the personal exploitations of one dependent worker and his family, but a single individual could hold several *colonicae* from Abbo in a variety of ways, and he could have *mancipia* who worked the land for or with him. These individual farms were spread throughout the Alpine valleys and along the arable areas of Provençal rivers, although the term does not appear in the extreme southern areas of Provence near Toulon, Arles and Marseille. Here instead one hears of *casae, campi, ortila, vineae, terrae, oliveta,* terms more specific to a different form of agriculture. Occasionally these *colonicae* seem to be grouped or Abbo seems to have acquired additional *colonicae* in areas where his family's holdings were already extensive. More often, however, these *colonicae* were widely scattered and depended through their tenant directly to Abbo's agents, not to a central vill.

While these small dependent properties, perhaps family farms, are found everywhere, they occasionally are formed into manors or estates. The most notable are his five *cortes* which were indeed bipartite estates resembling in some ways the classic manor.[48] These

---

[46] Störmer, p. 135. On the use of *mansus* and *colonia* in the eighth-century tradition-books of Salzburg see Herwig Wolfram, "*Libellus Virgilii:* ein quellenkritisches Problem der ältesten Salzburger Güterverzeichnisse," *Mönchtum, Episcopat und Adel zur Gründungszeit des Klosters Reichenau,* ed. Arno Borst, Vorträge und Forschungen vol. 20 (Sigmaringen: 1974), pp. 183–184, esp. note 23.

[47] Walter Schlesinger, "Vorstudien zu einer Untersuchung über die Huge," in *Kritische Bewahrung: Beiträge zur deutschen Philologie: Festschrift für Werner Schröder zum 60. Geburtstag,* ed. Ernst-Joachim Schmidt (Berlin: 1974), p. 19. On the use of the term *colonica* in Bavaria, pp. 50–57. See also his analysis of the uses of *mansus* and *Hufe* in "Hufe und mansus im Liber Donationum des Klosters Weißenburg," *Beiträge zur Wirtschafts- und Sozialgeschichte des Mittelalters: Festschrift für Herbert Helbig zum 65. Geburtstag,* ed. Knut Schulz (Cologne: 1976), pp. 33–85.

[48] See Ganshof, "Quelques aspects"; Verhulst, "Genèse"; Renée Doehaerd, *Le haut moyen âge occidental: Economies et sociétés* (Paris: 1971) pp. 176, 182. Although the term *villa* does not appear in the testament, it probably was in use in the region. On the *villa* of Chaudol, donated to the monastery of St. Victor of Marseille by the *patricius* Nemfidius in the seventh century, see Ganshof, "Les avatars". Ganshof remarks on the long territorial integrity of this estate which is returned to the monastery after several confiscations in 780. This contrast with the properties in Abbo's testament is probably due to the fact that for most of this time it was either church property or royal property conferred in benefice, and thus did not always undergo the divisions of inheritance or sale to which most of Abbo's property was subject. Percival, in "Seigneurial aspects," argues that the bipartite division of classical estates differs little from the bipartite manor of the late eighth and ninth centuries not only in the basic division into demesne/tenure but also in the existence of a similar superstructure including forerunners of the *banalité* and the importance of labor services owed by *coloni.* The latter, which are seen by Verhulst ("La Genèse", p. 140) as the decisive characteris-

cortes carried names, they were not simply located by reference to a village or settlement: Tallard on the Durance south of Gap;[49] La Salle near Briançon;[50] Upaix near Gap;[51] Valernes on the Durance near Sisteron[52] and Lavars in the area of Grenoble.[53] These estates included both *colonicae* dependent on them and *colonicae dominicale, terrae et vineae dominicales.*[54] The latter were apparently lands, vineyards and *colonicae* which formed a demesne. Thus these *cortes* were apparently bipartite, having both individual exploitations and a demesne presumably worked by *mancipia* or chattel slaves. However, as we shall see, there is no direct or indirect evidence that the tenants of the *colonicae* were required to provide labor on the reserve, a characteristic of the classical manor. Moreover, these *cortes* were not physically united units but rather units of production which could include geographically disparate properties and appurtenances. The estate at Lavars, for example, included in addition to the lands near Grenoble salt works along the river Verdon northwest of Aix-en-Provence.[55] The testament gives no indication of the relative size of the reserve and the tenancies of these estates, nor of the total size of any of them. However, since one, that at La Salle, apparently included whole alps, they would have been quite large. Superficiaty alone in a heavily forested, alpine region such as the area around Briançon would, however, have meant little in terms of economic value.

In addition to these *cortes,* Abbo had or shared parts of a number of smaller named locations termed *locella.* These included: part of a property probably near Susa called *Rogationes* which he had shared in indivision with his uncle and guardian Bishop Semforianus of Gap;[56] Bras-d'Asse near Digne;[57] *Voconciun* near Riez;[58] *Ruarmum* and Ambel near Gap;[59] and Memers near Venasque.[60] These "little places" which included lands,

---

tics of the classic Carolingian manor, Percival suggests, on evidence collected by Herlihy, "Rural Seigneury," to be declining, at least in Italy, in the first half of the eighth century. He stops short of insisting on a direct continuity, however, pointing out that similar systems of estate management may well have developed in different regions and at different times with only minimal actual relationship. The evidence, at any rate, is certainly inconclusive.

[49] "corte mea Talarno," par. 26.
[50] "corte mea Sallaris," par. 21.
[51] "corte mea Opaga," par. 28.
[52] "corte mea Valerignaca," par. 31.
[53] "in pago Segisterico Lauariosco, ... ipsa corte," par. 52.
[54] par. 26. Rouche, *L'Aquitaine,* p. 211, suggests that the term *"curtis indominicata"* which appears in the Donation of Nizezius did not imply a bipartite domain.
[55] par. 49.
[56] par. 49.
[57] par. 49.
[58] par. 50.
[59] par. 50.
[60] par. 50.

buildings and dependents, were probably small estates similar to these *locella* in documents examined by Ganshof[61] although there is no evidence that they were bipartite.

A final, important term encountered in the text is *portio*. Ganshof wished to see the meaning of this term in comparison with other, northern sources of the seventh and early eighth centuries, as portions or fragments of old estates.[62] In a sense this is true, but not in exactly the way he understood it. In Abbo's testament, *portiones* are shares in an inheritance but these portions were not necessarily parts of an actual estate (*villa* or *cortis*) in the previous generation. In nine of the ten uses Abbo makes of the word he is speaking explicitly of inheritances, either those which he had himself inherited, or those which he had been able to acquire from kin who had shared an inheritance in a previous generation.[63] This general use of the term as referring to a portion of an inheritance, and not of a particular estate, is found frequently in the *Formulae Marculfi* and other Merovingian formularies.[64] Of course, it is quite possible that these *portiones* would be inheritances from a single property, as in the case of the half of the *locella Rogationes* which Abbo termed a *portio* which his uncle had wanted to give to the church at Gap. However, the term cannot be used as evidence of a wide-spread system of villas as the fundamental unit of agricultural organization in the region. Manors, large and small, did exist, and some were bipartite, but these were the exception. The basic unit of organization was the *colonica*, which might exist isolated from others, grouped around a village, as part of an estate, or attached administratively and fiscally to a distant estate.

Dependents

The foregoing description of the lands and properties that made up the estate of a great aristocrat in the early eighth century is essentially incomplete. At every point in the testament, Abbo is concerned not just with the alps, fields, meadows, vineyards and olive groves that comprised his wealth, but with the men and women under his *patrocinium* (or in the terminology of the *Testamentum*, as in the *Lex Visigothorum*, his *obsequium*[65])

---

[61] Ganshof, "Quelques aspects," p. 79 n. 12.

[62] *Ibid.*, p. 89.

[63] par. 24, 38, 39 (3 times) 44 (2 times), 49 (2 times), 55.

[64] Especially *MGH Leges* V *Formulae Andecavenses*, 41, p. 18; *Marculfi formulae* II, 12, p. 83. Ganshof seems to have taken his definition from Fustel de Coulanges, *Histoire des institutions politiques de l'ancienne France: L'alleu et le domaine rural pendant l'époque mérovingienne* (Paris: 1927) pp. 238–252. The argument that *portio* means portion of a *villa* rests on the supposition that *villae* were the basic units of exploitation, a supposition which, as we have seen, is not supported by the text.

[65] *MGH Leges* I, p. 243, *Lex Visigothorum* V, 7, 18.

whom he considered essential appurtenances, the means by which these lands could be exploited. The description of the estate he left to his heirs includes then both the land and the people who inhabited it.

The farms and estates of the Rhône valley were inhabited and worked by a variety of persons referred to in the document as *liberti, ingenui, mancipia,* and *serui.* This terminology cannot be taken to be exhaustive for the persons so designated: the terminology is that of the patron and thus designates the status of his dependents in terms of their relationship to him, not necessarily their legal status. Thus except in formulaic descriptions of land one does not encounter the term *colonus,* although the *liberti* and the *serui* may well have been *coloni* from the perspective of law. In fact, as we shall see, their obligations are essentially those of the late classical colon. Nevertheless, their essential relationship with Abbo is their personal bond as his servants or freedpersons, not their legal category under public law. Moreover, the terminology is not entirely consistent: *ingenuus,* for example should mean free born in contrast to slave or freedperson. In fact in the barbarian kingdoms the term is often used interchangeably with *libertus* and has been seen by some scholars as perfectly synonymous with the various designations of freedmen.[66] In the testament the term is ambiguous: at times certainly designating freedpersons, at times having the usual, more traditional meaning of freeborn.

The social and legal status of those designated *mancipia* and *serui* in the *testamentum* is controversial and difficult to assess. The *testamentum* provides little insight into any dimension of their social status other than that directly related to their economic activity. One could suppose that the social status of Abbo's silk-worker Peter or of his harpist (appropriately named Iocos) was higher than that of ordinary *serui,* although the former was probably, and the latter certainly, a *seruus* prior to his manumission. Likewise Abbo's *ministeriales,* although most certainly *serui,* would have enjoyed a very different status from that of ordinary *serui.* The *mancipia* appear on *colonicae,* on the *cortes,* and elsewhere in the lands, sometimes apparently supplying the labor of the demesne, at other times entrusted to *liberti* to do the physical labor on smaller farms.[67] Normally they are not enumerated by name but appear as one of the improvements on property: "the land and the slaves at Savel,"[68] for example, or "together with the slaves, lands and all adjacencies looking to this place".[69] They make up part of the equipment of the property and are

---

[66] Particularly Fustel de Coulanges, *Ibid.,* pp. 341–42.

[67] On slavery see Charles Verlinden, *L'esclavage dans l'Europe médiévale.* I *Péninsule ibérique, France* (Bruges: 1955) and Hermann Nehlsen, *Sklavenrecht zwischen Antike und Mittelalter* (Göttingen: 1972). For more recent comparative material consult Rouche, *L'Aquitaine,* pp. 211–214, and, on slavery in Auvergne, Gabriel Fournier, "L'esclavage en basse Auvergne aux époques mérovingienne et carolingienne," *Cahiers d'Histoire* 6 (1961), pp. 361–375.

[68] par. 32.

[69] par. 34.

simply grouped with other *res*. The one exception to the anonymity of Abbo's *mancipia* is a case in which he names two domestic slaves, Rusticiu [*sic*] and Lupolina, in Gap.[70]

The testament distinguishes between *mancipia* and *serui* or *ancillae* both in the formulaic enumerations of appurtenances and in the descriptions of individual servants. At times *seruus* is simply juxtaposed to *libertus,* as in the description of property at Bezaudon, "which we acquired from Siagria together with freedpersons and slaves and its appendices …"[71] At other times both *seruus* and *mancipium* are included in enumerations as in the case of the property on Mont Cenis which he bequeathed to Novalesa "together with the free born, the freedpersons, the colons and servants, the lands, houses, buildings, slaves, fields, meadows, pastures, forests, vineyards and with all its adjacencies pertaining to it."[72] In this case, *serui* are included among the persons *(ingenuis, libertis ac colonis)* while *mancipia* are clearly among the things *(terris, domibus, edificiis, campis,* etc.), that constitute the inheritance. The specific mention of *serui* by name further confirms the impression that they were of quite different status from that of *mancipia*. Three *serui* and one *ancilla* are named in the testament. Of these three are associated with a particular farm where they are said to dwell *(manere)*. Probably then they are *serui casati,* that is, slaves settled on particular pieces of property. Although theirs were servile tenures, as settled slaves rather than household or chattel slaves they enjoyed higher status and more significant rights than mere *mancipia*.

Since, as we shall see below, a number of freedpersons are said "to dwell" on particular farms as well, these freedpersons had been probably *serui casati* prior to manumission. Thus the status of *seruus* may have been an intermediate one for slaves who had the hope of passing to freed status.

One might well question the appropriateness of translating either term as "slave", and indeed if one thinks in terms of classical Roman gang slavery or the slave economy of modern Europe and the Americas, these servants were clearly different. The geography and agriculture of this region hardly favored exploitation by means of great troops of slave laborers such as might have been found in areas better suited to large estates. However, the characteristics enumerated of these *mancipia* and *serui* and in particular their legal status and dependence on their owners seems to imply a higher degree of dependency than that usually associated with serfs. In particular, the apparent qualification of *mancipia* as *res* indicates that society retained much of the traditional legal and social stigmas of classical slavery. This is not to say, of course, that the economic circumstances of individual *serui* were necessarily harsh. Nothing is known of the size or value of the *colonicae* on which they dwelled, or of the relative kinds of payments to which they were obligated.

---

[70] par. 27.
[71] par. 39.
[72] par. 52.

The most frequently mentioned individuals in the testament are the freedpersons or *liberti*.[73] Over fifty of these are mentioned by name, and they and their families formed the most important social group among Abbo's dependents. They had charge of the disparate *colonicae,* supervised, along with his agents (who may well have also been freedmen) his estates, and formed the bulk of those under his *patrocinium.*

The terms *libertus* and *ingenuus* both appear in the testament in formulaic enumerations and in specific examples. In classical Latin and law the terms had quite different meanings, the former being a freedman and the latter one born free and hence not suffering from the obligations and impediments which continued to burden the freedmen. However, in the barbarian kingdoms the two were often used interchangeably, and one hears of *serui* who through manumission had become *ingenui.* Thus scholars such as Fustel de Coulanges have considered the two terms as synonyms in Merovingian charters.[74] The testament, however, employs them in such a way that while the meaning may have been at times equivalent, Abbo and his contemporaries had not lost all sense of distinction. Such enumerations as used to describe his property in the *pagus* of Macon, *una cum ingenuis, libertis ac colonis et seruis, uel omnes adiacentiis …*[75] may not imply any real difference of meaning. However, when he speaks of his property at Nanosces (St.-Julienne-de-Maurienne?) together with those *ingenuos de Amberto et liberto nostro de Alsede nomen Orbano, et ingenua nostra nomen Rigouera de Bognosco*[76] or when he bequeaths *liberta nostra Droctesenda cum filius suos, et habet ipsa liberta nostra homo ingenuus, nomen Radbertus,*[77] one must assume that he recognizes some distinction between *ingenuus* and *libertus.* In neither of these cases and certainly not in the case of formulae including *ingenuus* should one presume that the persons so designated are entirely free of Abbo's *patrocinium.*

The meaning of the distinction is not apparent from the testament itself. The most plausible explanation is to be found in Karl Bosl's discussion of "free dependence" in early medieval society.[78] The *ingenui* are presumably the "king's free" who originally stood di-

---

[73] On *liberti* see the article "Libertini" in Pauly-Wissowa, *Realencyclopädie der classischen Altertumswissenschaft* vol. 13 (Stuttgart: 1927), cols. 104–110. Also see Mary L. Gordon, "The Freedman's Son in Municipal Life," *Journal of Roman Studies* vol. 21 (1931) pp. 65–77; Arnold Mackay Duff, *Freedmen in the Roman Empire* (Cambridge: 1958); L. R. Ménager, "Considérations sociologiques sur la démographie des grands domaines ecclésiastiques carolingiens", *Etudes d'histoire du droit canonique dédiées à Gabriel Le Bras* (Paris: 1965) vol. II, pp. 1317–1335.

[74] *L'alleu,* pp. 341–42.

[75] par. 17.

[76] par. 11.

[77] par. 47.

[78] See Karl Bosl, "Freiheit und Unfreiheit: Zur Entwicklung der Unterschichten in Deutschland und Frankreich während des Mittelalters," in Karl Bosl, *Frühformen der Gesellschaft im mittelalterlichen Europa* (Munich: 1964), pp. 180–203, esp. pp. 184–190.

rectly under the king and his agents and who were differentiated from the rest of dependent society in that they had the right and obligation to participate in public courts and to provide military service. This sort of "freedom" does not mean that such *ingenui* were free from the variety of controls which Abbo, both as landowner and as *rector* of the region, would have been able to exercise.

In any case, the persons designated as *liberti* owe clearly defined and significant obligations to their former master and will continue to be in this relationship along with their children toward his heir. The specifics of this relationship had considerably changed since late Antiquity. Traditionally, the *patronus* continued to enjoy certain rights in regard to his *libertus:* he had a right of succession which carried with it the right of guardianship over underage *liberti;* he had the right to require respectful conduct from his freedpersons termed *obsequium.* This included the prohibition of the freedperson testifying against his patron, the prohibition of bringing any action involving the discredit of the patron or of his family, and the obligation to support the patron according to his means in time of need. The freedperson could also be required to perform *opera,* services, and to give *munera,* gifts, to the patron. The services were traditionally one day's work which at the freedperson's option could be transformed into a payment. The *munera* were more symbolic and were not major gifts. Although the obligations of the freedperson could to some degree extend to the parents and children of the patron, the children of the *libertus* did not inherit these obligations. A freedperson who failed to respect his obligations toward his patron might be forced to return to servitude.[79]

In Merovingian Gaul manumission could be made in a variety of ways and could result in a wide variety of obligations and duties on the part of the freedperson. From late Antiquity, the public disabilities of freed status gradually disappeared, leaving only the relationships with the former owner to distinguish between freed and free. These could be further eliminated if the master so chose. Early formularies provide examples of manumission which granted true *ingenuus* status: ... *vitam ducas ingenuam et nulli heredum ac proheredum nostrorum vel cuicumque servitium inpendas nec libertinitatis obsequium debeas nisi soli Deo;*[80] ... *nulle nulleve heredum hac proheredum meorum post hanc die nullum quicquam debeant servitium nec litimunium nec libertinitatis aut patrocinatus obsequium eorum nec ad posteritate ipsorum non requiratur.*[81] If the *patronus* was free to exempt the former slave from all obligations of *obsequium* and *servitium,* he was also free to require a variety of obligations, often rituals symbolizing the former status and intended to benefit the soul of the patron and to provide for his *memoria.* For example, in a testament prepared around 700 a certain Erminethrudis freed her *libertus* Mumolane: *cum omni*

---

[79] W. W. Buckland, pp. 87–90.
[80] *Marculfi formulae* II, 32. MGH *Leges Formulae* p. 95.
[81] *Formulae Bituricensis* 9, MGH *Leges* V *Formulae* p. 172.

peculiare suo ingenuam esse praecipio: luminaria tantum in ecclesia Bonisiaca ministare stodeat.[82]

Presumably the fact that Novalesa itself is constituted Abbo's heir and will thus serve to maintain his *memoria* explains why in this testament no freedmen are so charged. The duties of *liberti* toward their former masters could be much more than merely symbolic. The obligations could have considerable economic importance, and this is the case in the testament of Abbo. In only one instance does a freedperson appear without important obligations toward him and his heirs, and this person is a certain Tersia, the daughter of his freedwoman Honoria (and perhaps his own illegitimate daughter) to whom he gives property granted him by Theuderic IV which had been confiscated from rebels. Only here does he leave her the property and order *ut ipsa Tersia ipsas suprascriptas facultatis habere debeant.*[83]

The obverse of *obsequium* was of course the necessary protection a freed person needed. Normally the former owner was obligated to provide this protection, or else he made a church the protector and established the symbolic *munera* as evidence of the relationship which had been transferred to God *(nisi solo Deo)*. Such an emancipation provided the necessary protection for the *libertus* and brought the patron the spiritual reward of a good work. Since Abbo was donating his entire estate to the Church, such emancipations of his slaves were, from the perspective of his spiritual condition, unnecessary. In all other cases the relationship between freedpersons and Abbo and his heirs is closely connected with the status of the land which they hold. The overwhelming majority are settled on *colonicae* which they hold *sub nomen libertinitatis.*[84] Their obligations are quite explicit. They are to "belong to" Abbo's heir as they have done towards Abbo and his family, that is, they are to remain under the *patrocinium* of the monastery of Novalesa and are to owe the respect and deference implied in the duty of *obsequium*. In addition, they owe payments, *impensiones,* which they and their children are to pay to the *capitularius* or revenue collector.[85] If they fail to make these payments or to pay the proper *obsequium* to

---

[82] *PL* 88.1246; J. M. Pardesus, and L. G. O. Bréquiny, *Diplomata chartae et instrumenta aetatis merovingicae* II (Paris: 1849), p. 257. On the role of enfranchisements in the liturgical *memoria* of Merovingian testators see Michael Borgolte, "Felix est homo, ille, qui amicos bonos relinquit: Zur sozialen Gestaltungskraft letztwilliger Verfügungen am Beispiel Bischof Bertrams von Le Mans (616)," *Festschrift für Berent Schwineköper zu seinem siebzigsten Geburtstag,* ed. Helmut Maurer and Hans Patze (Sigmaringen: 1982), pp. 5–18; and "Freigelassene im Dienst der Memoria: Kulttradition und Kultwandel zwischen Antike und Mittelalter," *Frühmittelalterliche Studien* vol. 17 (1983), pp. 234–250.

[83] par. 56. On the terminology compare with Levy, *West Roman Vulgar Law,* p. 64.

[84] par. 48; Ganshof, "Quelques aspects," p. 86.

[85] par. 19, 23 on *capitularius* see: Walter Goffart, *Caput and Colonate: Towards a History of Late Roman Taxation* (Toronto: 1974) p. 25 and 142 note 11. On the effects of the transfer of *coloni* to landowners, effects which persisted into the eighth century, see Goffart, "Old and New in Merovingian Taxation", *Past and Present* vol. 96 (1982) pp. 8–9.

the monastery, the agents of the monastery are authorized to force payment or to prosecute them under the statute of Ungrateful and Contumelious Freedmen, and they are to revert to their former status of slaves and lose the farms which they held.[86] In addition, Abbo's *liberti* were bound to the *colonicae* which they held: he authorizes the agents of the monastery of Novalesa to seek out his slaves and his freedpersons who had been dispersed during the recent devastations of the region by the Saracens (and, no doubt, by the Franks) and to force them to return to the monastery's lands.[87] His repeated mention of penalties for failure to comply with these obligations, as well as the reference to runaways, suggests that the condition of *mancipia, serui,* and *liberti* was such that they sought and were expected to seek escape whenever possible.

The foregoing description of Abbo's freedpersons indicates that the reality of freed status was far removed from the legal concepts of Roman or Barbarian law. The duties of freedpersons, their relationship to the land they worked and the circumstances by which they were attached to it all indicate that their status was in fact that of colons. Perhaps they would have been so called in other documents referring to them, but for Abbo and his heir what mattered was their private relationship to him, that of freedman to patron. However, since Abbo was not simply a great landowner but also *rector* of the area of Maurienne and possibly later *patricius* of Provence,[88] the powers he exercised over his freedmen were a

---

[86] par. 45.

[87] par. 58. Discussions by Goffart, Percival, and others of the payments due to landlords by their *coloni* concentrate on the payments which arise from the nature of land tenure to the exclusion of possible obligations such as those observed in the *testamentum,* based in part at least on the personal relationship between *libertus* and *patronus.* No doubt this emphasis is proper for the late Roman period, but if one considers that the obligations of freedmen toward their master became increasingly onerous and may have become linked with obligations of tenure, this may help to explain both the increasing importance of services due by *coloni* and the acquisition by landowners of jurisdictional powers over persons residing on their estates. The decreasing services noted by Herlihy and Percival in Northern Italy during the early eighth century (see above, note 44) may be in part the result of the weakening relationship between *liberti* and their former owners, rather than purely an economic transformation. Percival suggests (pp. 468–72) that the gradual acquisition of the right to hold court is in part due to the long-term disintegration of public authority. And certainly, as Goffart points out in "From Roman Taxation," the categories of "public" and "private" had been merging from at least the fifth century (p. 382 and note 160). However, one must also realize that, when the cultivators of an estate were the owner's *serui* and *liberti,* he enjoyed considerable rights over their persons. Nevertheless, by 739 the tradition of public authority over *liberti* was not entirely lost: in the testament, par. 45, Abbo specifies that ungrateful or rebellious *liberti* who fail to make required payments are to be returned to servitude, *cum iudice interpellatione et distractione.* Even this allusion to public judicial authority is, however, tempered by his directive, par. 58, that the *agentes* of Novalesa should have the power to seek out and to force the return of any libertus "absque cuiuslibet contradictione."

[88] Cipolla I, 7, 10–11. On question of whether or not Abbo was later *Patricius* see above Chapter I, pp. 33–35.

combination of what at one time might have been called public and private. Perhaps the activities of the agents and *capitularii* of his heir, the monastery of Novalesa, would continue to confound the two.

Landholding

Throughout the preceding discussions of land and men, the relationship between persons and the land they work or inhabit has proved to be intricate. We must attempt now to distinguish among the various types of holdings which appear in the testament.

Few persons can be said to own land: those of Abbo's family and class, of course, and possibly the Tersia who received her property from Abbo without obligation to his heirs. Everyone else bears a relationship to the property which to some extent is defined by his social, legal and dependent status.

The relationship between *mancipia* and land is most simple. They are part of the appurtenances and have no rights to the property whatever. Hence their relationship is expressed in an impersonal, passive way, *ad ipsa loca pertinentes*.[89] Their situation is indistinguishable from other beasts which may belong to a particular farm or estate.

Eleven individuals are said to dwell (*manere*) in a particular location. These include the three *uerbicarii* (shepherds), a *faber* (smith), one *ancilla,* a *siricarius* (silkworker) and four *liberti*.[90] As suggested above, these persons have apparently no right to the property – they do not have (*habere*) it; they simply reside there. The *ancilla* certainly and the *uerbicarii,* the *faber* and the *siricarius* probably, are all slaves settled on particular lands, the former as *serui casati* and the others probably in order to support them while they practice their trades for the benefit of their owner. This hypothesis that *manere* implies a servile tenure is strengthened by examination of the two cases involving *liberti* who are said "to dwell" on particular properties rather than "to have" them. One is a freedman named Maroaldus whom Abbo's mother Rustica brought from the area of Geneva and settled near Die.[91] The description makes it likely that Maroaldus was a slave settled by Rustica in her husband's region who was subsequently freed. The second example is found in the disposition of a piece of property near St.-Jean-de-Maurienne which Abbo had given to a servant of that church "together with the *coloni, servi* and *liberti* dwelling together in that place."[92] Since the property had been given to the servant, one Bertelinus, *pro ingenuitatis* [*sic*], Bertelinus

---

[89] par. 15.

[90] par. 12, 16, 20, 25, 26, 35, 38, 46. comanere: 23, 26, comanentes: 51. See Schlesinger, "Hufe und Mansus," pp. 63–64.

[91] par. 32.

[92] par. 51. On qualifications of ownership in the early medieval kingdoms see Ernst Levy, *West Roman Vulgar Law* (Philadelphia: 1951) pp. 87–90.

and not the persons dwelling there presumably had the usufruct. Again, the wording implies that the distinction between those who "have land" and those who "dwell on land" was a real one, in part related to the present or past legal status of the person but essentially one of the type of tenancy, the latter being servile.

Ten pieces of property are held of Abbo *in benefitio,* that is, in benefice.[93] Much has been written on the practice of holding property in benefice in the Merovingian period, and in general the image presented by Abbo's testament conforms to the accepted notion of this sort of land holding.[94] The persons holding land in benefice in the testament are primarily Abbo's dependents and servants. They include four freedpersons, a *ministerialis,*[95] a *seruus* freed in the testament, and four persons whose legal status is not mentioned but who are possibly *liberti.* The properties held *in benefitio* include both acquisitions and inheritances and no general conclusion can be formed of what might be held in benefice based on the origin of the property. The nature of the holding is likewise not clear. However it seems that holding in benefice was less desirable than holding *sub nomen* [*sic*] *libertinitatis:* the difference was in part the permanence of the holding. While it appears in at least one case[96] that land held in benefice was inherited by the children of the original beneficiaries, the beneficent nature of such a holding would not guarantee the transmission of a holding to the next generation. Thus when Abbo freed his servant Poilonicus who had previously held land *in benefitium,* he changed the holding to a holding *sub nomen libertinitatis.*[97] The freedman's *peculium* was inherited (along with his obligations), and hence more secure than the possession of a benefice.

Most of the farms and other properties enumerated by Abbo in his testament and assigned to freedpersons are described as having been given to a particular freedperson (apparently as *peculium*) who is to have them and who is to belong to Abbo's heirs. Again, the precise nature of these tenancies is not clear, but the implications are that the freedperson exercises an active control over the property *(habet)* and that he must pay to Abbo or his heirs a fixed amount which is as much a part of his *libertus* status as it is a rent on his property. Together with *obsequium,* that is, the obligation to remain under the *patrocinium* of the heir, this payment or *impensio* is the only duty mentioned as incumbent upon the landholder other than that he must "look to the monastery," an obligation again of the freedperson to his patron rather than specifically an obligation of propertyholding.

---

[93] par. 11, 20, 24, 25, 32, 34, 35, 40, 48, 54.

[94] Fustel de Coulanges, *Histoire des Institutions* …: *Les origines du système féodal, Le bénéfice et le patronat pendant l'époque mérovingienne* (Paris: 1927); François Louis Ganshof, "L'origine des rapports féodo-vassiliques," *I problemi della civiltà carolingia.* Settimane di studio del cento italiano di studi sull'alto medioevo I (Spoleto: 1954) pp. 27–69; François Louis Ganshof, *Feudalism* (New York: 1961) 9–12 and the bibliography pp. xxvi–xxvii.

[95] On *servi ministeriales* see Nehlsen, *Sklavenrecht,* pp. 363–364.

[96] par. 32.

[97] par. 48.

This payment probably amounted to ten percent of the fruits, to judge from similar arrangements in Visigothic law.[98]

Conclusions

The nature of properties and the conditions of the persons holding, inhabiting, and working these properties vary widely in the region in the early eighth century. As we have seen, property changes hands rapidly through sales, inheritances, exchanges, and gifts. Partially due to the geography and partially due to the constant divisions and subdivisions of inheritances, the units of property are in general quite small. The individual *colonica* or farm is normally the basic unit in this process, and individual farms or groups of farms are constantly moving from one owner to another. The majority of these units are in the possession of freedpersons, and the obligations of the individual and his family toward his former master are inextricably linked with the obligations of land he holds. These apparently are combined into a payment (in kind or in money is not said) which is at once the old *impensio* of the Roman *libertus* and the rent, collected by a *capitularius,* of a colon. These freedmen, bound to their patron by this payment and by the general obligation of *obsequium,* risking to fall back into servitude if they do not perform faithfully their duties, form the basis for the lord's control of his lands. They hold one or more *colonicae,* they supervise the lord's slaves assigned to these properties, and they are able to pass their charges on to their descendants.

Less important but already in evidence are servile tenures inhabited by slaves and their families settled on *colonicae* over which they have no rights of possession. These tenures, distinguished from those of freedmen, are characterized by the fact that their occupants simply dwell on them *(manere)* and hence, etymologically, could perhaps be said to be *mansi.* Another small group of freedpersons and servants occupy properties in benefice – temporary and gracious holdings which are for the pleasure of the lord to grant and to withdraw.

Finally, in a few locations larger units, some which had long been in the family, others recently acquired, are beginning to resemble the manors of the central Frankish regions with their individual peasant holdings and their reserve. However, since most of the holdings are in the hands of freedmen whose obligations are limited largely to payments and the reserve is apparently worked by slaves who do not inhabit individual farms, the actual structure of the estates is far from that of the Frankish manors with their corvées performed by serfs.

Given the wide geographical dispersion of properties, the actual involvement of the lord in the management and control of his estates must have been minimal. Supervision of the

---

[98] *MGH Leges* I, 1, *Lex Visigothorum* X, 1, 19. See Poly, *Le Régime domanial,* pp. 62–63, esp. note 16.

vast holdings was in the hands of his unfree agents, *ministeriales* and *capitularii* who collected payments, sought out runaway slaves and freedpersons, and oversaw the freedpersons who in turn directed the work of the *mancipia* under their control.

CHAPTER IV
THE ARISTOCRACY: KINSHIP AND POWER

As kin, sources of his property, or secular and ecclesiastical officials, in all 55 persons of roughly the same status as Abbo are named in the testament and the foundation charter of 726. These hardly constitute a random sample of the landholding aristocracy of the region, but they do include a variety of persons which makes possible an examination of the social and political structures uniting, maintaining and transforming the aristocracy from the late seventh into the eighth century.

Ethnic Identity

The names indicate a slight preponderance of Germanic names: 55% as opposed to 45% names of Latin or Greek origin. However, one must not conclude that the bearers of these Germanic names are in some sense ethnic Franks, Goths or Burgundians any more than one can conclude that the others are pure Gallo-Romans — the appearance of Germanic names in "Roman" families had been frequent for well over a century, as had the occasional use of latinate names in "Germanic" families.[1]

However, one does find that in eighth century Provence the traditional use of ancient Gallo-Roman names common since the fourth century has continued. Among the names in the testament one finds a number identified by Karl Friedrich Stroheker as having been carried by senatorial aristocrats of the late antique period.

The name of Abbo's father, Felix, was well known in the Gallo-Roman aristocracy of Provence. According to Stroheker, the various bearers of this name in the region were probably descended from Agricola, praetorian prefect of the Gauls in 418 and consul in 421,[2] and Felix Ennodius, proconsul of Africa in 408 and again in 423. These included Magnus Felix Ennodius, the poet, who was probably from Arles and who became bishop of Pavia between 514 and 521;[3] Felix Ennodius, whose epitaph from the sixth century was found in Brignoles,[4] the Provençal Flavius Felix promoted consul in 511 by Theodoric the

---

[1] Martin Heinzelmann, "L'aristocratie et les évêchés entre Loire et Rhin jusqu'à la fin du VIIe siècle," *Revue d'histoire de l'église de France* vol. 62 (1975) pp. 75–90; *Bischofsherrschaft in Gallien: Zur Kontinuität römischer Führungsschichten vom 4. bis zum 7. Jahrhundert. Soziale, prosopographische und bildungsgeschichtliche Aspekte.* Beihefte der Francia, no. 5 (Munich: 1976), pp. 13–22.

[2] Karl Friedrich Stroheker, *Der senatorische Adel im spätantiken Gallien* (Darmstadt: 1970). Anhang, "Prosopographie zum senatorischen Adel im Spätantiken Gallien," no. 8. For property inherited by Abbo from his father's family see map A, p. 82.

[3] Stroheker, no. 112.

[4] Stroheker, no. 113.

Great[5] and the Felix who appears in the letters of Venantius Fortunatus as a senator from Marseille around the middle of the sixth century.[6]

Abbo's own mother, Rustica, carried a name frequent, in a variety of forms,[7] in the regions of Vaison and Lyons, as well as in the areas of Bordeaux and Limoges.[8] The most pertinent earlier figure who carried this name was Rusticula, the daughter of a Valerianus and Clementia born in the area of Vaison in the second half of the sixth century.[9] Her father died on the day of her birth and the young potential heiress, at a very early age, was kidnapped by a *vir nobilis* named Cheraonius who obviously wished to marry her for her fortune. However, by the intervention of Abbess Liliola of St. Caesarius of Arles and Bishop Siagrius of Autun before King Guntramn, she was freed and allowed to enter the monastery at Arles of which she became abbess. Although accused of participation in a plot to assassinate King Chlothar II sometime after 613, she was eventually allowed to return to her monastery. While there is no direct evidence to indicate that the family of this earlier Rusticula was connected with that of Abbo's mother, the geographical congruence (Vaison, Arles) and the obvious connections between her kindred and persons who in the late sixth century carried names which appear in the group with which Abbo's family was associated (Valerianus, Siagrius) suggests that the bonds uniting the aristocracy in the late sixth century had changed little over a century. A further suggestion of continuity between Rustica's family and earlier, powerful families in the region is provided by the mention in the testament of a freedman whom Rustica had brought to the area of Gap from Geneva. Geneva had, around 600, a Bishop Rusticus.[10] The coincidence of the names and of Rustica's connection in the area of Geneva suggests a possible link.

---

[5] Stroheker, no. 146.

[6] Stroheker, no. 147.

[7] Heinzelmann, "L'aristocratie" pp. 84–85; "Les changements de la dénomination latine à la fin de l'antiquité," in *Famille et parenté dans l'occident médiéval,* Actes du colloque de Paris 6–8 Juin 1974 ed. Georges Duby et Jacques Le Goff. Collection de l'Ecole française de Rome no. 30 (Rome: 1977) pp. 19–24, on the practice of varying forms of names in the late Empire. See also the works of Iiro Kajanto, *Onomastic Studies in the Early Christian Inscriptions of Rome and Carthage* (Helsinki: 1963); *The Latin cognominia* (Helsinki: 1965); *Supernomina. A Study in Latin Epigraphy* (Helsinki: 1966).

[8] Stroheker, no. 329–335. The fullest examination of Rusticus of Lyon and his family is that of Martin Heinzelmann, *Bischofsherrschaft,* Chapter II.2.1: "Rusticus: Das Bischofsamt als Abschluß einer staatlichen Laufbahn," pp. 101-113. Heinzelmann rightly concludes that one cannot demonstrate that all the families in the regions of Lyon, northern Burgundy, Limoges, and western Aquitaine in which the name Rusticus appeared were connected. For Abbo's property inherited from his mother's family see map B, p. 82.

[9] Stroheker no. 329. *Vita Rusticulae sive Marciae abbatissae Arelatensis, MGH SSRM* IV pp. 337–351. Note that her father was Valerianus, a name which as we have seen appeared among those dealing with Abbo's father. The likelihood that the persons among whom land was bought and sold were related by kinship is discussed below.

[10] par. 32. *SSRM* IV, 129. One should note also that a *Rusticius vir clarissimus* was the first signatory

Abbo's father had acquired property from a certain Valerianus.[11] This too was a name common to the area. Around 500 it had been carried by a *vir illustrissimus* mentioned by Avitus of Vienne[12] and, toward the end of the sixth century, by a noble in the region of Vaison.[13] Bishop Semforianus of Gap had acquired property near Grenoble from a priest Avolus.[14] This name appeared in the early sixth century in the person of the son of a Provençal noble taken as hostage to Italy in 507[15] and was also carried by a noble whose epitaph by Venantius Fortunatus described him as *nobilitate potens*.[16] The most important group of acquisitions made by Abbo in means other than inheritance were from a Siagria, the bearer of one of the oldest and most important names in the Rhône valley. The Syagrii appeared first in the region of Lyon and from the late fourth century until the eighth the name reoccurred in the Rhône valley, in Burgundy and Auvergne.[17]

In addition to names recognizable as those carried by senatorial aristocracy of the previous centuries, other names in the testament appear elsewhere in important families described in contemporary sources as of Roman origin. Most important are the names Wandalbertus, Waldebertus, and Crammelinus. These names, as Karl Ferdinand Werner has pointed out, appear in Burgundy in the sixth century and spread through this and neighboring regions, particularly at Besançon, where duke Waldelenus' son, Donatus, became Bishop and his other son, Chramnelenus, succeeded his father as duke.[18] This family, of

---

of Abbo's testament and hence certainly a relative. Also a domestic slave in Abbo's residence at Gap bore his mother's name, par. 27. On the tendency for unfree servants to carry the names of their masters in early medieval society see Wilhelm Störmer, *Früher Adel,* vol. I (Stuttgart: 1973) p. 33 and note18a; and Staab, *Untersuchungen zur Gesellschaft am Mittelrhein,* p. 335.

[11] par. 43.

[12] Stroheker, no. 401. See also Heinzelmann, *Bischofsherrschaft,* pp. 208–210.

[13] Stroheker, no. 402. Rusticula's father.

[14] par. 32.

[15] Stroheker, no. 62.

[16] *Ibid.,* no. 63. For an explication of the language of this epitaph see Heinzelmann, *Bischofsherrschaft,* pp. 57, 133, 157.

[17] Stroheker, no. 366–378; see also A. Coville, *Recherches sur l'histoire de Lyon du Veme siècle au IXeme siècle (450–800)* (Paris: 1928) pp. 5–29. For property acquired from Siagria see map C, p. 82

[18] See Karl Ferdinand Werner, "Bedeutende Adelsfamilien pp. 83–142; translated in T. Reuter, ed. *Medieval Nobility,* pp. 137–202. On the group including duke Waldelenus, see the translation, pp. 155–160. Werner's reconstruction of this group in the ninth and tenth centuries has been criticized, as for example, by Franz Irsigler, *Untersuchungen zur Geschichte des frühfränkischen Adels* (Bonn: 1969), p. 72. These criticisms do not, however, affect the validity of his argument for the seventh and eighth centuries. Likewise, the debate between Irsigler and Heike Grahn-Hoek *(Die fränkische Oberschicht im 6. Jahrhundert: Studien zu ihrer rechtlichen und politischen Stellung.* Vorträge und Forschungen, Sonderband 21 (Sigmaringen: 1976) concerning the existence of an early Frankish "nobility" is not germane to the consideration of seventh- and eighth-century Provence. For more recent work on this family of Juran *duces* and bishops of Besançon see Horst Ebling, Jörg Jarnut, Gerd Kampers, "*Nomen et gens:* Untersuchungen zu den Führungsschichten

apparently Roman origin, was closely allied and intermarried with other groups of Frankish nobles established in the region from the time of Chlothar II. In the later seventh century these included a bishop Chramlinus of Embrun deposed in 677 by Theuderic III
through the efforts of the mayor of the palace Ebroin.[19] As Werner shows, this group produced supporters of the Carolingians from the time of Charles Martel through the eighth
century and early ninth. The testament indicates that among Abbo's kin was a Wandalbertus abbas from whom he acquired property near Nyons. At several points he mentions
property acquired from a person (or persons) named Waldebertus and variously qualified
as *presbyter* and *episcopus*.[20] As we shall see, Abbo was probably connected to him by
somewhat distant kinship. Finally, Abbo's grandfather Marro had acquired property from
a Bishop Crammelinus at Mamers near Venasque.[21] The date of this acquisition is unknown, but the geographical similarity makes it possible that this Crammelinus was the
same bishop as the Chramlinus deposed from the see of Embrun in 677. Since property cir-
culated primarily among persons with some kin connection, one can suppose that this
bishop may have been related to Marro, who had other kin with property in the region.[22]
The hypothesis that Abbo was connected to this group of nobles is strengthened by the appearance, in the bishop list of Besançon, the traditional center of this family, not only of a
Wandelbertus sometime in the late seventh or early eighth century but also of his immediate predecessor Abbo, and a more distant predecessor who carried the name of Abbo's father Felix. Further, a *comes* in this region mentioned in Pseudo Fredegar in 609/610
carried the name Abbelenus. Finally, Abbo includes in his testament a donation to his
fidelis Protadius. This name likewise occurs in the Jura region in the early seventh century
in the persons of the *Dux* Protadius, who became mayor of the palace under Theuderic II
before his assassination in 605, and his apparent kinsman Protadius who was bishop of
Besançon in 614.[23]

---

des Franken-, Langobarden- und Westgotenreiches im 6. und 7. Jahrhundert," *Francia* vol. 8
(1980), pp. 700–701, and also Gerard Moyse, "La Bourgogne," p. 476; B. de Vregille, "Les
origines chrétiennes et le haute moyen âge," in *Histoire de Besançon,* directed by Claude Fohlen,
vol. 1 (Paris: 1964), pp. 182–185, and Gérard Moyse, "Les origines du monachisme dans le diocèse de Besançon (Ve–Xe siècles)" in *Bibliothèque de l'Ecole des chartes,* vol. 131 (1973), pp.
21–104 and 369–485, *passim.* The connection between Abbo's family and this group was first
pointed out by Jean-Pierre Poly in *La mutation féodale* p. 320 note 2. On Abbo's acquisitions from
Rigaberta and Waldebertus see map 4.

[19] *DMer.* 48; see below chapter V. p. 237

[20] par. 24, 52. It is likely that the descriptions of the properties in the testament were taken from the
records of their acquisition. Thus earlier transactions would have qualified Waldebertus as *presbyter,* later ones as *episcopus,* and these titles would have been carried over unchanged in the testament.

[21] par. 50.

[22] par. 36.

[23] Duchesne III, p. 198; Poly *La mutation* p. 320 note 2. The donation to Protadius was of property

In conclusion, the family connections of Abbo place him in two long traditions of aristocratic importance in the region: the Gallo-Roman senatorial tradition which had dominated the area south of Lyon from the end of the third century well into the sixth, and the tradition of families of some Roman origin but quickly allied with Frankish central power in the region from the sixth.

Until quite recently, the dominant understanding of the fusion of Germanic and Gallo-Roman elements of aristocratic society had been that the two ethnic groups had begun to merge even before the time of Clovis and that by the eighth century this process was complete. After roughly 700, Eugen Ewig and others have argued, designations such as Roman, Goth, Frank, were more territorial than ethnic, and the real distinctions in society were those separating aristocrat and peasant, not Frank and Roman.[24] More recently, in both France and Germany, this position is coming under reexamination as some scholars argue that ethnic differences in the aristocracy persisted well into the eighth, if not even into the tenth and even eleventh, centuries.

J.-P. Poly and E. Bournazel have pointed out that, while by the eighth century intermarriage may well have made it impossible to speak of biological descendants of Franks or Romans, individuals continued to be designated by some texts, both legal and "historical"

---

confiscated from the cleric Maurengus, who was probably a rebel allied with the *dux* Maurontus (see below, p. 130). par. 55. The fact that the property was a royal grant from confiscation rather than allodial or inherited may suggest that the bequest to Protadius was in return for his assistance in suppressing the revolt. On Abbelenus, see *Continuator,* 37 p. 29, and Gérard Moyse, "La Bourgogne," p. 476. On Protadius, 475, 479.

[24] The old studies of G. Kurth, *Etudes franques,* 2 vols. (Paris-Brussels: 1919), while containing some intelligent ideas, are no longer adequate discussions of medieval ethnicity. More important are Eugen Ewig, "Volkstum und Volksbewußtsein im Frankenreich des 7. Jahrhunderts," first published in *Caratteri del secolo VII in occidente* 2. Settimane di studio del Centro italiano di studi sull'alto medioevo 5 (Spoleto: 1958) and reprinted in Eugen Ewig, *Spätantikes und fränkisches Gallien;* Reinhard Wenskus, *Stammesbildung und Verfassung: Das Werden der frühmittelalterlichen gentes* (Cologne-Graz: 1961); "Die deutschen Stämme im Reiche Karls des Großen," *Karl der Große,* 179–219; R. Sprandel, "Struktur und Geschichte des merowingischen Adels", *Historische Zeitschrift* 193 (1961) pp. 33–71; Walther Kienast, *Studien über die französischen Volksstämme des Frühmittelalters* (Stuttgart: 1968) (to be consulted with caution); Karl Ferdinand Werner, "Les nations et le sentiment national dans l'Europe médiévale," *Revue historique* 244 (1970), reprinted in *Structures politiques du monde franc VI–XIIe siècles. Etudes sur les origines de la France et de l'Allemagne* (London: 1979); and the essays in *Aspekte der Nationenbildung im Mittelalter,* ed. Helmut Beumann and Werner Schröder (Sigmaringen: 1978); a particularly insightful understanding of the symbiosis of Frankish and Gallo-Roman society is that of Giovanni Tabacco in "I processi di formazione dell'Europa Carolinga," in *Nascita dell'Europa ed Europa Carolingia: un'equazione da verificare.* Settimane di studio del centro italiano di studi sull'alto medioevo 27, vol. 1 (Spoleto: 1981), pp. 17–43. On the later Frankish principalities see Karl Brunner, "Der fränkische Fürstentitel im neunten und zehnten Jahrhundert," *Intitulatio II: Lateinische Herrscher- und Fürstentitel im neunten und zehnten Jahrhundert,* ded. Herwig Wolfram, *MIÖG* Ergänzungsband 24 (Vienna: 1973), pp. 181–191.

(as for example in the *Gesta episcoporum* of Auxerre) as Franks, Romans, Goths, Burgundians, etc.[25] The important question is not then whether these individuals were really descendants of the people of the migration period, but rather how the individuals so designated and their societies identified and perceived them. Poly and Bournazel concentrate on onomastic and legal data, primarily from Aquitaine and Provence, in order to determine the bases for these ethnic designations.

They conclude that, through the eleventh century, there persisted a "conscience nobiliaire 'à la romaine'" in the aristocracy of the Midi.[26] This memory was based in a living genealogical tradition of descent from senatorial or even imperial families on the part of these southern aristocrats. This vertical group identity, Poly and Bournazel argue, reinforced by a separate legal tradition, a claim to a monopoly on access to the sacred, and a tradition that only Roman origins could confer nobility, was in sharp contrast to the more horizontal kin identity of the Frankish imperial aristocracy. During the period of Carolingian ascendancy the latter obscured from view but did not eliminate entirely the former, which was able to reemerge in the tenth and eleventh centuries. Only then did the two really form an amalgam as the old Roman nobility forgot, at least in part, their origins and the Frankish aristocracy began to adopt a more linear form of kinship structure.

These two traditions, Poly and Bournazel further argue, were not only distinct but hostile to each other, and this hostility continued as long as the two nobilities represented radically different cultures from which developed the society of the High Middle Ages.

A more modest revision of the hypothesis of an early fusion of Frankish and Roman aristocracies has been advanced by a student of Eugen Ewig, Horst Ebling, who, likewise basing his investigations on anthroponymy, argues that an amalgamation of these two groups did not take place before the middle of the eighth century.[27] His examination of secular and religious officeholders in Francia between 511 and ca. 741 indicates that Germanic or Romance names, far from being the result of naming fashions *(Namenmode)* were highly reliable indications of ethnic identity. Of the 271 secular officeholders between 613 and 741, he finds that 90% (245) carry Germanic names and only 10% (26) Roman names. Of the persons in these groups whose ethnicity is given in texts, he finds no Franks who carry Roman names. All those of Frankish origins (15) carry Germanic names, and only one of Roman origin carried a Germanic name. A similar examination of bishops' names produced comparable results. Here Ebling studies 813 bishops between the sixth and the first half of the eighth centuries. Of these, 319 (40%) carried Germanic names, and they became more and more frequent as time went on. Of the 494 bishops with Roman names, fully 90% (450) were also designated as of Roman origin.

---

[25] *La Mutation*, pp. 315–335.
[26] *Ibid.*, p. 324.
[27] Ebling, *Nomen et Gens*, pp. 689–701.

These two revisionist examinations of ethnicity in the Frankish empire are most appropriate points of departure for consideration of the ethnic identity of the aristocracy in the Rhône valley. Indeed, Poly and Bournazel cite the family of Abbo as an example of a "senatorial family in the first half of the eighth century." Likewise, one of the kindreds with which Ebling must deal at some length, since it does not conform to the general pattern he finds, is that of the *Dux* Waldelenus, with whom, as Poly points out, Abbo is connected. Before considering the testament in detail, however, it would be well to point out certain characteristics of these arguments which these histories share with the preceding scholars whose works they are criticizing.

With few exceptions, studies of early medieval ethnicity tend to accept five general suppositions: 1. Ethnicity is closely related to language (either in spoken language or in anthroponymy) and law. 2. Everyone had a specific ethnic identity. 3. Everyone should be able to recognize this one ethnic identity – Welfs should not be called Franks by one source and Bavarians by another – one source must be right, the other wrong. 4. Except over long generations, ethnic identity is very difficult to change, largely because of the personal nature of inherited law. 5. Ethnic identity was a source of friction – for instance, the title of Poly and Bournazel's chapter reads "Political unity and ethnic opposition".

These suppositions create an "objective" model for examining ethnicity which may simplify the problem but simultaneously distort the phenomenon of ethnicity itself. Sense of ethnic identity was probably never so clear-cut, neither in the migration period nor in the subsequent four centuries. From the earliest period the identity of peoples, both Gallo-Roman and Germanic, was fluid, potentially changeable, and, to an extent, contradictory.

In the migration period, as Herwig Wolfram and Reinhard Wenskus[28] have shown, the *gentes* or peoples were composed of various groups who could and did change their identity and be identified by others differently depending on circumstances. The clearest example of this ethnic complexity is found in Priscus' description of a meeting while on a diplomatic mission to the Huns between the author and a man who had begun life as a Greek but was at the time of the meeting a Scythian Hun. By changing his dress, marrying a barbarian wife, and fighting alongside the Huns, he had become in fact a barbarian. This change was remarkable for a Roman but natural for the Scythian "people" described by Priscus in the Thucydidean term ζύγκλυδες meaning essentially a group of rabble thrown together by chance.[29] Priscus further describes the Scythians as speaking their own

---

[28] Herwig Wolfram, *Geschichte der Goten* (2nd edition Munich: 1979). Wenskus, *Stammesbildung*, esp. pp. 81–98, 113–124, and *passim*.

[29] Priscus in Constantine Prophyrogenitus in *Excerpta de Legationibus Romanorum ad Gentes*, ed. Carolus de Boor (Berlin: 1903), vol. 1, p. 135. Priscus, *fragmentum 8, Fragmenta Historicorum Graecorum* 4, 86–88. See Wolfram, *Geschichte der Goten*, p. 451, n. 12, and Falko Daim, "Das 7. und 8. Jh. in Niederösterreich," *Germanen Awaren Slaven in Niederösterreich: Das erste Jahrtausend nach Christus* (Vienna: 1977), p. 90.

language as well as Hunish, Gothic, and Latin: "The Scythians, a jetsam of peoples, speak in addition to their own barbarian dialect, Hunic, Gothic, or latin."[30] For Thucydides as for Priscus, ξύγκλυδες had an essentially negative connotation and is used by Gylippus to shame his troops into defeating "human jetsam."[31] Thus language, dress, and kinship were, for these migration period barbarians multiple, arbitrary, and changeable.

If we examine post-migration sources, we find that a similar complexity continues. Those very elements on which contemporaries placed the most importance for determining membership in a *gens, natio,* etc., are to some extent arbitrary or at least changeable. The most famous, cited by Zöllner and Wenskus, is that of Regino of Prüm: "diverse nations of peoples differ among themselves in origin, customs, language, and laws." *(diversae nationes populorum inter se discrepant genere, moribus, lingua, legibus).*[32] This list is not greatly dissimilar from that in the Diet of Verona in the following century: "a coming together of Saxons, Suevs, and Bavarians, Lotharingians, Italians and of others dissimilar in birth, language, custom." *(conventum Saxonum Suevorum et Bawariorum Lothariorum Italicorum aliorumque, natione, lingua et habitu dissimilium),* cited by K. F. Werner,[33] or indeed the lament of Ado of Vienne over the battle of Fontenoy at which, for the first time, Christian Frankish armies met in disastrous confrontation: "Not dissimilar in arms or distinct in the custom of peoples, but only opposed in their camps" *(Non armis dissimiles, non habitu gentis distincti, solum castris obversi).*[34] Finally, even when an author placed in the forefront the distinction of laws, as does Agobard in his *Liber adversus legem Gundobadi,* he does not imply that law is either essential or immutable. He argues that all Christians are one in Christ; paraphrasing Coll. 3, 9–11, "Where there is no gentile and Jew, circumcised and uncircumcised, Barbarian and Scythian, Aquitainian and Lombard, Burgundian and Alaman, slave and free, but all in all in Christ" *(Ubi non est gentilis et Iudeus, circumcisio et preputium, barbarus et Scitha, Aquitanus et Langobardus, Burgundio et Alamannus, servus et liber, sed omnia et in omnibus Christus).*[35] Further, he states that in the area of Lyon, distinctions of law are found not only among inhabitants of the same regions or civitates, but even within the same households: … "there are as many differences of law as there are not only in each region or in each city, but even within many

---

[30] ξύγκλυδες γὰρ ὄντες πρὸς τῇ σφετέρᾳ βαρβάρῳ γλώσσῃ ζηλοῦσιν ἢ τὴν Οὔννων ἢ τὴν Γότθων ἢ καὶ τὴν Αὐσονίων,

[31] Thucydides, VII.5, pp. 9–13.

[32] *SSR Germ. ep. ad Hathonem.* The text was emphasized, in a different way from the present treatment, by Erich Zöllner, *Die politische Stellung der Völker im Frankenreich* (Vienna: 1950).

[33] Werner, "Les nations", p. 291.

[34] *PL* 123.136.

[35] *MGH Ep.* 5, 158–64. Helmut Beumann, commenting on this text in "Die Bedeutung des Kaisertums für die Entstehung der deutschen Nation im Spiegel der Bezeichnungen von Reich und Herrscher," *Aspekte der Nationenbildung,* p. 329, suggests that the *Franci* are not included because they are already identical with the *Imperium Christianum.*

houses" (... *tanta diversitas legum quanta non solum in singulis regionibus aut civitatibus, sed etiam in multis domibus habetur*). And finally he suggests that Louis the Pious could as emperor change the legal identity of those "perpauci" still living by Burgundian law to the law of the Franks: "If however it should be pleasing to our most wise lord emperor that he would transfer them to the law of the Franks" *(Si autem placeret domino nostro sapientissimo imperatori, ut eos transferret ad legem Francorum).*[36]

If we take in turn those elements on which contemporaries seem to have placed the greatest importance, we find that they are relatively fluid and in a sense arbitrary. Regino lists first *genus*-origin, similar to the *natio* of the Diet of Verona. Origin can include in a narrow sense personal ancestors, but also the common origins of a people. Both are, in anthropological terms, fictive, in that a selection must be exercised to determine from which of the myriad possible origins one wishes to choose. This process is very clear among the Franks and Goths, whose national histories and genealogies present a past which is formed to be comparable with that of the Romans, and parallel to them.[37]

The second characteristic emphasized by Regino, *mores,* corresponds to the *habitus* of Verona and of Ado. *Mores* can, in one sense, mean law: "The difference between *lex* and *mores* is that *lex* is written, *mos* is custom tested by tradition and/or unwritten *lex*" (*Inter legem autem et mores hoc interest, quod lex scripta est, mos vero est vetustate probata consuetudo, sive lex non scripta*).[38] However, since Regino also mentions *leges,* and other texts written before and after Regino speak of *habitus* (appearance, dress, deportment), it is reasonable to understand *mores* here in that same sense. This emphasis (in the second place of the list) on custom recalls Charlemagne's care to dress his young son Louis as a Gascon when sending him to be king of the Aquitanians, and suggests the importance of distinctive custom, most evident in dress and tonsure, as a sign of belonging to a distinct group.

Language is the third characteristic mentioned by Regino, the second by the Diet.[39] Much has been written on the growing significance of language and recognition of language as a characteristic of different peoples. However, bilingualism and multilingualism were characteristic of large populations, particularly in such regions as the Rhône valley,

---

[36] Herwig Wolfram, *Intitulatio II.*, pp. 82–83.

[37] In particular, the *Liber historiae Francorum* I *SSRM* 2, 241–242; and the *Origo Francorum duplex SSRM* 7, pp. 517–28.

[38] *Etymologiae*, ed. W. M. Lindsay II, x, 2; V, iii, 2–3.

[39] Wenskus argues in "Die deutschen Stämme," 207–210, that the distinction between those speaking *lingua theodisca* and *lingua Romana* was increasingly important by the ninth century. This may be so concerning the eastern and western parts of the Empire, but since, as Haimo of Auxerre (died 855), cited by Wenskus, pointed out, those speaking *lingua Romana* included the *Romani, Itali, Aquitani, Franci, Burgundiones,* and *Gotthi,* language could hardly be a factor in differentiating among these peoples.

and *gentes* like Burgundians had lost their own language in the transformations of the migration period; language, like other ethnic characteristics, was therefore at best relatively fluid, particularly in aristocratic circles.

Regino mentions *leges* last in his list; others do not mention them at all. In the ninth and tenth centuries references to the particular law of individuals occur with decreasing frequency, and when they appear at all it is in such areas as Catalonia-Septimania or Italy. However one should not conclude from this rarity that the ancient "personality principle" which once clearly specified the immutable, non-territorial nature of Germanic law passed from father to son, was finally breaking down. In fact, the so-called "personality principle" was never as universal or as clearly ethnic as some legal and social historians have presented it to be. As Heinrich Brunner pointed out long ago,[40] the personality of Germanic law did not precede the establishment of Germanic peoples in the Roman Empire. The appearance of the "national laws" themselves, as we now know, were for the Goths, Salic Franks, and Burgundians, the result of their contact with and adaptation of Vulgar Roman Law. While containing elements of migration-period custom, they are largely dependent for form, categories, and structure on Roman law and are pacts or covenants written to provide for harmonious coexistence of Barbarians and Romans living in the same areas. Laws such as those of the Bavarians and the Alamanni are pacts imposed on groups of peoples by the Franks and are to a high degree derivative.[41] Hence at no time were the "national laws" actually timeless statements of tradition. They were recent in origin and subject to amendment, particularly in the eighth and ninth centuries.

According to Brunner, the earliest Germanic laws, such as the *Lex Salica,* provided that Romans and non-Salic barbarians be judged according to Salic law. The first indication of the personality principle among the Franks occurs in the *Lex Ribuaria,* but it is hardly evidence of an immutable, inherited legal personality. It specified that in judicial proceedings the accused was to respond "according to the law of the place where he was born" *(in iudicio interpellatus, sicut lex loci contenit, ubi natus fuit, sic respondeat).*[42] This sort of

---

[40] Heinrich Brunner, *Deutsche Rechtsgeschichte* vol. 1 (2nd ed. Munich-Leipzig: 1906), no. 35, pp. 382–399. On this complex and much debated subject, see also L. Stouff, "Étude sur le principe de la personalité des lois depuis les invasions barbares jusqu'au XIIe siècle," *Revue bourguignonne de l'enseignement supérieur,* vol. 4,1 (1894), pp. 1–310; and Hermann Nehlsen, "Aktualität und Effektivität der ältesten germanischen Rechtsaufzeichnungen," *Vorträge und Forschungen,* vol. 23 (Sigmaringen: 1977), pp. 449–502.

[41] On the relationship between barbarian law and Roman law see Levy, *West Roman Vulgar Law,* pp. 14–17, and in general Rudolf Buchner's *Beiheft* to Wattenbach-Levison, *Deutschlands Geschichtsquellen im Mittelalter: Vorzeit und Karoliner, Die Rechtsquellen* (Weimar: 1955).

[42] 35, 3. However, in the Visigothic and Burgundian kingdoms some sense of personality of law must have existed from the early sixth century to judge from the legal codifications for Goths and Burgundians on the one hand and for Romans on the other. See Wolfram, *Geschichte der Goten,* pp. 239, 258 n. 67, 402, 456.

personal law is based then not on the law of the parents but on the individual's place of birth.

A sense of law as a heritage from parents regardless of the place in which one was born developed only with the expansion of the Salian Franks and their domination over other peoples. It is the retention of the law of a conquering and ruling elite among members of that elite in outlying corners of the realm. But even this sort of personality of law was subject to variation and limitation. Mixed marriages could lead to circumstances in which an individual might have more than one law. A woman in Italy, for example, controlled property from her own inheritance not according to the law of her husband which had, through marriage, become her personal law, but rather by the law in which she was born. More important, from the late eighth century, some disputes between persons of different laws were increasingly to be settled according to the law of the place where the crime was committed.[43] When, in those areas such as Italy, Burgundy, and Septimania, one finds judges inquiring into the law of the individuals involved in legal proceedings, one should not build this "professio iuris" into a technical declaration of ethnicity. The *Capitulare missorum*,[44] which orders the *missi* to inquire into the birth law of the individuals, is vague on whether the law was acquired from the parents or from the place of birth: "And let them ask each person what law they have from birth" *(et per singulos inquirant, quale habeant legem ex nomine* (corr.: *natione). Thus law, like the other characteristics of peoplehood, is hardly a sufficient distinction on which to assign ethnic identity. True, it is personal, but personal in a variety of ways which are in constant flux through the early Middle Ages.

In conclusion, we find that those characteristics used by contemporaries to distinguish among *"nationes"* or *"gentes"* are all partial, to a large extent subjective, and difficult for the historian to perceive, in part because of our scanty documentation but primarily due to their essential ambiguity. No one characteristic, be it law, language, custom, or birth, can be considered a sufficient index by which to assign ethnicity, nor was it any different for contemporaries. Self-perception, and perception of others, represented a choice in a variety of somewhat arbitrary characteristics, which could be seen differently by different people. The real, although not entirely impenetrable, barriers were between slave and free, free and noble. Within the elite a person or faction could be Burgundian by birth, Roman by language, and Frankish by dress. Likewise, someone born of a father from Francia and a mother from Alamannia could properly be termed a Frank or an Alamannian by different authors considering him from different perspectives. His own perception of himself might change during his lifetime, depending on how he viewed his relationship to the Frankish king and his local faction. Or the specific legal identity of an individual might be unimpor-

---

[43] Capitulare Haristallense (779) *MGH Capit.* vol. I, p. 49 no. 20, c. 10. On similar Saxon laws for the ninth century see Brunner, vol. I, pp. 386–87 and n. 19.
[44] *MGH Capit.* vol. I, p. 67, no. 25, c. 5.

tant to him except under very specific circumstances, such as inheritance, at other times being subordinated to his other group associations.[45]

With these general considerations in mind, let us return to the case of Abbo and the specific arguments of Poly and Ebling.

The individuals connected with Abbo as explicit or implicit kin include roughly equal percentages of Germanic and Roman names. Nevertheless, Poly and Bournazel argue that "the partial Germanization – or rather the Frankization – of the anthroponymy of this aristocratic group is far from signifying the absence of a Roman consciousness which is evidenced here by the usage of the Roman testament, the use of noble titles (*vir clarissimus*) fixed by imperial protocol and the devotion to saints issued from old senatorial families (Veranus), saints who are also probably ancestors."[46]

Thus far one can agree, and in light of the wider suggestions of association with the great senatorial families of the region which we have made above, one could even expand on this argument. Likewise, not only is Veranus, who might be the bishop of Vence or Cavillon,[47] a patron of an oratory in Abbo's possession, but one could argue that Pancrasius, patron of a church also belonging to him, reflected and enforced the regional ties of Abbo's family with the Roman traditions of the region. The relics of Pancrasius had been brought to Marseille, after all, by the deacon of none other than Gregory of Tours in the sixth century.[48]

However, this is only part of the picture. Certainly Abbo's ties were strong with the Gallo-Roman aristocracy, but his Frankish contacts were no less important. The onomastic tradition in his family was, as we have seen, roughly equally divided between Roman and Germanic names. His involvement with Charles Martel was essential in his political position and for the growth of his power. We do not know how long before him the names of Saints Veranus and Pancrasius had been used as titular patrons of his oratory and church, but his selection of Saint Peter as principal patron of his new foundation in 726, four years after the initial involvement of Charles Martel with the papacy, might suggest a Frankish orientation in his patronage policies. Again, Abbo's connections with the family of Waldelenus of Besançon suggest that his ties to important families of the region were not exclusively Gallo-Roman. This family is usually seen as Gallo-Roman because the Dux Chramnelenus is said by Fredegar to have been *ex genere Romano,* but it must be remembered that two other *duces* closely connected with Chramnelenus, Wandalmarus, and

---

[45] Perhaps the best example of such complexity is the much debated origins of the Welfs. Judith, the second wife of Louis the Pious, was of Bavarian, Saxon, and Alemannian origin. See most recently Karl Brunner, *Oppositionelle Gruppen,* pp. 102–103.

[46] *La mutation,* pp. 320–21.

[47] Par. 4 note 14.

[48] Par. 10 note 43.

Waldericus, are said in the same sentence to have been *ex genere Francorum*.[49] Taken as a whole, one must conclude that Abbo was Frankish as well as Gallo-Roman, and manipulated both elements of his background for his purposes. Certainly one cannot find in him a trace of any opposition or hostility between Frankish and Gallo-Roman ethnicity. A more loyal supporter of the *dux Francorum* Charles (who likewise carried the Roman title of *vir inluster*) would be difficult to find.

The cases of Abbo, and as we shall see below, that of his enemy Maurontus, also seem to contradict the conclusion Ebling draws from his examination of names of officeholders in the Frankish kingdom. Abbo was, after all, at least rector if not *patricius,* and thus a "Gallo-Roman" officeholder with a Germanic name. Likewise, as Ebling admits, the *Dux* Chramnelenus *ex genere Romano,* seems to have been an exception. But rather than adding up exceptions, it might be well to reexamine the methodology and conceptions which underlie Ebling's work as a whole.

First, the data on the Franks are taken largely from Ebling's important but limited *Prosopographie der Amtsträger des Merowingerreiches*[50] which omits certain other important officeholders and overlooks kinship ties among others, ties which confuse the image of naming patterns suggested in his article. Second, the sample upon which much of the argument rests is simply too small to be considered reliable bases for statistical interpretation. Of the 271 names of secular officeholders from 613–741, 245 are Germanic. It is possible to demonstrate the Germanic ethnic identity of only 15, or 6%, of these. Since one has no reason to suppose that this tiny number is in any way a statistically random sample, the figures are meaningless.

In addition to these flaws in method, the examination may also suffer from weaknesses of interpretation. He and his coauthors, Jörg Jarnut and Gerd Kampers, working respectively on Lombard and Visigothic officeholders, propose that the names are evidence of a specific ethnic identity of the individuals who bear them or that they are the result of a "Namenmode".[51] Rather than "Namenmode" one might posit "Namenstrategie". Considering the very real importance of individual names in Merovingian society, one might expect that sons destined for high public office in the service of Germanic kings would carry names in the tradition of the ruler and the kingdom which they would serve. This does not mean that their brothers and sisters need all have carried such names or that all of the 230 individuals about whose ethnic backgrounds nothing is known were ethnic Franks. Likewise, the predominance of Roman names among bishops need not be proof

---

[49] *Chronicle of Fredegar,* 78, p. 65: "Quod cum decem docis cum exercetebus, id est Arinbertus, Amalgarius, Leudebertus, Wandalmarus, Waldericus, Ermento, Barontus, Chairaardus ex genere Francorum, Chramnelenus ex genere Romano, Willibadus patricius genere Burgundionum, Aigyna genere Saxsonum ..."

[50] Beihefte der Francia 2 (Munich: 1974).

[51] *Nomen et Gens,*" p. 690.

that the old Gallo-Roman aristocracy held on to Church office into the eighth century to the extent that the authors assume. At least in theory, *Ecclesia vivit lege Romana,* and it may well be that not only Roman but also Frankish and Franko-Roman families were inclined to give Roman or Latin names to sons destined for careers in the Church.[52]

Underlying all the assumptions of Ebling is of course the presupposition that everyone (or almost everyone) was clearly and unambiguously either a Frank or a Roman. However, the "exceptions" he cites, such as Bodegisel and Waldelenus, as well as those we have identified, such as Abbo, may have been more common than he realizes. In the Rhône valley of the early eighth century, families of great aristocrats seem to have had both Roman and Frankish backgrounds. In such families, strategic choices about which aspects of a complex ethnic heritage to emphasize could be made depending on circumstances, expectations for particular children, and other families which were objectives directed at manipulating one or another part of the family's ethnic and regional contacts. This does not mean that to someone like Abbo ethnicity was unimportant; it may well have been extremely significant, although never is he or indeed anyone with whom he is associated or with whom he is in conflict identified as "Roman" or "Frankish." However, this importance need not have been predetermined or limited to one ethnicity. Abbo, with his complex relationships within a traditional patronage structure, his urban ties, his silk clothing, and his Roman law, certainly drew on this rich heritage for part of his status and position. But his intimate involvement with *Romania* did not determine either the sphere or the direction of his political involvement.

Equally important to him were his personal and familial ties with Francia: those most clearly manifested in the anthroponymy which characterized his kin, his connections with the Juran and trans-Juran families such as that of Waldelenus, and, most important, his service to Charles Martel. Within this perspective, Abbo's "ethnicity" was probably closer to that described by modern historians and sociologists as "ethnic leadership," that is, political ethnicity rather than folkloric traditions, although the latter, too, could be called upon to mobilize groups to political ends.[53] As Wsevolod W. Isajiw suggests, "In contrast to the objective approach by which ethnic groups are assumed to be existing, as it were 'out there' as real phenomena, the subjective approach defines ethnicity as a process by which individuals either identify themselves as being different from others or belonging to a different group or are identified by others, or both identify themselves and are identified by others as different."[54] In this sense, surely, should one understand the real importance of ethnic identity in the Rhône valley at the beginning of the eighth century.

---

[52] On the exceptions and limitations to the theory that clerics and in particular bishops lived according to Roman law see Carl Gerold Fürst, *"Ecclesia vivit lege Romana? Zeitschrift der Savigny-Stiftung für Rechtsgeschichte. Kanonistische Abteilung"* vol. 61 (1975), pp. 17–36.

[53] As in, for example, *Ethnic Leadership in America,* ed. John Higham (Baltimore: 1978).

[54] *Definitions of Ethnicity* (Toronto; 1979), p. 9.

Kindred of Abbo

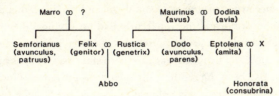

Kinship Patterns

The recognition of possible connections between Abbo and these two traditions based on naming patterns is insufficient to demonstrate that Abbo himself, or indeed the various persons who carried either old senatorial names or names of the Waldelenus/Chramnelenus group, felt themselves part of these traditions. Naming was important, but its specific meaning is not self-evident. In order to understand the perceptions Abbo and his contemporaries had of their kinship we must look more closely at the way various persons in the testament are identified and related explicitly by the testator.

The precision mentioned above with which Abbo specified the origins of his properties makes it possible to examine something of the actual perception of kinship ties uniting the aristocracy of early eighth century Provence. Of the thirty-four persons he names from whom he acquired property, nine are close relatives, and a number of others can be inferred to have been connected with Abbo by ties of kinship. The testament, augmented by the foundation charter of Novalesa, makes possibly the stemma on this page.

In addition to these, Abbo speaks of a "parens" Goda who shared inheritance with Dodo and a Wandalbertus abbas whom he also terms *parens noster*.[55] Finally one of the signatories to the foundation charter of 726 a Bishop Eusthacius, termed himself "quosinus" or cousin of Abbo.

Abbo's terminology is somewhat confused. He alternates between *auunculus* and *patruus* for his paternal uncle Semforianus, bishop of Gap (classical Latin: *patruus*) and he calls Eptolena who is clearly a maternal aunt (classical Latin: *matertera*) by the term for paternal aunt, *amita*. Both shifts, which are quite normal throughout the Middle Ages, suggest a weakening in the perceived distinction between maternal and paternal kin with perhaps an increased value placed on the position of maternal uncle.

The system by which Abbo states the origins of his estate suggests that he viewed somewhat differently the two sides of his ancestry. In the bequests, he is careful to distinguish the individual maternal kin from whom he had inherited, while properties from his father's side are less clear in their origin. The latter are said simply to be from his *parentes* except when he further clarifies their origin by mentioning from whom his uncle Sem-

---

[55] par. 36. In addition, the Virgilia in par. 52 could well be a daughter. See above, Ch. I note 68.

forianus[56] or his father[57] acquired them. One can offer two explanations for this difference. First, inheritance *ex parentibus* may simply mean from his father and since these inheritances were the most normal (he apparently had no siblings) they needed no further explanation. On the other hand, property from his maternal relatives came to him through less obvious successions, and hence he was careful to state exactly the origins of each piece. This care may have also been the result of the relative importance of his maternal and paternal families. His father's lands were almost entirely in the Hautes-Alpes, and while by the seventh century germanic names cannot be taken in any ethnic sense, the total lack of such names in the known members of this family before Abbo suggest that the family may have not been closely tied to the Frankish lords of the region. His mothers's family, on the other hand, had most of its holdings in the areas of Arles and Marseille below the Durance where the Franks had long maintained an interest in the wealth to be obtained through duties on shipping. In this family, the names Dodina, Dodo, Goda all suggest closer involvement with Frankish Austrasia.[58] Abbo's own career, moreover, was spent in the service of the Franks, both in the area of the Rhône and possibly in Francia. Thus he may have owed his rise to the continuation of connections through his mother's family which may have been more important than that of his father in terms of his career as follower of Charles Martel, and, possibly, *patricius* of Provence. Finally, his mother's family was apparently closely connected to some of the greatest families in the Rhône valley. Thus his care to enumerate inheritances and acquisitions from maternal kin may have been due to the relative importance of these persons in Provençal and Frankish society.

A second significant pattern in Abbo's designation of kin is that *only* those persons from whom he had inherited property are so designated. He had also purchased or otherwise acquired property from a great number of persons, some of whom shared inheritances with his maternal kin, particularly with his uncle Dodo and his *parens* Goda.[59] However, these persons are never referred to as kin. This omission suggests that in the landed aristocracy kinship was largely defined as inheritance kin, although efforts to acquire portions of previous inheritances from these distant connections suggest that outside of this strict inheritance kin there existed a privileged circle of persons who exchanged and sold property among themselves in order to reunite constantly fragmenting estates.

A closer examination of this circle within which land changed hands indicates that it

---

[56] par. 28.

[57] par. 43.

[58] The names Dodo and Godo recall in particular the family of the Dodo *domesticus … principes Pippini* in the *Vita Landiberti* (SSRM VI cap. 24, p. 377) and his kinsman Godobald in the *Miracula S. Dionysii* (*Neus Archiv* vol. 18, 1893, p. 601), who were important supporters of the Arnulfingians in the region of Liège and Maastricht in the early eighth century. See Matthias Werner, *Der Lütticher Raum,* pp. 121–139. In spite of the coincidence of names and the similar orientation, the evidence is insufficient to connect the family of Abbo with this important Austrasian clan.

[59] par. 39.

was composed of three groups. First were Abbo's closest kin, his parents, grandparents, and uncles from whom he inherited property. Next were those from whom he both purchased and inherited property: again uncle Dodo, his kinswoman Goda, and Wandalbertus. The third and largest group, 12 in all, were those from whom he purchased or otherwise acquired property through private transactions.[60]

Among the members of the last group a considerable number were individuals from whom isolated purchases had been made, often increasing holdings where inheritances had been significant. In other instances the pattern of acquisitions suggests that Abbo was reuniting property which had been divided by inheritance in previous generations. Often these properties were still held in indivision, just as Abbo continued to hold, with his cousin Honorata, property the two had inherited from their grandparents Maurinus and Dodina.[61] Among the persons holding property in indivision were Abbo's kinsmen Goda and Dodo,[62] Bishop Waldebertus and Rigaberga, Avolus and Freberga, and in the previous generation, Abbo's mother Rustica and her brother Dodo. By combining the information concerning Abbo's properties in certain locations, it is possible to construct an image of property dispositions over several generations in some instances. For example, in the valley of Orcières near Embrun Abbo's property was formed as follows:[63]

His maternal great grandparents had apparently left property in the valley divided into three portions, one at Brintico which had been divided further into three portions, one going to his mother, one to his maternal relative Goda, and one possible in indivision to Waldebertus and Rigaberga. In the other location, Moccense, the property was held among Siagria, Dodo and Goda in indivision, and again Waldebertus and Rigaberga. The final portion at Albariosco had gone to Abbo's kinsman Dodo. In time Abbo had purchased the portions of Waldebertus and Rigaberga as well as that of Siagria. He either inherited or purchased the portions of Goda and Dodo as well, thus reassembling much of the initial inheritance.[64]

---

[60] See above, chapter III, for the meaning of *conquiro*. Archibald R. Lewis, in his *The Development of Southern French and Catalan Society,* p. 10, confuses the image of Abbo's acquisitions considerably by translating *conquiro* simply as *conquer:* "… just as Abbo's will mentions land, in 739, which he had acquired by conquest."

[61] par. 44.

[62] par. 24, 34.

[63] par. 24.

[64] There probably had existed other portions that Abbo had not acquired. Although it is impossible to determine exactly the relationships among the inheritors, the fact that Dodo, Goda, Waldebertus and Rigaberga had each inherited two portions while Rustica and Siagria had only one each might suggest that the first four were of a previous generation to that of Rustica and Siagria. Dodo and Goda, who shared elsewhere inheritances were probably brother and sister, as would be likely for Waldebertus and Rigaberga. Their parents may have been siblings of Rustica's mother Doda. The individual portions inherited by Siagria and Rustica suggest that they might have received their portions only after further division upon the death of their parents, making them possibly first cousins.

Another inheritance, this time in the area of Gap, was shared by Waldebertus, Siagria, Widegunda and Rigaberga.[65] Abbo had purchased all of the portions. If these persons are then recongnized as more or less distant members of the same inheritance group, then the circulation of property among them becomes more understandable. Abbo's acquisitions were, in order of importance, after those from his father and mother (*de parentes nostros* in the text) from Siagria, who sold or otherwise transferred property to him in the Valley of Maurienne, in the area of Grenoble, Vienne, Macônnais, Gap, Die, and Sisteron. The vast extent of her property and in particular the northern portions of it support the hypothesis, suggested by her illustrious name, that she was in some way connected with the ancient and widespread family of the Syagrii whose importance from the Lyonnais to the Bordelais and south to Cahors and Provence had been enormous for generations. From his kinsman Waldebertus Abbo had land in the *pagi* of Sisteron, Riez, Gap and Embrun. From the above mentioned Widegunda with whom he was apparently connected, he acquired considerable property in the *pagi* of Briançon, Gap, Vaison and Venasque. From Goda he had purchased or inherited land in the *pagi* of Embrun, Riez, Arles, and Die and, in apparent indivision with Dodo, in Gap as well. Dodo, Abbo's maternal uncle, was his source for property in Embrun, and in indivision with Abbo's grandmother at Marseille and Arles and with his mother in the pagus of Cavaillon.

In all the given examples of acquisitions, the same strategy is apparent. Roman testamentary law strongly encouraged, not to say required, the division of estates very widely.[66] In each generation, therefore, children, both male and female, shared their family's inheritance in such a way that the estate was threatened with constant division and dispersion. Abbo, who by his political position was a powerful and leading member of a diffuse kindred, was able to undo the parceling, at least to some extent, by acquiring anew the lands so divided. Clearly his acquisitions were focused on the *portiones* inherited through the previous two generations by his kin.

Reacquisition was only one means of preserving the estate. A second, which we have already seen, was the practice of maintaining property in indivision. This was practiced by Abbo, by his close and explicitly named kin, and also among some wider and more distant connections. By maintaining the unity of the farms and estates and dividing simply the revenue, the efficiency of the agricultural units could be preserved and the complicated rights to the persons working the estates did not have to be settled. Only when property passed outside the family, as in the case of Abbo's own testament, did the division have to take place, as in the case of the division between Abbo and his cousin Honorata made in the testament.[67]

---

[65] par. 52. See map E, p. 82 for property acquired from Wideguda.

[66] On Roman inheritance in general see Buckland, pp. 334–404.

[67] par. 44. On women consecrated to God in the Merovingian church see most recently Suzanne Fonay Wemple, *Women in Frankish Society: Marriage and the Cloister 500 to 900* (Philadelphia: 1981), pp. 127–148.

A third means of preserving the patrimony was the limitation of heirs through the practice of dedicating children to the Church. In a powerful family such as that of Abbo, of course, this also served to enhance the power and prestige of the family, especially when members became bishops of important sees. Among Abbo's own kin, we find a paternal uncle, Semforianus, bishop of Gap; a connection Waldebertus progressively (?) priest, and then bishop (of Arles?); a kinsman Wandalbertus who was an abbot, and a cousin, Eusthacius, a bishop. Although it is not entirely inconceivable that some of these may have ascended to the episcopal dignity after a secular career which had produced legitimate children and heirs, there is no indication that this was the case. More than likely, then, these men had no legitimate heirs other than their nieces and nephews, and thus their portions of their parents' estates would have returned to the children of their siblings. The same is probably true of some of the women in Abbo's family. Ricuberta[68] is termed *"deo sacrata femina,"* and while this could mean that she took the veil after the death of her husband, the fact that Abbo seems to have acquired considerable amounts of her inheritance would suggest that she had no heirs. More likely she was vowed to religion at an early age and hence had no children of her own.

A final means of preserving the family patrimony was the failure of other members of the family, whether by design or by chance, to produce heirs. The most remarkable example of this is Abbo himself, who never makes the slightest allusion to a wife or to legitimate children living or dead. Abbo however is not the only one: his uncle Dodo has left him property, thus implying that he may have had no children who survived him either. The same may have been true of Siagria, given the amount of property which she sold or otherwise transferred to Abbo. However, one must be very cautious about drawing any conclusions about the extent to which this practice may have endangered the perpetuation of aristocratic families in the region: a testament would naturally mention those persons lacking children whose property thus passed to another relative or was otherwise alienated; Abbo could have had numerous, prolific kin who are not mentioned in his testament precisely because they did leave their property to their children. Nevertheless, the testament does indicate that the tendency to disperse the family patrimony integral to Roman testamentary law was partially overcome through a variety of means to limit offspring and to reunite estates.

Officeholding

The relationships which we have to this point examined served to maintain the importance of the family in the Rhône basin. Marriages with other important families in the area, widespread distribution of property through inheritance coupled with frequent

---

[68] par. 32.

purchases to reunite it, various strategies for limiting the numbers of heirs, all tended to maintain the social and economic position of the family. Abbo was however a man on the move. His fortunes were rising, and this was due not simply to his inherited position in the Rhône valley but rather to his contacts with the wider world of Frankish politics. One can only speculate on the origins of his relationships which brought him into the camp of Charles Martel. They may well have been through his kin in the area of Besançon discussed above.[69] Already around 719 one Amalbertus, whom Karl Ferdinand Werner has identified as probably a member of this kin group, was an important follower of Charles Martel.[70] It is conceivable that Abbo's appearance among Charles followers only a few years later in 722[71] was either prepared by his kinsman's position or continued a family alliance with the Austrasian Arnulfingians.

Certainly Abbo, with his family's extensive connections in the Alpine region, was a valuable regional ally for Charles. Not only was he connected with the family of Waldelenus and his descendants which controlled the episcopal see of Besançon and which was widely spread through Burgundy; his uncle Semforianus had been bishop of Gap before his deposition by enemies (possibly during the revolt of Antenor); his cousin Eusthacius was a bishop and his kinsman Wandalbertus an abbot. If one expands this list of ecclesiastical officeholders to include the likely kin of Abbo's mother Rustica, one finds important bishops, abbots and abbesses from Geneva to Arles. Finally, this tradition of officeholding by members of his family would be continued in his monastery: the first abbot, Godo, carried a name which, in a feminine form, was the name of one of Abbo's relatives from whom he had acquired considerable property. Godo, who disappears before 739, was succeeded by an abbot who bore the same name as the testator himself, Abbo.

Abbo's family, with its combination of Frankish and senatorial traditions, its strategic position in the alpine passes, and its control of episcopal sees and the office of *rector,* bears extremely close resemblance to another alpine family, that of the so-called Victoriden of Chur.[72]

This family, known, like that of Abbo, primarily through an eighth-century testament

---

[69] see above, p. 180 and Werner, "Noble Families, pp. 158–69.

[70] D Arn. 10; Heidrich, "Titulatur," p. 240. A 8

[71] D Arn. 11; Heidrich; "Titulatur," p. 241. A 10.

[72] See in particular the works of Otto P. Clavadetscher, "Die Einführung der Grafschaftverfassung in Rätien und die Klageschriften Bischof Viktors III. von Chur," *Zeitschrift der Savigny-Stiftung für Rechtsgeschichte, Kanonistische Abteilung* vol. 39 (1953), pp. 46–111; "Zur Verfassungsgeschichte des merowingischen Rätien," *Frühmittelalterliche Studien* vol. 8 (1974), pp. 60–70; and "Churrätien im Übergang von der Spätantike zum Mittelalter nach den Schriftquellen," in *Von der Spätantike zum frühen Mittelalter: aktuelle Probleme in historischer und archäologischer Sicht,* ed. Joachim Werner und Eugen Ewig, *Vorträge und Forschungen* vol. 25 (Sigmaringen: 1979), pp. 159–178.

(actually a *donatio post mortem*),[73] dominated the region of Raetia from the sixth through the middle of the eighth century. As Otto P. Clavadetscher has shown, the family traced its origins to one Zacco, probably a Frank who had been placed in the region during the sixth century to command the strategic alpine passes. In the seventh and eighth centuries the family controlled both ecclesiastical and secular offices in Chur: ca. 660 one Vigilius held the title of *tribunus*. His sons Victor and Jactadus were, respectively, bishop and *praeses*. In the next generation the sons of Jactadus, Vigilius, and Victor were bishop and *praeses*. In the following generation Victor's son Tello was bishop while another son, Zacco, was *praeses*.[74]

Clavadetscher suggests that this family, which was at once closely tied to the Roman traditions of the region and to the Franks, owed its position to an early marriage alliance between the Frankish commander and a local family. The nature of the offices held by various members of the family remains unclear. *Tribunus* suggests a military office and may have been the local designation of the Frankish military commander.[75] *Praeses* indicates a civilian office, and it is possible that as Raetia became virtually independent during the seventh century the office of *praeses* absorbed that of *tribunus* as the family consolidated its position and independence.[76] Although in sources originating outside the region, the *praeses* Victor is termed *comes*,[77] Clavadetscher argues with reason that the title was not bestowed by Frankish kings but rather transmitted within the family and self bestowed.

In the 770s, one finds, instead of the title *praeses*, that of *rector*, the same title held by Abbo. In a diploma of 773/74 Charles the Great took under his protection the Bishop and *rector* of Raetia Constantinus.[78] Whether the change in title from *praeses* to *rector* indicates a change in political structure in Chur is unclear. Clavadetscher argues that, in spite of the fact that in diploma of Charles the Frankish king states that he had established Constantinus as *rector* of Raetia (*... quem territurio Raetiarum rectorem posuimus*), the fact that Constantinus is termed *rector* and granted as such royal protection indicates that he was not a royal officeholder.[79] Abbo, too, apparently held his position of *rector* by virtue

---

[73] *Bündner Urkundenbuch*, ed. Elisabeth Meyer-Marthaler and Franz Perret vol. 1 (Chur: 1955), no. 17, pp. 13–23.

[74] Clavadetscher, "Zur Verfassungsgeschichte," p. 62.

[75] *Ibid.*, p. 69.

[76] *Ibid.*, p. 69. On the use of *praeses* to designate the mayor of the palace Grimoald see Ingrid Heidrich, "Titulatur," p. 101.

[77] In the *Vita S. Galli* auctore Walahfrido SSRM IV, c. 10, pp. 319–20; c. 11, p. 321; c. 12, p. 321. Clavadetscher, "Churrätien," p. 174.

[78] *DKar.* 78. Theodor Sickel suggested that the diploma was prepared in 773 in order to maintain the support of the Raetiens during his Italian campaign (Reg. 235 K 25). This hypothesis, if correct, would further confirm the strategic importance to the Carolingians of maintaining the cooperation of local magnates in the alpine passes. Charles' grant of immunity to Novalesa on March 25, 773, was certainly part of his preparations for his campaign (*DKar.* 74).

[79] Clavadetscher, "Die Einführung," pp. 79–82. He bases his argument on the fact that the diploma

of his inherited position in the Susa region, rather than as an appointee of Charles Martel. In the foundation charter of 726, although he states that the establishment of Novalesa was made *pro nos uel stabiletatem regno Francorum,* he claims his office not by Frankish grant but by grace of God: *Ergo una cum consensum pontificum uel clerum nostrorum Mauriennate et Segucine civitate in quibus nos Deus rectorem esse instituit …*"[80] Thus, just as in the case of Constantinus and his Victoriden predecessors, Abbo owed his position to a long history of family control over a crucial border region in the Alps.

Charles certainly needed the support of such families because his opponents in the region were at least as well established. The same pattern of landholding, of widespread estates worked or managed by freedmen under the supervision of agents, and of political power bases founded on a combination of kin alliances and lay and ecclesiastic officeholding created the strength of the so-called rebels who would oppose the Carolingians in the series of wars in the 720s and 30s. The probable relationships between this group and other enemies of the Arnulfingians will be discussed in the next chapter. However, for local power they seemed well established not only in the positions of *patricius* or *dux,* but also in important episcopal sees such as Vienne and as abbots of regional monasteries. The extent to which this control of ecclesiastical offices may have been widespread can be indirectly grasped from the signatures on the two documents prepared by Abbo; the first, the foundation charter of 726, was witnessed by four bishops, two abbots, an archdeacon, two deacons, a priest and a simple cleric. The testament prepared fourteen years later contains no signatures of ecclesiastics. Perhaps this was due to an incomplete transcription of the signatures or to the different nature of the documents: a religious foundation rather than a personal testament. However, since one of the signers, the archbishop of Vienne, was a relative of the Merovingian royal family,[81] whose successor abandoned his see rather than accept the confiscations accomplished by Charles Martel,[82] another, the abbot Maorongos was quite probably a rebel,[83] and given the widespread disruption of episcopal succession and confiscations from anti-Carolingian ecclesiastics throughout the region, one can imagine that the ecclesiastical powers may have been even more allied with the re-

---

indicates that Charles took Constantinus and the Raetien people under his protection, not as bishop but as *rector.* Were Constantinus merely a *comes,* such a protection would have been meaningless: the king did not guarantee the protection of a count and a population against outsiders; it was rather the duty of a count to provide protection in the name of the king. Thus Constantine must have held a position in some way independent of the Frankish king.

[80] Cipolla, I, p. 7.

[81] On the rôle of episcopal sees in the familial politics of the Merovingian period see Heinzelmann, *Bischofsherrschaft in Gallien* and, most recently, Georg Scheibelreiter, *Der Bischof in merowingischer Zeit* (Vienna: 1983), pp. 16–50.

[81] Archbishop Aeochaldus. Duchesne, I. p. 198.

[82] *Ibid.,* 199. See below chapter V, notes 56–59.

[83] 13, 9. See below Chapter V, p. 130.

bels than with Abbo and his faction. Thus Charles would have needed local supporters like Abbo.

Abbo was also important to Charles because of the strategic location of his extensive family properties and the center of his family's power. The region of the Alps, valleys and coastal expanses in which Abbo held property, although distant from the Frankish heart-lands to the north and east, was nevertheless vital for Frankish commerce and defense. Obviously the Rhône was the great highway connecting the interior of the realm with the Mediterranean world. So vital was this region to the welfare of the Merovingian economy that at an earlier period, the area of Provence had been divided in order to assure that each of the Frankish kingdoms would have access to the Mediterranean.[84] Into the eighth cen-tury this water route functioned as the primary line of communication and trade with the civilized world.

Perhaps equally important from a Frankish perspective was the overland route into Italy that passed through Susa. From the north, one traveled through St.-Jean-de-Maurienne before crossing the Alps in the Dora Riparia valley; from the south the way passed through Gap, Embrun, and Briançon, at which town one was joined by travelers from the west arriving via Grenoble, and then on to Susa and Lombardy.[85] If the Rhône was primarily the route of trade, the valley of the Dora Riparia was the route of war: the Romans had understood well the strategic importance of Susa in guarding the access to the pass, and the walls of the Roman *castellum* still protected the city in the eighth century. The city along with its surrounding territory had been ceded to the Franks by the Lom-bards around 574[86] and had since that time been an important strategic city in the Frank-ish-Lombard border. In the later eighth century, Pepin III would turn back a Lombard in-vasion in the valley.[87] Thus the position of *rector* of Maurienne and Susa which Abbo held in 726 was an important position from a strategic perspective, and his loyalty to Charles Martel must have been important in assisting the suppression of the revolt in the region.

The clash which pitted Abbo as a supporter of Charles against the *Dux* Maurontus and his followers in the Valley was not the first between Abbo's family and the *dux* or *patricius* of the region. The Chronicle of Fredegar ends with a detailed although confused account of a battle between the *Patricius* Willebad of Burgundy and five members of the Wal-delenus/Chramnelenus group in 642 in which the *patricius* lost the field and his life.[88] As Werner points out, the description implies that the battle was a feud between the families,

---

[84] See Buchner, *Die Provence,* chap. 1 and 2, and Eugen Ewig, "Die fränkischen Teilungen und Teil-reiche (511–613)" in *Spätantikes und fränkisches Gallien,* pp. 131–33; and "Die fränkischen Teilreiche im 7. Jahrhundert (613–714) *Ibid,* pp. 172–230 *passim.*

[85] See above, chapter I, p. 13 and p. 20 note 19.

[86] Fredegar, IV, 45, pp. 37–38.

[87] *Ibid., Continuator,* 37, pp. 105–106.

[88] Fredegar, IV, 90, pp. 76–79.

since others kept out of it.[89] Just as this mid seventh century battle eliminated the family's last rivals in Burgundy, the battles between Abbo and Maurontus eliminated Abbo's remaining rivals in the lower Rhône. Viewed from such a perspective, it is extremely probable that the Abbo who was the last *patricius* of Provence was the author of the testament. By judicious choice of the winning side in the decades-long struggle between Charles Martel and his opposition within his family and then throughout the periphery of the Empire, Abbo had managed to consolidate his own position and to reach the pinnacle of power in the valley. Thus the revolt of Provence takes on the dual image of a struggle between pro- and anti-Arnulfingians and between rival local groups, both of which have important connections in the wider world of Frankish aristocratic society. Such internal, local rivalries, which, as Peter Brown has often characterized the Gallo-Roman aristocracy every bit as much as the Frankish, became the local background for the great European-wide rise of the Arnulfings.[90]

However, the final suppression of anti-Arnulfingian groups in Provence changed the way power was distributed and maintained in the region. The result of the final pacification of the region was not the establishment of Abbo's family as the new local rulers of a quasi-independent *regnum*. Abbo himself may have been rewarded with the office of *patricius,* but if so the office died with him. In fact, as we have seen, Abbo had no sons or, apparently, close kin to whom he could have left either his private fortune or for whom to attempt to secure his office in the next generation. This very lack of kin probably made him an attractive supporter and a secure governor of Provence in the eyes of Charles Martel. Although raised to the highest office, he would have no successor to claim his estate or his position. In fact, if he had any real heir, in the long run it was the family of Charles Martel.

The abbot in whose care Abbo left the monastery, as we have seen, was another Abbo, probably a kinsman. However, he made provisions in his testament for authority over the community, its spiritual and its material life, to pass to Bishop Walchunus (of Maurienne?). What was to become of this charge upon Walchunus' own death was not stated, although as Josef Semmler has accurately pointed out, there is no reason to suppose that his episcopal successors were to inherit this position.[91] Clearly Walchunus' long-time involvement with Novalesa and with its founder, not his official position, had been the cause of Abbo's designating him to administer the monastery. The personal nature of this commission is assured by the confirmation of the freedom from episcopal interference in the

---

[89] Werner, "Noble Families," p. 156.

[90] See below, Chapter V. Peter Brown, "Relics and Social Status in the Age of Gregory of Tours," in *Society and the Holy,* esp. pp. 243–250; "Eastern and Western Christendom in Late Antiquity: A Parting of the Ways," *Ibid.,* p. 186 and note 71.

[91] Josef Semmler, "*Episcopi potestas* und karolingische Klosterpolitik," *Mönchtum, Episcopat und Adel zur Gründungszeit des Klosters Reichenau,* ed. Arno Borst. Vorträge und Forschungen Vo. 20 (Sigmaringen: 1974) pp. 339–340.

election of the abbot granted in 770 by Carlmann.[92] If the bishops of Maurienne did not continue to enjoy the *potestas* over the monastery, this *potestas* probably passed to the royal family, as is suggested in its mention in the *Notitia de servitia monasteriorum* of 818/19 among those monasteries which owed the emperor *militia, dona,* and *orationes,* that is, military service payments and liturgical services for the support of the military.[93] Likewise, as Semmler also observed, the continued Carolingian control of the monastery may explain the seemingly impossible tradition at Novalesa that Charles the Great's illegitimate son Hugo became a monk and then abbot at Novalesa.[94] This report in the *Chronicon* would be unworthy of serious consideration were it not that the date of Hugo's death, 14 June, is recorded in the necrology of Novalesa's priory San'Andrea di Torino, on 13 June: *Depositio domni Ugonis abbatis Novaliensis.*[95] The reasonable implication that Semmler draws is that while the actual account of Hugo's entry into the monastery as told in the *Chronicon* is obviously legendary, Novalesa was probably one of the several monasteries of which Hugo was absentee abbot.

The implication of this Carolingian control of Novalesa after the deaths of Abbo and Walchunus is clear.[96] The role which Abbo's family played in the region, both as landowner and as protector of the passes into Lombardy, passed to the new royal house. The continued support for and protection of the monastery by the Carolingians from Pepin III was actually strengthening the new dynasty's own power in this area. The power and influence built up over long generations by the families of Rustica and Felix had been grafted onto the family of Charles Martel.

---

[92] D. Karlmann no. 52.

[93] Semmler, "Episcopi potestas," p. 340. *MGH Capit.* I, 171, p. 350.

[94] *Chronicon Novaliciense,* IX, 25, ed. Cipolla II, p. 193. As Semmler points out, this tradition has been much disputed and is not mentioned either in Werner, "Die Nachkommen Karls des Großen" p. 445 or in Otto Gerhard Oexle, "Le monastère de Charroux au IXe siècle," *Le Moyen Age* vol. 76 (1970) pp. 193–204. G. Penco, "Tradizione mediolatina e fonti romanzi nel Chronicon novaliciense," *Benedictina* vol. 12 (1940) p. 6, accepts the tradition as genuine. The Annales of Lobbes (*SS* II, p. 195) state that in 825 Louis the Pious gave his half brother Hugo "cenobia Sancti Quintini et Laugiense et pluria alia." He was abbot of St. Bertin and Saint-Quentin. However Oexle, "Le monastère," p. 202 note 30, suggests that this entry is possibly a confused amplification of Thegan's Vita Hludowici, c. 24: Eodem tempore iussit fratres suos tonsuare, Druogonem, Hug et Theodoricum ... quos postmodum honorifice constituit ... et Hugoni coenobia multa [dedit.]" This could well be, but Novalesa might have been one of these monasteries given Hugo.

[95] ed. Cipolla, I, p. 341.

[96] The close relationship between Novalesa and the Carolingians and their religious reformers is shown by the presence of Abbot Asinarius of Novalesa at the reform council of Attigny in 762. See Eugen Ewig, "Saint Chrodegang et la reforme de L'église franque," in *Spätantikes und fränkisches Gallien* vol. II, pp. 238–250.

CHAPTER V

THE REVOLT OF PROVENCE

Abbo's testament was written at the very moment which saw the end of a protracted and extremely destructive series of wars in the Rhône valley. Throughout the early eighth century, during the very time that Abbo was acquiring land and making arrangements for his monastery at Novalesa, the area was rocked by a series of uprisings involving the local aristocracy, their Saracen supporters, and the armies of Charles Martel. In 739 the situation was far from restored to order: we have seen that in his testament Abbo authorizes the agents of Novalesa to seek out those slaves and freedmen who were necessarily dispersed throughout the region during the period of Saracen invasion and destruction.[1] We know, in addition, from documents preserving the record of efforts made by the bishop of Marseille in 780 to recover properties of St. Victor confiscated by the rebel *Patricius* Antener and then subsequently confiscated from him by Charles Martel, that this period of turmoil had brought widespread disruption to the region.[2] Even after the suppression of the so-called revolt, the area south of Vienne lay largely in ruin: the Bishop of Vienne, Willicarius, went into voluntary exile following the plundering of his see's property by both sides.[3]

Obviously these revolts were part of a much wider phenomenon: during the dispute which followed the death of Pepin II within the Arnulfing family for the succession, most of the *regna* of the Frankish Empire – Aquitaine, Provence, Bavaria, Frisia, and Alamannia, took the opportunity to develop into largely autonomous unities under their dukes or *patricii*.[4] However, although this much is generally accepted, the question of whether these revolts were caused by the hostility of the indigenous populations of various regions toward the Franks has been the subject of much debate. This has been particularly true of the revolts of Aquitaine and of Provence, and the traditional interpretation of the revolt of Provence has been that it was one more index of the long-standing ethnic sense of separateness and hostility to things Germanic on the part of the Gallo-Roman aristocracy of

---

[1] par. 58.

[2] Cart. St. Victor de Marseille I, 45; *Gallia Christ. noviss.* II, 33; see Buchner, *Die Provence,* pp. 100–101. Buchner gives a satisfactory interpretation of the sense of these two confusing documents although for reasons we have discussed above, he stubbornly and wrongly refuses to recognize the Abbo *Patricius* in the documents as the Abbo of the Testament.

[3] L. Duchesne, *Fastes episcopaux de l'ancienne Gaule* I (Paris: 1907), p. 209, based on the *Liber episcopalis Viennensis ecclesiae* of Legerius published by Duchesne, Ibid., p. 199.

[4] In general see Eugen Ewig, "Die fränkischen Teilreiche im 7. Jahrhundert," pp. 172–230. Also Jörg Jarnut, "Untersuchungen zu den fränkisch-alemannischen Beziehungen in der ersten Hälfte des 8. Jahrhunderts," *Schweizerische Zeitschrift für Geschichte* 30 (1980) pp. 7–28; Hagen Keller, "Fränkische Herrschaft und alemannisches Herzogtum im 6. und 7. Jahrhundert," *Zeitschrift für die Geschichte des Oberrheins* 124 (1976) pp. 1–30; Archibald R. Lewis, "The Dukes in the *Regnum Francorum,*" *Speculum* 51 (1976) pp. 381–410.

the region.[5] Thus the revolts of the *Patricius* Antener and the *Dux* Maurontus have been seen as part of a final effort of this indigenous aristocracy to oppose the Franks. The French historian Michel Rouche has emphasized the Roman character of the revolt and has suggested that the accusation of a pact between Maurontus and the Moslem *wāli* of Septimania "only corroborates the general spirit of fundamental hostility of the Franks toward the Romans," since such an accusation is in his opinion unfounded and unacceptable.[6] Even Erich Zöllner described the revolt as "a resistance of the Roman population against Frankish lordship."[7]

This view seems supported by the traditionally used sources analyzed to examine the revolt, and indeed there is nothing in the bare outlines of Charles Martel's expeditions into the Rhône valley to suggest another interpretation. The subjugation of the region was a long and difficult process which occupied the greater part of the 730s and left the area devastated for over a generation.[8] The first revolt actually occured under the *Patricius* Antener during the lifetime of Pepin II, but in the early years of the century he and his bastard son Charles were too occupied with problems elsewhere, particularly in Aquitaine, to deal with Burgundy and Provence. Only after the Battle of Poitiers in 732 was Charles free to lead his first expedition against the Lyonnais in 733–35. Although our primary source, the so-called Continuator of Fredegar, says that he handed the region over to his *fideles,* his victory was ephemeral. In 735, if the Continuator is to be believed, the *Dux* (probably *Patricius*) Maurontus made a pact with the *wāli* Yüsuf of Narbonne and as a result Saracen garrisons were established at Arles and at Avignon.[9] Charles then made a second expedi-

---

[5] The traditional image of a sharp distinction between ethnic perceptions translated into political actions (what sociologists call "ethnic leadership") south of the Loire is presented by Michel Rouche, "Les Aquitains ont-ils trahi avant la bataille de Poitiers? Un éclairage événementiel sur les mentalites,'" *Le Moyen Age* 74 (1968) pp. 5–25 and *L'Aquitaine des Wisogoths aux Arabes (418–781)* (Paris: 1979); and in a much less extreme form by Erich Zöllner in *Die politische Stellung der Völker im Frankenreich,* Veröff. des Instituts für österreichische Geschichtsforschung 13 (Vienna: 1950).

[6] Rouche, "Les Aquitains," p. 24.

[7] Zöllner, p. 94.

[8] Ramón de Abadal y de Vinyals, "El paso de Septimania des dominio godo al franco a través de la invasión sarracena 720–768," *Cuadernos de historia de España* 19 (1953) pp. 5–54 provides a summary of the events in Provence and reproduces the essential texts.

[9] Recently some southern French scholars have suggested that the account of Muslim assistance requested by the leaders in Provence is but more Frankish propaganda aimed at discrediting the indigenous Roman rebels. This argument seems frankly based more on feelings of anachronistic regional patriotism than historical reality. It is particularly difficult to support given the unanimity of the sources: not only does the pro-Carolingian Continuator state "Denuo rebellante gente ualida Ismahelitarum quos modo Sarracinos corrupto uocabulo nuncupant inrumpentesque Rodanum fluuium insidiantibus infidelis hominibus sub dolo et fraude Mauronto quidem cum sociis suis, Auennionem urbem munitissimam ac montuosam ipsi Sarracini collecto hostile agmine ingrediuntur, illisque rebellantibus, ea regione uastata"; (*Continuator,* 20 pp. 93–94) but the involvement of the

Kindred of Maurontus

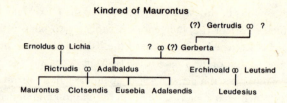

tion as far south as Arles and Marseille, but if he was as victorious as the Continuator states, the victory was indeed short lived. In 738 he had to make a final expedition with the support of the Lombard king Liutprand.[10] This time, with the assistance of the Lombards, he was more successful. By 739, the year Abbo wrote his testament, he had achieved complete submission of Provence and the expulsion of the Moslem forces. This year marked the definitive absorption of the lower Rhône into the Frankish kingdom.

If these events permit an interpretation from the perspective of Romance-Germanic antagonism, however, they do not require it. In fact, in light of a prosopographic investigation based on Abbo's testament, this traditional interpretation must be discarded. The revolt must be seen rather in the context of anti-Arnulfingian, Frankish opposition to the

---

Saracens is stated by Abbo in his testament written one year after the supression of the revolt (par. 58). More significantly, the *Chronicon moissiacense,* which should probably be viewed as a chronicle of Narbonne since it is essentially centered on that city and unusually well informed about its history (see Patrick J. Geary, "Un fragment récemment découvert du *Chronicon moissiacense" Bibliotheque de l'Ecole des chartes* 136 [1978] 69–73) is extremely explicit: His temporibus (734) Iusseph Ibin Abderaman Narbona praeficitur; alio anno Rodanum fluvium transiit, Arelato civitate pace ingreditur, thesaurosque civitatis invadit, et per quatuor annos totam Arelatensem provinciam depopulat atque depraedat." (*SS* I, 291). The explicit statement that the Muslems entered Arles peacefully confirms the accusation that their initial arrival in the area was accomplished with local cooperation. Moreover, the term "pace" may be equivalent to the Arabic term meaning "under treaty of conquest", a normal Islamic mode of occupation by negotiation with local notables. (The author is grateful to Peter Brown for this observation.) Michel Rouche, in his attempt to deny that the charge of cooperation between the rebels and the Muslems ("Les Aquitains", p. 24 note 66), argues that in contrast with the Frankish sources, the *Chronicon moissiancense* is "beaucoup moins précis." However, in quoting the passage given above he inexplicably omits the key words *pace ingreditur thesaurosque. ...* The explicit statement that the Muslems entered Arles peacefully confirms the accusations that the Aquitanians had entered into an alliance with the Saracens or that the Provençal aristocrats had cooperated with the *Wāli* should be compared with the alleged and quite probable dealings of Tassilo with the Avars later in the century. Such arrangements, although often disasterous for the initiators, were within a long tradition of late Roman and early medieval military alliances – consider the invitations to the Berbers to become involved in Visigothic affairs in 711. Moreover, against the Arnulfings the only reasonable hope for the regional opposition groups lay in alliances with their neighbors. To conclude that such alliances were treasonable or immoral is to accept the biased perspective of the Carolingian party.

[10] Paulus Diaconus VI, 54 *SSRL.*

Kindred of Waratto

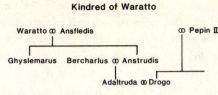

growing power of Pepin and Charles, and in particular the events must be compared with related movements in Aquitaine and in Bavaria which involved similar if not identical Frankish families. In the Rhône valley, opposition leaders in the 730s seem to have been related to anti-Arnulfingian groups in Neustria, and their role in the region at the turn of the century must lead to a revision of the traditional image of the composition of regional aristocratic groups in the Frankish Empire.

The passages in question are three of the four instances in which Abbo describes acquisitions by judgment or precept:

1. *... et colonica in ipso pago Viennense, Baccoriaco super fluuium Carusium ubi faber noster Maiorianus mansit et filius eius Ramnulfus de Balciaco, quem incontra Ardulfo per iudico Agnarico patricio euindicauimus.*[11]

2. *Colonicas in Velentio, quem per preceptionem dominica de ratione Riculfu et germano suo Rodbaldo ad nos peruenit.*[12]

3. *Dono fidele meo Protadio res illas in pago Vuapencense, ubi dicitur Semprugnanum, cum adpendices suas, quem de Agloaldo conquisiuimus, et illa portione, quem de Maurengo clerico pro sua infidelitate, quod nobis mentiuit, et per uerbo dominico conquisiuimus, dum et ipse nobis mentitus fuit, ipsas res palatius nobis cessit, uolo ut habeat.*[13]

4. *Donamus Tersię filię Honorię liberti nostrę, quem Teudaldos de Seguciu huxorem habuit, res illas quę fuerunt Riculfum filium Rodulfum condam quem pro preceptione domno Theoderico rege, et illuster uero domno Karolo in pago Diense, Vuapencense et Gratianopolitano conquesiuimus; preter colonicas in pago Ebredunense, in Velencio, quem ad monasterio sancto Petro herede meam delegauimus, dum et ipse Riculfus apud gente Sarracenorum ad infildelitatem regni Francorum sibi sociauit et multa mala cum ipsa gentem pagana fecit.*[14]

The first acquisition from Ardulf is unclear. It may simply have been a court case involving purely civil matters. The others, which were "per preceptionem dominica" or "per uerbo dominico" refer to property confiscated from individuals judged guilty of *infidelitas*,

---

[11] par. 16.
[12] par. 25.
[13] par. 55.
[14] par. 56.

that is, of rebellion.[15] Numbers two and four are clearly related and involve the same judgment and disposition since the property in two is exactly that which is excepted from the bequest in four (*colonicae* in Velentio). The persons mentioned in these passages are then most probably (and those in two and four explicitly) participants in the revolt of Provence which had only just ended. With the addition of the leader, Maurontus, we have then a list of five rebels from the period of Charles' conquest of the region. The names must be examined carefully to determine the probable origins and alliances of these rebels.

Maurontus, Maurengus. Both names are hypocristics of the element *Maur.* Their appearance together as participants in the revolt might suggest that they were related, since in the eighth century aristocratic families often used similar name elements (as in the case of the other group of rebels, Riculfus, Rodbaldus and Rodulfus) if it could be shown that like Maurontus, who as a *dux* or *patricius* came from the highest level of society, the Maurengus *clericus* was more than a simple cleric.[16] Maurengus does not appear elsewhere in the testament; however, a *Maorongos abbas* was one of the signatories to the foundation charter of Novalesa in 726.[17] His name immediately follows the names of bishops among the signatures, suggesting his important status, although his monastery is unknown. It is quite possible, then, that this *Maorongos abbas* was an important ecclesiastic with a close relationship to Abbo prior to the revolt of Maurontus and his followers. For his participation in the revolt, he was deprived of his office and appears in the testament as a simple cleric condemned for breaking faith. While the testament does not say explicitly that his *infidelitas* was toward the Franks and not simply a personal affront to Abbo, the fact that the grant of his property to Abbo was done by royal decree implies that if he had lied and rebelled against Abbo, it was in the latter's capacity as *rector* of the region of Maurienne and Susa.

Maurontus is a name of Romance origin. However, there is no reason in the eighth century to suppose that the Maurontus who led the revolt against Charles Martel was a local notable of mere Gallo-Roman origin.[18] By the seventh century, as we have seen above, no

---

[15] The delicate question of terminology used in eighth- and ninth-century sources to designate anti-Carolingian opposition and the complex evolution of the opposition groups has been studied by Karl Brunner, *Oppositionelle Gruppen im Karolingerreich* (Vienna, Cologne, Graz: 1979). See especially Chapter I, "Die Sprache der Quellen," pp. 14–39. For the confiscated property see map F, p. 82.

[16] Here and elsewhere I have used the card file *Prosopographia Orbis Latini (PROL)* compiled under the direction of Professor Karl Ferdinand Werner at the German Historical Institute in Paris. I am grateful to Professor Werner and to his colleagues for their assistance and welcome at the Institute. On Mauring, duke of Spoleto, see Ed. Hlawitschka, *Franken, Alemannen, Bayern und Burgunder in Oberitalien* (Freiburg i. Br.: 1960).

[17] In Dei nomen Maorongos abbas rogetos subscripsi," Cipolla I, p. 13, 9.

[18] Buchner was suspicious of this hasty conclusion, often repeated in the French literature on Maurontus. See *Die Provence*, pp. 28–29, n. 85. The name Maurontus first appears in the Rhône region in 683 when a Maurontus Archidiaconus was signatory to an episcopal confirmation. Arch. dép. Bouche du Rhône, 1H1 rouleau. See below, p. 141.

differentiation in this region between Germanic and Roman ethnic identities can be made on the sole basis of names. In fact, if one looks elsewhere for persons bearing the name Maurontus, one must look to an old, illustrious Neustrian family which had in the past opposed Arnulfingian expansion. As Maurice Chaume noted years ago, at least two Mauronti are known in the seventh century, but they appear in the upper stratum of Neustrian aristocracy.[19] In order to demonstrate that this family was quite likely active in the Rhône valley and that the rebel leader was probably connected with it, we must first examine briefly the Neustrian aristocracy in the final decades before Arnulfingian consolidation.

Neustrian Mayors of the Palace

The leading aristocracy in Neustria during the seventh century faced two major threats to their control of the kingdom following the death of Dagobert I (d. 639). The first was from Ebroinus, a man of low or at least lower birth (*et infimo genere ortus*)[20] whose rise to power in Neustria-Burgundy as *maior domus* on two occasions (658–673 and 675–680) broke the continuity of Neustrian aristocratic power. His death in 680 however paved the way for a restoration of the old aristocratic family which had controlled this position prior to him. The second danger, that of the ambitious Arnulfingian family and their Austrasian supporters, led to a long period of crisis and warfare which ultimately ended in conquest of Neustria and its unification with Austrasia under Arnulfingian control. Through this tumultuous period, the appearance of anarchy and confusion presented by the largely pro-Arnulfingian sources masks important continuity: the mayors of the palace from the death of Dagobert until 688 when Pepin II assumed control of Theuderic III and Neustria, a period of 49 years, except for the years of Ebroinus' power, all came from the same family – the same family that probably produced the Maurontus *dux* in Provence.

This family first appears in the court of Dagobert I in the person of Erchinoaldus who was related to the Merovingian royal family through Haldetrud, the mother of Dagobert.[21] According to a very late notice in the *Annales marchienenses* probably based on a dedicatory inscription and hence reasonably trustworthy, he was the brother of Adal-

---

[19] Maurice Chaume, *Les origines du duché de Bourgogne*, vol. 1, p. 35.

[20] Ebling, CXLIX, pp. 131–133. *Passio Ragneberti MGH SSRM* V, pp. 209–210, "… Ebroinus nomine ex infimo genere ortus, Deo et sanctis contrarius, in maiordomatus honore fuerat sublimatus." On Ebroin see J. Fischer, *Der Hausmeier Ebroin* (Bonn: 1954).

[21] Ebling, CLVI, pp. 137–139. *Fredegar* IV, 84, p. 71. "Post discessum Aegane Erchynoaldus maior domus, qui consanguaeneus fuerat de genetrici Dagoberto, maior domi palacium Chlodouiae effecetur."

baldus,[22] *Francigena … natalibus ortus praeclaris* in the court of Dagobert who married Saint Rictrudis, a noble woman of Gascon origin brought to the Neustrian court.[23] This couple had a son named Maurontus who early in his life was at court *"prudens notarius*

---

[22] *Annales Marchianenses, MGH SS* XVI, p. 611: "Mortuo Erchenoldo maiore domus palatii, Franci Ebroinum cura pastoralia sublimant, et sanctus Amatus Senonensi ecclesiae praesidebat archiepiscopus. His Erchenoldus frater Adalbaldi patris sancti Mauronti reedificavit Duacum castrum, et infra castrum edificavit ecclesiam in honore Dei genitricis virginis Mariae que nunc sancti Amati dicitur." This late notice, inserted into the chronicle in the thirteenth century, should be given little credence were it not that the statement is related directly to the reconstruction of the castle of Douai and the construction of the Church of St. Amand, previously, the Church of the Virgin. Given this relation, it is likely that the authority was a dedicatory inscription within the church itself and hence quite likely the information on the relationship between Erchinoaldus and Adalbaldus should be accepted. On the historical tradition at Marchiennes and its preservation of Merovingian traditions, see Karl Ferdinand Werner, "Le rôle de l'aristocratie dans la christianisation du Nord-est de la Gaule," *Revue d'histoire de l'Eglise de France* 62 (1975) pp. 45–73 and, most important, "Andreas von Marchiennes und die Geschichtsschreibung von Anchin und Marchiennes in der zweiten Hälfte des 12. Jahrhunderts," *Deutsches Archiv* 9 (1952), pp. 402–463. Rolf Sprandel in *Der merowingische Adel und die Gebiete östlich des Rheines* (Freiburg i. Br.: 1957) p. 59. Note 59 dismisses similar evidence for the relationship between Adalbaldus and Erchinoaldus presented by P. Latrin, "L'influence colombanienne à l'abbaye de Moroeuil en Artois", *Mélanges colombaniennes* (1950) pp. 243–46. Latrin's evidence was an eleventh-century manuscript from Maroeuil containing the office of Saint Bertille, founder of Maroeuil. Although Sprandel considered "Diese Überlieferung ist aber wohl zu spät, um voll ernst genommen werden zu können," the fact that both liturgical tradition at Moroeuil and apparently a dedicatory inscription at Douai preserved this tradition makes it quite likely true.

[23] *Vita S. Rictrudis, AASSOSB* II, 937; *AASS* Maii III, 81–89; Pl 132.827–848. The Prologue is edited in *SSRM* VI, 91–94. The *vita* was written in 907 by Hucbaldus of St. Amand at the request of the monks and nuns of Marchiennes, Rictrudis' monastery. At first Hucbaldus refused to write the *vita* because the religious were unable to provide him with any sure material on her life because of the destruction by the Normans. However he later agreed when they were able to provide him with both oral and some written material, the former filling in what had been lost: "Cumque renitenti mihi quaedam historiarum exemplaria suis ostenderent concordantia dictis, de cetero illis quorum non contemnendae videbantur personae, mihi fidem facientibus, quod haec quae referebant eadem olim tradita litteris fuerint, sed insectatione Northmannicae depopulationis deperierint." (*SSRM* VI, 93). As L. Van der Essen showed in his *Étude critique et littéraire sur les vitae des saints mérovingiens de l'ancienne Belgique* (Louvain, Paris: 1907) pp. 260–265, these written sources included, among others, the *Vita Arnulfi* (*SSRM* II, 426–446), the *Vita S. Amandi I* (*SSRM* V, 395–449) Pseudo-Fredegar, and Isidore of Seville's *Etymologiae*. The most important source, for our present purposes, was the *Vita S. Richarii* of Alcuin (*SSRM* IV, 381–401) which Hucbaldus followed extremely closely in reporting a miracle in which Richarius saved the unnamed son of a certain *Deo devota femina Richtruda* whom Hucbaldus identified with the founder of Marchiennes. In the two texts (Alcuin, *SSRM* II, 394–5) and Hucbaldus (*PL* 132.840–41) the only major changes are the identification of the infant as Maurontus, son of Rictrudis, and the suggestion that the miracle was the evidence of the merits of both Rictrudis and Richarius rather than only of the latter as in Alcuin's text. The close verbal and structural similarity of the two makes it impossible that Hucbaldus could have found the story in the first *Vita Richarii* (*Vita Richarii sacerdotis Cen-*

regalium praeceptorum conscribens edicta,"[24] but who later retired to a monastery he had established on his own lands at Breuil-sur-Lys (dép. Nord near Douai).

Contemporary with the generation of this Maurontus' parents was another Maurontus who appears in the *Vita Richarii sacerdotis Centulensis primigenia*[25] and, probably, in the eleventh century *Vita Walarici*.[26] He reappears in Alcuin's version of the life of St. Richarius[27] and from that source in the Chronicle of St. Riquier by Hariulf, who confused this Maurontus with the later abbot of Breiul-sur-Lys.[28] In the *Vita Richarii primigenia*, he and his *propinquus* Ghyslemarus are credited with intervening with Nanctilda, the widow of Dagobert I, to grant Richarius the property of Forest Montiers between 639 and 642. Both men are clearly from the highest level of Neustrian society: *vir nobilis scilicet Ghys-*

---

tulensis primigenia, (SSRM VII, 438–453), which presents a much simpler and more direct account, and which nevertheless is clearly Alcuin's source. Van Der Essen, who did not know the *Vita Richarii primigenia*, supposed that Alcuin's passage had come from an earlier *Vita Rictrudis* now lost. While the existence of the earlier *Vita Richarii* makes this unlikely, it would appear that while Hucbaldus followed Alcuin's text, he did have other sources that allowed him to show remarkable independence from his source. As Van Der Essen pointed out, one chapter after this miracle story so faithful to Alcuin's text, Alcuin tells of the Maurontus he describes as "nobilis quidam vir et terrarum vel silvarum ad regem pertinentium servator praebuerunt locum manendi in silva Chrisciacense, qui et ipse Maurontus postea, saeculari habitu deposito, monachus factus est in eodemque loci." (pp. 396–97). If Hucbaldus had no other sources, the temptation to identify this Maurontus with his saint's son would have been tremendous. Another later writer, Harulf of St. Riquier, indeed made this error in his Chronicle (ed. F. Lot, *Collection de textes pour servir à l'étude et à l'enseignement de l'histoire* vol. 17 (Paris: 1898) chap., 19 bk. 1, p. 32 note 2 and p. 14). Hucbaldus' description of Maurontus' service at court leaves no possibility that he confused the son of Rictrudis with the other Maurontus mentioned by Alcuin: "Et ut clara editus prosapia, regis quoque praeclarus fulsit in aula, regia honoratus bulla, utpote prudens notarius regalium praeceptorum conscribens edicta. (PL 132.842) Hucbaldus was in fact correct: they could not be the same since the first was born during the reign of Dagobert I (623/29–38) while the second was already an important and influential person at Dagobert's court. There is no basis then for identifying them as the same persons or for accusing Hucbaldus of so doing, as did Krusch in his edition of Albuin's *Vita*, p. 394, n. 1. In conclusion, it appears that Hucbaldus knew not only Alcuin's *Vita Richarii* but other texts which spoke of Maurontus as well, and that hence his *Vita S. Rictrudis* probably conserves elements of now lost Merovingian hagiographical texts. On Hucbaldus, see F. Dolbeau, "Le dossier hagiographique de S. Amé, vénéré à Douai, Nouvelles recherches sur Hucbald de Saint-Amand," *Analecta Bollandiana* 97 (1979) 90–110. For a general discussion of the place of such noble families' saints, see Friedrich Prinz, "Heiligenkult und Adelsherrschaft im Spiegel merowingischer Hagiographie," *Historische Zeitschrift*, vol. 204 (1967), pp. 529–544.

[24] PL 132.842.

[25] See above n. 23. On the value of Alcuin's text one should consult Krusch's introduction in *SSRM* 7, pp. 438–444 and p. 449 n. 5–10 as well as Friedrich Prinz, *Frühes Mönchtum im Frankenreich* (Munich: 1965) p. 128.

[26] *Vita Walarici abbatis Leuconaensis*, SSRM IV, pp. 157–175.

[27] SSRM IV, p. 396.

[28] see above, n. 23.

lemarus, sive et alius propinquos similiter nobilis et palatinus nec dissimilis genera Maurontusque nomine.[29] Maurontus' intervention was apparently in his capacity as guardian of the royal forests, *servator terrarum et silvarum ad regem pertinentium,*[30] according to Alcuin. This must be the same Maurontus as the brother of one Ursinus who was the beneficiary of a miracle attributed to St. Walaricus (died ca. 622). The *vita* describes Ursinus as ... *de alta satis fuerat prosapie. Germanus quidam erat cuiusdam nobilissimi Mauronti, qui et ipse summos inter proceres palatii et dignitatem aulae regiae illo in tempore cunctos suo ingenio praecellebat.* Although this text is quite late, miracles of Saint Walaricus were reported circulating already in the ninth century by Ado of Vienne,[31] and this account may be one of those. Maurontus later entered religious life as a monk at Forest Montiers, establishing a monastery at the site.

This Maurontus may be the same as the abbot of St. Florent le Vieil whose death is reported in the *Vita Ermenlandi abbatis Antrensis.*[32] However, his death ca. 695 would suggest that this is another man, since the Maurontus in the *Vita Richarii* was already an important person in the entourage of Dagobert I in the 630s, making him a very old man indeed at his death.

In the generation following the death of Dagobert, two other men from the highest level of Neustrian aristocracy carried the names of the *propinqui* Maurontus and Ghyslemarus. They are not identified explicitly as kin, nor are they identified as related to the previous bearers of the same names, but a number of convergences make this quite likely.

The first is the Maurontus, son of Rictrudis and Adalbaldus, discussed above. Some time after Dagobert's death the fortunes of his family fell: his father was murdered while visiting his mother's estates in the South,[33] and his mother entered religious life at Marchiennes in the convent she founded. Later she was followed by her three daughters and, as we have seen, by her son.[34] These events could correspond with the rise of Ebroinus and the bitter fighting between this relative upstart and the older Neustrian aristocracy of which the family of Erchinoaldus and Adalbaldus was so important a part.

The Ghyslemarus of this next generation is well known as the Neustrian Burgundian

---

[29] *SSRM* VII, p. 449.

[30] *SSRM* IV, p. 169.

[31] Ado of Vienne, PL 123.243: April 1: "Et in pago Wimnoensi S. Walerici confessoris cuius sepulchrum crebis miraculis illustratur." On the martyrology of Ado see Henri Quentin, *Les martyrologes historiques du moyen-âge. Etude sur la formation du martyrologe romain* (Paris: 1908). See also Jacques Dubois and Geneviève Renaud, *Edition pratique des martyrologes de Béde de l'anonyme lyonnais et de Florus* (Paris: 1976), I–III.

[32] *SSRM* V, pp. 693–694.

[33] *Vita S. Rictrudis*, PL 132.835.

[34] PL 132.838. Maurontus' sisters were Clotsendis, said to have been baptised by St. Amandus; Eusebia, goddaughter of Queen Nanthildis; and Adalsendis. The stemma on page 128 may be of help in following the arguments concerning the families of Maurontus son of Rictrudis.

maior of the palace during the turbulent reign of Theuderic III.[35] After the assassination of Ebroinus in 680, Ghyslemarus' father Waratto took his place.[36] However, the Neustrian conflicts of the previous decade had worked to the advantage of the Austrasian Arnulfingian family and Waratto was faced with compromise or resistance to the growing power of Pepin II. Waratto chose accommodation, and almost immediately Ghyslemarus, who violently opposed his father's rapprochement with Pepin, overthrew his father and established himself in his place. Only after Ghyslemarus' death (according to the *Liber historiae Francorum* and the Continuator) did his father return to his position, which he occupied until his death in 686.[37] His successor was again part of this family: his son-in-law Bercharius,[38] the husband of Anstrudis, daughter of Waratto and Ansfledis. Bercharius resumed the policies of his late brother-in-law Ghyslemarus by opposing Pepin and met with the same fate. He was defeated by Pepin at Tértry in 687 but allowed to remain in his office until his murder (according to later, pro-Carolingian sources, at the instigation of his mother-in-law) the following year.[39]

Circumstantial evidence connects the Ghyslemarus Mayor of the Palace with the Abbot of Breuil-sur-Lys, and connects both of these to the Maurontus and the Ghyslemarus in the court of Dagobert.

First and most evident are their names, which are extremely rare in the seventh century, appearing apparently only in these persons. Second, Maurontus son of Rictrudis and Adalbaldus was said to have had as godfather Richarius,[40] the founder of St. Riquier who had benefited from the intervention of the Maurontus "servator terrarum et silvarum." This coincidence suggests that Adalbaldus and Rictrudis were part of the party around Richarius as were the earlier Ghyslemarus and Maurontus. Third, the geographic origins of Erchinoaldus, Adalbaldus, and Ansfledis suggest that the suggestion that they were related is likely: Erchinoaldus had properties around St.-Wandrille and Jumièges, on the Marne at Lagny and at Péronne on the Somme.[41] Adalbaldus, his brother according to the

---

[35] Ebling, CLXXXVII, pp. 159–160; *Liber Historiae Francorum SSRM* II, p. 321.

[36] Ebling, CCCVIII, pp. 234–235. On the family of Waratto, see Ewig, "Die fränkischen Teilreiche im 7. Jahrhundert," pp. 223–224, n. 204, and Prinz, *Frühes Mönchtum,* p. 140.

[37] *SSRM* II, 321; *Vita Audoini* II *SSRM* V, p. 562 n. 1.

[38] Ebling, LXIX, pp. 77–78.

[39] *SSRM* II. p. 322. See the stemma on page 129. Ebling, following the *Gesta ss patrum Fontanellensium,* thought that Drogo, Pepin II's son, had married Anstrudis, the widow of Bercharius, and cites in edition the diploma of 697 in which Drogo and Adaltruda his wife contest property with St. Denis. In fact, the diploma (*LS* 27) makes Bercharius the *socer* or father-in-law of Drogo. Hence, it would appear that Drogo had married the daughter of Bercharius and Anstrudis, Adaltruda, and not Anstrudis herself. See Werner Bergman, "Untersuchungen zu den Gerichtsurkunden der Merowingerzeit," *Archiv für Diplomatik,* vol. 22 (1946), no. 16.

[40] *PL* 132.838.

[41] On property of Erchinoaldus see Ebling, CLVI, p. 137. See map p. 137.

Annales Marchianensis, were found in the area of modern Douai,[42] and those of Ansfledis not far away in the departments of Seine-Maritime, Oise and Somme.[43] Waratto's, like those Erchinoaldus, were in the area of Caux north of Rouen.[44]

The final evidence connecting the families of Waratto and Maurontus son of Adalbaldus is their cooperation in the affair of Bishop Amatus of Sion.[45] Amatus, along with Bishop Chramnelenus of Embrun and Abbot Filibert of Jumièges had supported the opponents of Ebroinus and Theuderic III in Neustria and Burgundy who had recalled Dagobert II and enthroned him in 676. This effort to establish a rival Neustrian king under the control of the old Neustrian aristocracy had failed and most of the aristocracy remained faithful to Theuderic, leaving these ecclesiastics guilty of *infidelitas.*[46] Amatus was condemned and ordered imprisoned at Péronne in the custody of Abbot Ultan.[47] Although Péronne had been under the control of Erchinoaldus,[48] this was clearly not done at the orders of and under the authority of Ebroinus. Ultanus died in 680, the same year that Ebroinus was killed and succeeded by Waratto. At this time Amatus was transferred into the custody of Maurontus at Breuil-sur-Lys where, according to the *vita Rictrudis,* the abbot acted toward the bishop not as a jailor but as a servant.[49] This choice of Breuil-sur-Lys and of Maurontus as a new and altogether light form of detention suggests a close connection between the family of the new *maior domus* and that of Maurontus, as well as a favorable view of Amatus' actions, although as long as Theuderic III was king Amatus could not recover his liberty. A final suggestion of a connection between these families is the appearance of a last "Ghyslemarus *comes palatii*" at the turn of the century in the same area that was the territory of Adalbaldus and Maurontus of Breuil-sur-Lys – at Valenciennes and Quierzy.[50]

In conclusion, all evidence points to the hypothesis that from Erchinoaldus and his son Leudesius (briefly able to regain the title of Neustrian *maior domus* in 675)[51] through Waratto, his son Ghyslemarus, to his son-in-law Bercharius, Neustrian opposition to Ebroinus and later to the Arnulfingians was led by one powerful aristocratic family which

---

[42] *Vita Rictrudis PL* 132.835.

[43] *Gesta ss patrum Fontanenellensis coenobii,* ed. F. Lohier and J. Laporte, (Rouen, Paris: 1936) bk. IV, 2. pp. 40–41.

[44] *Vita Filiberti, SSRM* V, p. 600.

[45] On Amatus see Paul Edmond Margin, *Etudes critiques sur la Suisse à l'époque mérovingienne 534–715* (Geneva, Paris: 1910), pp. 271–4 and most important Louis Dupraz, *Contribution à l'histoire du Regnum Francorum pendant le troisième quart du VIIe siècle (656–680)* (Fribourg: 1948), pp. 102–103; 310; 365.

[46] DM. 48 "… qui in infidilitate nostro fuerant inventi …"

[47] *Vita S. Rictrudis PL* 132.842.

[48] *Vita Fursei Abbatis Latiniacensis, SSRM* IV, 439; 444.

[49] *PL* 132.842–43.

[50] Ebling, CLXXXVIII, p. 160. *DM* 66 (*LS* 23) *DM* 73 (*LS* 29).

[51] Ebling, CCXXVI, p. 181. *SSRM* II, 318.

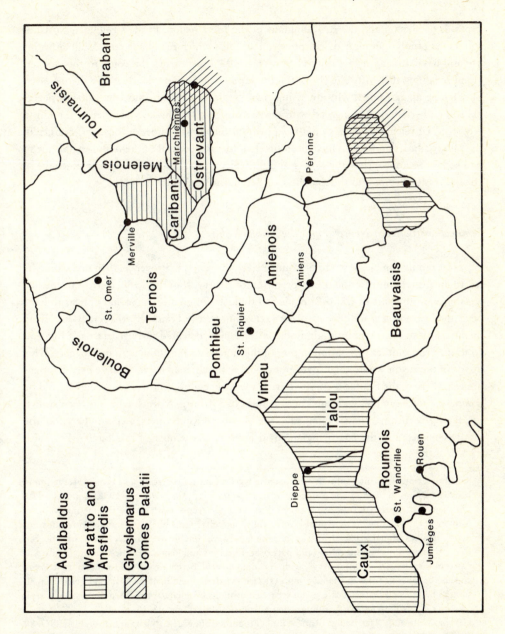

had risen to prominence in the court of Dagobert I and was related to the Merovingian family through his mother. Moreover, the two Mauronti and the Ghyslemari were members of this dominant kin group, which had been formed by an alliance of aristocratic groups between Rouen and Douai, not unlike the earlier alliance in Austrasia between the

Pepinids of Herstal and the Arnulfingians of the Metz region. In the struggle against Ebroinus the family temporarily lost power, a struggle which may have cost Adalbaldus his
life and have driven, at two different times, the Mauronti from the court to the cloister.
Upon regaining their office in the 680 s, the family was bitterly divided over the necessity
of reaching an agreement with the rising Arnulfingians – Waratto saw the value of peace;
his son and son-in-law disagreed with disasterous results. The last member of the kin in
Neustria, Ghyslemarus *comes palatii,* appears to have maintained a local importance in
the family's heartland but to have been firmly under the control of the Arnulfingians, who
had sought to appropriate the power and influence of the family through the marriage of
Drogo, son of Pepin, and the daughter of Bercharius and Anstrudis.[52]

Connections between Neustria and the Rhône Valley

If this family can be shown to be connected to the rebels in Provence, then one would be
led to an entirely untraditional interpretation of the revolt in the 730s. Instead of the last
resistance on the part of Gallo-Romans to Frankish domination, it would appear to have
been the last act in a long series of struggles among the Frankish aristocracy involving
members of an anti-Arnulfing kindred that had been defeated in Neustria itself but had
continued for another generation in the southern parts of Burgundy and in Provence. This
image of the revolt would then correspond well with what is known to have been happen-
ing elsewhere in the Frankish empire during the early eighth century. The rebels should be
compared, for example, with the kin of Rupert of Salzburg-Worms, who has been shown
by Herwig Wolfram to have belonged to the Neustrian Rupertiners, a very old aristocratic
family connected to the Merovingian royal house.[53] A member of this family, Folchaid,

---

[52] See above, note 46. This continuity in Neustria would contradict Archibald Lewis' observation in
his "The Dukes in the *Regnum Francorum,* A. D. 550–751," *Speculum* 51 (1976), pp. 581–410,
"In Neustria, expect [*sic*] for a brief period in the mid-seventh century, we find a succession of
Mayors of the Palace who were unable to establish hereditary rule but who seem to represent com-
peting families of magnates." It is true that the family was unable to establish hereditary rule, but
the only mayors during this period not part of it, Ebroinus and Pepin, indicate that the family was
close to success. Drogo's marriage with the daughter of Bercharius would suggest that Pepin
considered marriage into this family important for the strengthening of his position in Neustria, although Drogo's premature death again created enormous problems for the Arnulfings. See Joseph
Semmler, "Zur pippinidisch-karolingischen Sukzessionskrise," pp. 1–36.

[53] Herwig Wolfram, "Der heilige Rupert und die antikarolingische Adelsopposition," *MIÖG* 80
(1972) pp. 4–34, and more recently, the modification of his position in "Vier Fragen an die Geschichte des heiligen Rupert," *Studien und Mitteilungen zur Geschichte des Benediktiner-Ordens,*
vol. 93 (1982), pp. 14–17; "Vier Fragen zur Geschichte des heiligen Rupert: Eine Nachlese,"
Festschrift St. Peter zu Salzburg 582–1982 (Salzburg: 1982), pp. 2–25; "Der Heilige Rupert in
Salzburg", *Frühes Mönchtum in Salzburg,* ed. Eberhard Zwink (Salzburg: 1983), pp. 81–92.

was married to the Agilofing duke of Bavaria, Theodo, and this connection led Rupert to seek refuge in Bavaria when he fled Worms following the consolidation of power by the Arnulfings. Likewise, the resistance of the Thuringian *Dux* Radulfus to the Carolingians was in no way part of a "national or ethnic" uprising of Thuringians against Franks: Radulfus was himself a member of an important Frankish family installed by the Merovingians among the Thuringians. This family under Radulfus was simply refusing to accept domination by the Arnulfings.[54] Closer to the Rhône region, the opposition of the Alemannian Dukes Gotfrid and, later, Wilihari to Peppin II in the late seventh and early eighth century is yet another example of the attempt by leaders of an old Frankish family established in their position by the Merovingians, to oppose the growth of Carolingian power.[55]

Provence and lower Burgundy in the early 700s resembled in many ways Bavaria in the second half of the seventh century: both regions had acquired considerable autonomy as Neustria and Austrasia had been embroiled in the struggle for the control of the Merovingian kings. During this time the Frankish *duces* were able to establish themselves locally and to increase their distance from the Arnulfingians. The *Patricius* Antener had been able to consolidate the region of the Rhône valley from Lyon to the sea into a largely autonomous *regnum* just as had the Agilofingians in Bavaria, Eudo in Aquitaine and, at an earlier date, Radulfus in Thuringia.[56]

Considerable evidence indicates that this autonomy involved persons and institutions with strong ties to Neustria and, in particular to the regions associated with the Neustrian family of *maiores domus* examined above. The first indiction is the Bishop Chramnelenus of Embrun who, as we have seen, was one of the principal supporters along with the bishop of Sion and the Abbot of Jumièges, of the opposition to Ebroinus.[57] Chramnelenus

---

[54] Karl Ferdinand Werner, "Les principautés périphériques dans le monde franc du VIIIe siècle," *l'problemi dell'Occidente nel secolo VIII*, Settimane di studio del Centro italiano di studi sull'alto medioevo, vol. 20 (Spoleto: 1973), p. 503; "Bedeutende Adelsfamilien," p. 106–107 (translation, p. 163); Ewig, "Die fränkischen Teilreiche im 7. Jahrhundert," p. 205, esp. note 132.

[55] On the Alemannian dukes see Jörg Jarnut, "Beiträge zu den fränkisch-bayerisch-langobardischen Beziehungen im 7. und 8. Jahrhundert (656–728)," *Zeitschrift für bayerische Landesgeschichte* vol. 39 (1976), pp. 331–352; Herwig Wolfram, *Intitulatio I, MIÖG* Erg. Bd. 21 (Vienna: 1967), pp. 144, 161, 157, and most recently Hagen Keller, "Fränkische Herrschaft"; and Jörg Jarnut, "Untersuchungen zu den fränkisch-alemannischen Beziehungen."

[56] Lewis, "The Dukes"; Ewig, "Die Fränkischen Teilreiche im 7. Jahrhundert." The name Antener is often taken as *prima facie* evidence that the *Patricius* was of local, Gallo-Roman origin. However, even apart from the questionable method of determining "ethnic identity" on a basis of anthroponomy discussed above, Antener, it must be noted, was by the late seventh century an important name in Frankish tradition. In the myth of the Trojan origin of the Franks which begins the *Liber Historiae Francorum*, Antener, along with Priam, is one of the two Trojan leaders who found the Frankish people. *MGH SSRM* II, p. 241, 244.

[57] See above, p. 136 and note 46.

was not the only bishop of the region with such Neustrian ties. Archbishop Aeochaldus of Vienne, one of the witnesses to the foundation charter of Novalesa in 726, was known to have been *"affinis Francorum regibus,"* that is, to have had some kinship to the Merovingian royal house.[58] His successor (immediate or after one other; the evidence is unclear) was Archbishop Austrobertus, whose coinage dates him circa 726–730,[59] that is, during the revolt of Provence prior to Charles Martel's intervention. He was Neustrian, a native of Normandy, and was buried at his estate near the Seine at *Vilidiacus,* near the estates of Waratto and Ansfledis.[60] We do not know the origin of his successor Willicarius, but he was clearly not a supporter of Charles Martel: after the conquest and confiscations Willicarius left his see and spent the remainder of his life in the monastery of St. Maurice.[61] To these anti-Carolingian ecclesiastics should also be added the Abbot Maurengus deprived of his office and his property by Theuderic IV in the aftermath of the Carolingian conquest. Finally, as Friederich Prinz has argued, the close relationship between select religious institutions in the Rhône valley and Neustria can be seen in the introduction of the mixed rule of Benedict and Columbanus in three Provençal monasteries in the last third of the seventh century.[62] The first was Lérins, the great center of the old Gallic monastic life, reformed ca. 660–667 by Aigulf, who came to Lérins from Fleury-sur-Loire.[63] The second was Grosseau (Grasellus), which, in a confirmation by Bishop Aredius of Vaison, was said to contain monks living according to the rules of Benedict, Macarius, and Columbanus. This confirmation is particularly interesting because it was written, at the order of Aredius,

---

[58] Louis Duchesne, *Fastes épiscopaux de l'ancienne Gaule* vol. 1 (Paris: 1894) p. 199: Le Livre épiscopal de Léger: "Erat (Eoldus) enim affinis Francorum regibus."

[59] On the coinage of Austrobertus, Reinhold Kaiser, *Bischofsherrschaft zwischen Königtum und Fürstenmacht. Studien zur bischöflichen Stadtherrschaft im westfränkisch-französischen Reich im frühen und hohen Mittelalter.* Pariser historische Studien 17 (Bonn: 1981) p. 72 note 90.

[60] Duchesne, pp. 200–201. "Hic episcopus sanctus in villa quadam proprietatis suae Vilidiaco, non longe a Sequana fluvio supultus est." Ado of Vienne provides the variant Vidiliaco, which is probably to be identified as the modern Vélizy (Yuelines, arr. Versailles, can. Viroflay) or Vesly (Eure, arr. les Andelys can. Gisors). On the importance bishops attached to burial in their "propria patris" see Scheibelreiter, *Der Bischof,* pp. 245–246.

[61] "... cum furioso et insano satis consilio Franci res sacras ecclesiarum ad usus suos retorquerent, videns Viennensem ecclesiam suam indecenter humiliari, relictu episcopatu, in monasterium sanctorum martyrum Aguanensium ingressus, vitam venerabilem duxit." Duchesne, p. 201.

[62] On the introduction of Irofrankish monasticism into the Rhône valley, see Friedrich Prinz, *Frühes Mönchtum,* pp. 275–278.

[63] Prinz, *Frühes Mönchtum,* p. 276; Prinz argues that the opposition to Aigulf, led by Columbus and Arcadius, which led to the execution of Aigulf under Mummolus of Uzès, was more likely based on the opposition to the introduction of the mixed rule than, as some have argued, as a Frankish-Gallo-Roman opposition. (See the *Vita Aigulphi, AASS* Sept. 1, pp. 743–747). Certainly his hypothesis is more likely than one which posits an ethnic opposition, but one might suspect that the opposition to the introduction of the mixed rule might have been tied with the intense political conflicts as well.

by one "Maurontus archidiaconus."[64] The final monastery was Douzère, founded as by Abbot Landbertus of St. Wandrille, on land granted the important Neustrian monastery by Theuderic III between 673 and 678.[65] Again one sees the geographical connection between the Rhône valley and the lower Seine where the family of Waratto held its estates.

Alongside this evidence of old Neustrian ties and of anti-Carolingian *potentes* in the Rhône valley, one must consider the evidence that although to later, Carolingian historiographers the region was in rebellion, it maintained important ties with Neustrian religious institutions supporting the anti-Carolingian king Chilperic II. In March of 716 during the height of the struggle in Neustria, Chilperic granted St. Denis immunity from 100 *solidi* of tolls in the port of Marseille and reconfirmed charters of exemption granted by his predecessors.[66] The next month he granted freedom from duties payable at Fos on a wide variety of Mediterranean commodities to the monastery of Corbie.[67] The two charters suggest that, although in Neustria proper Chilperic and his Neustrian nobles were fighting for their lives, he could still command the officers of the royal fisc in distant Provence – hardly evidence of a state of rebellion by anti-Frankish Gallo-Romans. This apparent recognition of the power of the distant king (even if only as a convenient focus of anti-Arnulfing activity) should be compared to the welcome given to Rupert of Worms in Bavaria by the Agilofings. As Herwig Wolfram has demonstrated, this support was based on a common opposition to the rising Arnulfingian power and which saw Chilperic II as a useful rallying point from which to control Arnulfing ambition.[68] When, to all of this evidence of close ties between the region in rebellion and Neustria, is added the detail that the leader of the rebellion, a *dux* and hence a man of the same social rank as the old Neustrian mayors of the palace, bore the name Maurontus, then the hypothesis that he and his supporters were part of this Neustrian party continuing the efforts of his kin for one more generation in Provence becomes most plausible.

An analysis of the other rebels whose names appear in Abbo's testament further strengthens the hypothesis that the revolt was an internal Frankish quarrel, not an interethnic one. They are Rodulfus, Riculfus, and Rodbaldus. These names, designating two

---

[64] Archiv. Bouches du Rhône 1H1 Rouleau; edited, Pardessus, *Diplomata*, no. 401, pp. 191–192. Prinz, *Frühes Mönchtum*, p. 277 note 51. On the importance of the office of archdeacon, which was second only to that of bishop and was often held by the heir apparent, see Scheibelreiter, *Der Bischof*, pp. 101–107.

[65] Prinz, *Frühes Mönchtum*, pp. 277, 312; *Vita Ansberti*, c. 9; *MGH SSRM* V, p. 625.

[66] *DM* 82; Semmler, "Zur pippinidisch-karolingischen Sukzessionskrise," p. 12; François Louis Ganshof, "Note sur les ports de Provence du VIIIe au Xe siècle," *Revue historique* 183 (1938) 28–37; "Les bureaux du tonlieu de Marseille et de Fos. Contribution à l'histoire des institutions financière de la monarchie franque," *Etudes historiques à la mémoire de Noël Didier* (Paris: 1960) pp. 126–133.

[67] *DM* 86 and bibliography above, note 66.

[68] Wolfram, "Vier Fragen," p. 17.

generations of the same family, are composed of the Germanic elements Rod (Hroth, Rot, Ruad) and ulf (olf). From the description of them in the testament, they do not seem to be of the same class of Maurontus, that is ducal of *viri inlustres*. Rather they are probably *comites* of the "rebel" *dux*. In spite of their germanic names that follow the traditional division of radicals (each son's name containing one radical of his father's name), it is unlikely that they were among the "iudices" established by Charles in 736. The infidelity of which they were convicted should be seen rather in light of Charles' first pacification of the Lyonnais in 736. The Continuator of Fredegar states that "Charles ... now went with his army into the land of Burgundy against the city of Lyon. He subjected to his rule the chief men and officials of that province and placed his judges over the whole region as far as Marseilles and Arles." (... *partibus Burgundie dirigit Lugdunum Gallie urbem maiores natu atque praefectus eiusdem prouintie sua dicione rei publice subiugauit, usque Marsiliensem urbem uel Arelatum suis iudicibus constituit*) ...[69] Hence he subjugated rather than replaced the prefect and the nobles of the region. This reference should probably be seen as referring to Maurontus (who has been supposed to have been *dux* or *patricius* of Provence, but who could better be seen as a *dux* in the Lyonnais who had extended his power south) and his party, including the sons of Rodulfus, who were bound to Charles by oath. The revolt in 737 would then be represented by Abbo as an act of infidelity to that oath.

Even more conclusive of the presence of this family in the region prior to the eighth century is an epitaph, recovered at Briord (dép. Ain) of one Riculfus and his wife Guntello. Although the epitaph is not dated, Le Blant places it on formal grounds as sixth or seventh century.[70] The extremely gross way in which formulae are combined in it without regard for syntax or grammar would suggest the latter date, and the fact that it is in verse, according to Dr. Martin Heinzelmann, would suggest that the individuals were of considerable but not highest social standing: lesser personages would not have had verse epitaphs, greater would have had them better composed. Thus by the 730s, the rebel Riculfus and his kin should be seen not as newly arrived but rather as part of the lower aristocracy long established in the region. One might speculate that they may have arrived along with the ancestors of Maurontus under Dagobert I, but soon established connections in the region by marriage.

That the rebels Riculfus and Rodbaldus were quite likely connected to Maurontus by kin ties is suggested by onomastic evidence of a later date. In the ninth century these same name elements reappear in one of the most important aristocratic families of Burgundy

---

[69] *Continuator*, 18, p. 93.

[70] E. Le Blant, *Recueil des inscriptions chrétiennes de la Gaule anterieurs au VIIIe siècle* 2 vols. and supplement (Paris: 1856 and 1892) vol. 2, no. 380, p. 18. On the inscriptions of the region see Ingrid Heidrich, "Südgallische Inschriften des 5.–7. Jahrhunderts als historische Quellen," *Rheinische Vierteljahrsblätter*, vol. 32 (1968) pp. 167–183.

and Alemannia, the Welfs. The appearance in the rebels' names of the elements *Rod* and *ulf,* which Fleckenstein has shown to be typically Welf, particularly in the name of the rebels father, Rodulf, suggests that while the rebels certainly should not be viewed as Welfs, they may have come from the same aristocratic group which later produced the historical Welfs.[71] This hypothesis is strengthened if both of the rebel name groups are compared with the Welf entry in the Reichenau *Liber Memorialis* studied by Gerd Tellenbach: Ruadpreht-Heilwig-Chuonrat-Hemma-Morentio.[72] Here one finds not only *Rod* and *ulf* but *Mor* as well. The editors of the *Klostergemeinschaft von Fulda* have recently commented, *a propos* of a Morenzo who was a monk at Fulda from ca. 781 to 829, on the likelihood that this is a Welf name. "The identification of the M. in the Welf entry with the Fulda monk of the same name is in no way certain; that there existed a cognatic kin connection of the two is entirely thinkable ..."[73] One must immediately caution against a facile assimilation of the names Morentio and Maurontus – linguistically they are quite, or should be quite different. However both are formed from the same prefex Maur-Mor, as in for example the *Annales Laurissenses minores,* where the duke of Provence's name is preserved as Morontus.[74]

Nevertheless, the appearance of the prefix *Maur* in the names of two of the five known rebels (Mauringus, Maurontus) and the Welfish elements *Rod* and *olf* in three of the five suggest that the same aristocratic group which produced anti-Arnulfing Franks in Neustria and Burgundy in the seventh and eighth centuries produced this important ninth-century family which, prior to the marriage of Louis the Pious with the daughter of Welf, seems to have been somewhat outside the inner circle of great aristocratic families allied with the Carolingians.

---

[71] Josef Fleckenstein, "Über die Herkunft der Welfen und ihre Anfänge in Süddeutschland," *Studien und Vorarbeiten.* pp. 71–136; 101–102. I am grateful to Professors Tellenbach and Karl Schmid for their advice and suggestions on how to understand the very important difference between posible distant continuity as evidenced in names and perceived continuity, the only historical sense in which persons could be said to form a family. These early bearers of "Welf" names are certainly not Welfs, although they, like many other aristocratic families, pursued policies designed to establish their independence from central power, just as would the Welfs in the tenth and eleventh centuries. For the finest reflection on the importance of self-perception in aristocratic "mentalité" see Karl Schmid, "Welfisches Selbstverständnis," *Festschrift für Gerd Tellenbach* (Freiburg: 1968) pp. 389–416.

[72] *Das Verbrüderungsbuch der Abtei Reichenau,* p. 98.

[73] *Die Klostergemeinschaft von Fulda im früheren Mittelalter,* ed. Karl Schmid et al. (Munich: 1978) Münstersche Mittelalter-Schriften vol. 8/3, p. 473. That the names Rupert-Hrodpert examined by Wolfram in the context of Bavarian and Neustrian opposition groups can be related to this name group in Provence must raise the possibility of not only a parallelism but possibly even relationship among these various groups of Carolingian opponents.

[74] *MGH SS* I, pp. 112–113.

Conclusions

The foregoing discussion of the revolt of Provence as seen through the testament of Abbo leads us to two general conclusions. The first and most specific concerns the nature of the revolt itself. Maurontus and his followers, including Riculfus, Rodbaldus, and Mauringus, should not be seen as Gallo-Romans rebelling against a Frankish yoke, but rather as members of the old Frankish aristocracy continuing a tradition begun in Neustria over a generation previously of opposing the upstart Arnulfingians. Moreover, Charles Martel, it must be noted, was able to crush this revolt with the assistance of "Romans" like Abbo. Again one sees the similarities with Bavaria. Within this great duchy the Agilolfings and their supporters in the East can be seen as closely parallel to Maurontus and his supporters in the Rhône valley. Both groups were closely connected to events in Neustria but sought autonomy from rising Arnulfing power. Parallel to Abbo one sees such Bavarians as Bishop Arbeo of Freising, who, as Friedrich Prinz has recently pointed out, was a leader of a western Bavarian family oriented toward "Frankish" (that is, toward centralist, Carolingian) alliances.[75] The parallels between Maurontus and Tassilo III on the one hand and between Abbo and Arbeo on the other go beyond the mere fact of their pro- or anti-Carolingian positions. In Burgundy-Provence as in Bavaria, the rival groups built their positions and manifested their political and cultural orientations through the foundation and support of religious institutions and in the choice of *patrocinia* for their foundations. In this comparative perspective, the foundation of Novalesa and the choice of St. Peter as principal patron indicates much more than mere "private" piety on the part of Abbo: such a foundation was a statement of cultural and political identity as clear as those of the western Bavarian nobility who would ultimately abandon their duke for Charles the Great. Likewise one should interpret in this context the statement in the foundation charter of 726 that the monks of Novalesa were to live *"secondum [sic] euangelica normam et regola [sic] Benedicto."*[76] The antique traditions of Gallic monasticism had survived in the lower Rhône as the normal form of monastic life in the face of growing Benedictine and Irofrankish monasticism which, by the eighth century, was largely the norm in the North.[77] Thus Abbo's decision to place his new foundation under the Benedictine Rule was a clear indication that its destiny, like that of its founder, was to be tied to the central Frankish, that is, Carolingian, party.

The more general and in many ways more interesting conclusion concerns the nature of the Neustro-Burgundian aristocracy in the later seventh and early eighth centuries. The

---

[75] Friedrich Prinz, "Bayerns agilofingische Kloster- und Adelsgeschichte und die Gründung Kremsmünsters," *Die Anfänge des Klosters Kremsmünster,* ed. Siegfried Haider, *Mitteilungen des oberösterreichischen Landesarchivs,* Erg.-Bd. 2 (Linz: 1978) pp. 25–50.

[76] Cipolla, ed., pp. 8–9.

[77] Prinz, *Frühes Mönchtum,* pp. 277–278. For the three exceptions to this tendency to retain Gallic monastic traditions, see above. p. 140–141.

"kindred" which included Adalbaldus, Waratto, Maurontus *dux* and others is hardly a family in any modern or high medieval sense: certainly one could not argue that the generations represent an agnatic descent group. Nor could one suggest that the Rodulfus and the Maurontus were brothers or even necessarily close kin. Instead what we are seeing is a very wide, fluid group, admission to which is gained not simply by blood but also by marriage, as in the case of Bercharius, son-in-law of Waratto and the case of Drogo, son of Pepin II who, by marrying Bercharius' daughter himself became part of this family. Perhaps as significant as kin connection in the group is a sense of party connection – a sense of belonging to the leading aristocratic group in Neustria jealous of its position and determined to defend it against parvenues, be they Ebroin or Pepin. However, even here, as the case of the Mayor of the Palace Ghyslemarus indicates, the group did have its internal cleavages.

This group, which well fits the general outlines of the *Sippe* described by Karl Schmid and others,[78] had its origins in an alliance sealed by marriage with the Neustrian royal family and rose to prominence in the court of Dagobert I, who was the cousin or nephew of Erchinoaldus. In fact, Erchinoaldus was the last Mayor of the Palace to be described as having been appointed by the king – thereafter mayors, whether of this family or of other families, would be "elected" by the aristocracy.[79] The expansion of this *Sippe* into Burgundy and Provence can perhaps also be explained by its position at the court of Dagobert. It was part of that old aristocracy described by Karl Ferdinand Werner as "Frankish nobles of probably Neustrian origin," which would spread throughout the Frankish empire in the later seventh and eighth centuries.[80]

Even after the Arnulfingian victories in Neustria and in Provence, the rebels' *Sippe* was not exterminated. In Neustria, the Arnulfingians married into it, and possibly it was through Drogo's marriage with Adaltruda that he came to be, in addition to Duke of Champagne, Duke of Burgundy.[81] Likewise, the last Ghyslemarus appears to retain his

---

[78] The classic formulation remains that of Karl Schmid in "Zur Problematik." Other recent studies by Schmid and other European scholars have appeared, for example, in the volume edited by Timothy Reuter, *The Medieval Nobility,* and *Famille et parenté dans l'occident médiéval,* ed. Georges Duby and Jacques Le Goff (Rome: 1977).

[79] Fredegar IV, 84, p. 71.

[80] Werner, "Bedeutende Adelsfamilien." The quotation is from the Reuter translation, p. 168.

[81] A number of convergences suggest that the marriage of Drogo with the daughter of Bercharius strengthened the family of Pepin II not only in Neustria but in the region of lower Burgundy and Provence as well. The judicial proceeding involving Drogo and Adaltruda (*LS* 27) was witnessed by Agnericus, the *patricius* mentioned in Abbo's testament (16) who was probably *patricius* of Burgundy (see Buchner, Die Provence, p. 104) and by Antener, the *patricius* of Provence who later revolted against the Arnulfingians (see Buchner, p. 98). On the document, dated March 14, 697, see Bergmann, "Untersuchungen", no. 16, p. 70–71. Further, although Drogo is said in the *Liber historiae Francorum* to have been the duke of Champaigne ("Drocus ducatum Campaniae accepit" *SSRM* II, p. 323), in the Annals of Metz he is termed "Burgundionum dux," and it is probably he who is implied to have been the "Burgundionum ducem" in the *Vita Boniti* who is reconciled with

local authority in the region where his ancestor Adalbaldus had his estates. In Provence Maurontus escaped;[82] Riculfus, Rodbaldus, and Mauringus were deprived of their estates but not of their lives. In fact, ironically enough in 780 it was a Bishop Maurontus of Marseille who petitioned Charles the Great for the return of property confiscated in turn by Antener and by Charles Martel that had belonged to the Monastery of St. Victor of Marseille.[83] Likewise, the name appears in the list of living and dead entered in the Reichenau *Liber memorialis* during the ninth century from Abbo's own Monastery of Novalesa.[84] Finally, if there was in fact some connection between this early *Sippe* and the later Welfs, the ninth-century establishment of the Welf Rudolf in Burgundy by the Carolingian may have been facilitated on a local level by the preexisting position of kin in the region.[85]

This image of the resilience of the *Sippe* accords well with Karl Schmid's observation that, owing in large part to the fluid, non-linear nature of these kin groups they were not so easily exterminated, but rather tended to reappear under slightly different forms from generation to generation in spite of major reversals.[86] It also supports Karl Ferdinand Werner's thesis of the necessity of Carolingian cooperation with older aristocratic families.[87] In Neustria, in Burgundy, in Provence, and elsewhere, local ties to the aristocracy were essential for effective control and the Carolingians needed both to maintain their contacts with local supporters such as Abbo[88] and also to co-opt the elements of their enemies such as the family of Maurontus.

Until now we have emphasized the Frankish, Neustrian character of this great *Sippe*, and this image is essentially correct. However, if the *Sippe* was Frankish, it was probably

---

the bishop of Lyon by Bonitus (*SSRM* VI, p. 130; see introduction p. 111). Lewis, "Dukes," p. 402, note 136, rejects the thesis, defended by Ewig, ("Teilreiche", pp. 229–230), that Drogo was Duke of Burgundy. He does not defend this position other than to say that "it seems improbable that Pepin II had any effective control over Burgundy after he defeated the Neustrians in 687." He ignores, however, the evidence of the *Vita Boniti* and of course is unaware that the marriage of Drogo to Adaltruda might have given Drogo at least some support in the region.

[82] *Continuator* 21, p. 96 "… Fugato duce Mauronto inpenetrabilibus, tutissimis rupibus, maritimis munitionibus."

[83] *Cartulaire de S. Victor de Marseille,* ed. B. Guérard, vol. 1(Paris: 1857) no. 30; *Gallia christiana novissima* II, col. 33.

[84] *Liber memorialis,* p. 9.

[85] On the proximate origins of the Welfish Rudolfingians in Burgundy see Theodor Schieffer's introduction to his MGH edition, *Die Urkunden der burgundischen Rudolfinger* (Munich: 1977), in which he describes them as an Austrasian family which had no prior connection to the region.

[86] Schmid, "Zur Problematik," p. 4.

[87] Werner, "Bedeutende Adelsfamilien."

[88] Abbo was by no means unusual as a local supporter of the Arnulfingian family who assisted it in its consolidation in his area. He should be compared with the Leo who facilitated Charles the Great's consolidation of Italy in the next generation. See Donald A. Bullough, "*Leo qui apud Hlotharium magni loci habebatur,* et le gouvernement du Regnum Italiae à l'epoque carolingienne," *Le Moyen Age* 67 (1961), pp. 221–245.

likewise Roman. To understand this apparent paradox we must return to the origins of the family in the court of Dagobert. Adalbaldus, it will be remembered, married Rictrudis, a noble woman from "Gasconia," according to her *vita*.[89] The meaning of "Gascon origins" for an eleventh century *vita* for seventh-century reality is uncertain, but the image of Southerners brought up at the royal court in the seventh century and then involved in Merovingian politics and social alliances is in total conformity with other well-known examples. The most important is that of Desiderius of Cahors, the son of prominent Gallo-Romans Salvus and Haerchemfreda, and brother of Rusticus, Siagrius, Selina and Avita.[90] He and his brothers Siagrius and Rusticus lived at the royal court during their adolescence and from there were returned to the South to fill important lay and ecclesiastical offices: Rusticus became bishop of Cahors, Siagrius *Patricius* of Provence,[91] and Desiderius briefly followed his brother in Provence before succeeding his other brother Rusticus as bishop of Cahors.[92] Just as the Merovingian kings found in these Southerners loyal administrators whom they could return to the Midi to govern, one can imagine that the choice of ancestors of Maurontus to fill important positions in the region was probably facilitated by Rictrudis' meridional origins which were not lost by her marriage with a well connected Frank. Such marriages of important families from different regions effected in the royal court during the early seventh century were part of the more general cultural and social mixture of Frankish and Roman society which took place through the influence of Irofrankish monasticism, particularly that of Luxeuil. As Friedrich Prinz has shown, the monastery of Luxeuil and the court of Clothar II and Dagobert I in Paris were the two foci of this process, drawing together such leading political and ecclesiastical figures of Frankish and Gallo-Roman background as Arnulf and Abbo of Metz, Eligius of Noyen, Audoenus of Rouen and Sulpitius of Bourges. The result of marriage alliances such as that between the families of Rictrudis and Adalbaldus was that these kindred became at once Frankish and Roman.[93] Its members, particularly in Neustria, were part of the important Frankish aristocracy fighting for control of the position of mayor of the palace and hence

---

[89] *Vita S. Rictrudis*, II, *PL* 132.831. While the traditions concerning the Neustrian relationships centered around Marchiennes reported by Hucbaldus may be given credence for the reasons outlined above, n. 23, it is impossible to say to what extent the details of Rictrudis' own background may reflext reality. The *vita* states: "Haec (Rictrudis) claro satis exstitit oriunda germine, Ernoldo nobili edita, genitore, et Lichia genitrice ex agili pugnacique Wasconum gente."

[90] *Vita Desiderii Cadurcae urbis episcopi*, SSRM IV, pp. 547–602.

[91] *Ibid.*, 568; Buchner, 96–97; Ebling, CCLXXVII, pp. 214–215; Stroheker, *Der senatorische Adel*, no. 378, p. 222.

[92] *SSRM* IV, 568.

[93] On intermarriage of Franks and Gallo-Romans at court see Rouche, *L'Aquitaine*, p. 174–175, although Rouche minimizes its importance in Aquitaine. See also Ebling, et. al., *Nomen* et *gens*, pp. 698–701 on intermarriage. For the reasons outlined in note 1, Chapter IV above, one must view this latter study with caution. On the influence of Luxeuil on the Frankish aristocracy see Prinz, *Frühes Mönchtum*, pp. 121–151.

control of the kingdom. Simultaneously, through their local ties they were regional aristocratic families and gathered support for their lordship through the networks of kinship and
alliance uniting old Gallo-Roman families.

Thus for certain purposes, such as opposition to Charles Martel and his puppet
Theuderic IV, it is conceivable that when "Frankish" meant supporters of the Frankish
mayor and his king, families such as that of Maurontus were perceived as Romans or Burgundians, although they had possibly better Frankish blood than did Charles. Similarly,
Abbo, who lived by and knew well Roman law, and was deeply connected to the remains
of Romano-Provençal society identified himself and was identified with Charles, that is to
say, with the Franks, and this good Gallo-Roman aristocrat founded his monastery specifically for the "stability of the *regnum Francorum*."[94]

Thus we can conclude on the example of these rebels that the principalities which
emerged at the end of the seventh century had their roots both in the pan-European world
of the Frankish aristocracy and in particular, local traditions, both of which were interre-
lated, since this "international" aristocracy was at every moment rooting itself through
marriage and land with local magnates. The successful maintenance of family power, a
combination of land, office, and followers, required careful balance and interplay of both,
at various times emphasizing membership in the Frankish aristocracy, at times asseting a
local, particularist tradition. In the late seventh century, as later in the tenth, more appeared to be gained from the latter than from the former. In the first instance, Pepin and
his successors were able to build, from his position of local, Austrasian power, a new sense
of European unity at the expense of other, equally "Frankish" and equally "local" leaders
such as Maurontus. In the tenth century, no Pepin or Charles Martel appeared, and those
who attempted to appropriate the universal tradition, the Ottonians and Capetians, were
unequal to the task.

---

[94] Cipolla I, p. 9.

CONCLUSIONS

Dodina, Abbo's maternal grandmother, would undoubtedly have been familiar with a type of small earthenware vessel called an "olla" which had been, since the late Empire, the typical form of container used in the areas in which she and her husband Maurus had their estates. These paleochristian "ollae" were found not only in Provence but all along the coast from Italy to Catalonia and were part of the artisanal continuity of form and style uniting this region for centuries. By the year that Abbo prepared his testament, he would surely have been more familiar with the "pégau": a grey, non-glazed sort of vessel typical of regions farther up the Rhône valley into the area around Geneva more identified with "barbarian" pottery production than with late classical traditions. By the early 700s, this more northern form of container had largely replaced the more classical form and would dominate pottery production until the thirteenth century when they would be displaced by finer imported pottery and by new forms of local production.[1] This evolution in such simple things as pottery forms is indicative of the transformations of the entire Rhône basin during these generations. By the end of Abbo's lifetime, the orientation of the region was, as we have seen, no longer along its horizontal but rather along its vertical axis – not looking to the traditional areas of Roman culture but to the Frankish and Germanic areas of political power.

However, this image is deceptive if one understands by it any radical change in the region. We must remember that Dodina's daughter, and quite likely Dodina herself had close contacts with the region of Geneva, and it is likely that these contacts were already long established. The more northern traditions of Burgundy, the Transjuran and Francia were by no means new to the lower Rhône in the eighth century, they had simply become more fashionable. The new fashion dictated that one look less to the Mediterranean and more to the North. Like the change in pottery, much of the change that took place between the late Merovingian period and the early Carolingian one in the region were of this nature: long before Charles Martel's arrival in the lower Rhône the elements of the new order, economic, social and political were in place. The real change was one of emphasis, of style: crucial, to be sure, but extremely difficult to assess.

Economy

In the testament, we see the different systems of late Roman and classic medieval agricultural organization existing side by side. Abbo's estates can be seen as a well preserved

---

[1] Jacqueline Rigoir, "La ceramique paléochrétienne sigillée grise," *Provence historique,* vol. 10 (1960), pp. 1–92; "Les sigillées paléochrétiennes grises et orangées," *Gallia,* vol. 26 (1968), pp. 177–244. Gabrielle Demians d'Archimbaud, "Ceramique médiévale en Provence," *Archeologia* vol. 72 (1974) pp. 37–49.

example of late Roman agriculture and landlordship, with his *liberti, mancipia,* his *colonicae;* his estates supervised by his agents; and his revenue collectors, backed up by public judges. At the same time, he can be seen as a precursor of the manorial system, with his slaves settled on individual plots of land, his bipartite estates and his properties parceled out in benefice. Had he been able to pass along to lay heirs his lands, one might have seen the process of division and reunification of property continued for generations. In fact, the act of bequeathing his lands to a monastery greatly affected the course of their future organization. Unlike Abbo, Novalesa would never die, it would never feel called upon to free its *mancipia* as meritorious works, it would not experience the fragmentation of its estates across generations. Instead, it would hold what it had and would continue to add to its holdings in each generation. With this new and unaccustomed stability, the possibility of slowly restructuring and uniting properties over generations would become possible. No polyptique from Novalesa exists, but if one did, by 800 one might have seen a more unified system of *villae* replacing the multitude of small holdings or *colonicae* that one finds in Abbo's testament. Estates like Abbo's five *cortes* may have become the rule rather than the exception. This process needed only a change in the process of constant divisions to take place.

This change took place not only through the donation of land to monasteries, but also through the process of granting it in benefice. We see already that Abbo is granting land to his fideles *in benefitio.* That such a grant could help maintain the integrity of economic units is clear from the example of the *villa* of Chaudol claimed by St. Victor of Marseille in 780. As Ganshof noted, this estate maintained its integrity for at least a century, in large part, no doubt, to the fact that it was first held by the Church and then given in benefice to the *fidelis* of the Carolingian agent (probably count) Ardingus. True, the fullest expression of the Carolingian manor would not appear in Provence until much later and the estates of Provence might never be identical to those of more northernly regions, but the effects of the Carolingian conquest of the region freed common elements already present in the two systems to begin to work toward this end.

Thus far we have spoken only indirectly about the maritime commerce which was of such great importance in the prospertiy of classical Provence. After the second decade of the eighth century, we hear no more of the commerce from Marseille and Fos for over a century. To the valid arguments pointing to long term decline in the East-West commerce, one must also add another factor: the apparent lack of interest in the southernmost parts of Provence on the part of its Frankish lords through the eighth and most of the ninth centuries. None of the early Carolingians seems to have visited the region between the last expedition of Charles Martel and the appearance of Lothair I in the 840s. What interest there was in the region was in the Alpine areas and in particular the passes, such as that through Susa into Lombardy. Is this cause or effect of the declining importance of the international trade through the region? Probably the answer is a mixture of both. Certainly control of the commerce through Marseille and Fos in the late Merovingian period had been in the hands of royal agents, and apparently its beneficiaries were, by the early eighth century, largely the great monasteries of Francia. The early Carolingians had other sources of revenue and other concerns than the dwindling international trade up the Rhône. The property confiscated from rebellious lay and ecclesiastic opponents and then the booty from the wars of conquest against the Franks' neighbors, not tariffs on luxury goods, were their sources of wealth. They may have seen little value in reestablishing the facilities of the ports which were quite likely destroyed in the wars against the rebels and the Saracens. What commerce remained was largely the slave trade handled by Jews, and it was not until the reign of Louis the Pious, after the prosperity due to military expansion was over, that the kings of the Franks looked again to these merchants for support.

Society

The same mixture of the old and the new that we have seen in the economy of Provence in the early eighth century was present in its aristocratic society. Families like that of Abbo were legitimately part of the old senatorial tradition and had continued the great names of the Gallo-Roman aristocracy into his own day: those of the Syagrii, the Aegidii, the Avoli, etc. At the same time these families are part of Germanic society characterized by different names, likewise common in the region fo over a century: Waldebertus, Chramnelenus, Abbo, etc. Should one suppose that the old senatorial families disappear along with their names? There is certainly no reason to think so. What does disappear is the fashion to continue to use these names and thus to emphasize this part of families' dual tradition. Thus the Germanic names which had appeared alongside the Gallo-Roman names will continue to reemerge across the eighth, ninth, and tenth century, as will such Romance names as Maurontus and Maurengus which had resonance in Francia as well as in Provence. Like aristocracies elsewhere, that of the Rhône basin adapted itself to new conditions, identified itself with the new sources of power, and endured.

This dual orientation of the aristocracy is most clearly seen in its involvement in the so-called revolt of Provence. As we have seen, at one level this series of conflicts was the continuation of familial efforts to achieve dominance in their regions: Abbo stands in the tradition of Flaochad, eliminating the *Dux* Maurontus in the 730s just as Flaochad had eliminated the *Patricius* Willibad in the 640s. However simultaneously Abbo is a supporter of Charles Martel and as such involved in a much wider struggle for the dominance of the entire Frankish realm. Within this struggle, Maurontus represented not simply a local aristocratic group seeking autonomy but a much wider anti-Arnulfing party resisting the son of Pepin II throughout the Empire.

Government

Much has been made of the transformation of the Romano-Ostrogothic constitution of Provence following Charles Martel's final victory. Again, these transformations can be seen either as a radical departure or the continuation of long-established traditions. The positions of *rector* and that of *patricius* are abolished, it is true, and the Carolingians establish counts drawn apparently from Alemannia and elsewhere as governors of the region. Property confiscated from the churches of the region is granted in benefice to these new authorities and their followers. All is changed. And yet, much remains the same. The disappearance of the *patricius* continues for no more than a century: in 844 Fulcradus will be termed *dux* of Arles, a recognition, if not of the continuity of an office, certainly of the reality of power in this distant part of the empire. The *Alemanni* established by the Carolingians in the region also, represent less an innovation than continuity: from where else was Abbo's family with their connections in Grenoble and Geneva, and indeed probably the family of Maurontus, if not from that area called in the extreme south Alemannia? In the 780s Ardingus and others may have seemed new arrivals, but they could no doubt be quickly assimilated into the regional society as had other outsiders before them. Already by 812 the Count of Arles Leibulf seems to have been established in the area for at least two generations. Once more the imperial aristocracy was simultaneously a local aristocracy as it had been in the seventh century.

The foregoing is not intended to deny that the early eighth century marked a turning point in the transition from Merovingian (or if one will, from late Roman) to Carolingian society either in Provence or in other areas of Europe, such as Raetia and Bavaria. Rather, it simply indicates that the transition is less a question of a physical transformation than a psychic one. The structures of land, blood, and labor remain, but they are used differently and, still more important, seen differently. To say that the change is just in style or taste is not to deny its significance. These changes are extremely important because new perceptions bring a new reality: those who remain in power do so by changing their self-perceptions. It is by no means the first time that this has happened in the region, nor will it be the last. The old structures remain but are given new meanings and new functions in the society. The best example of this is Novalesa itself, Abbo's family monastery. It will continue to protect the passes into Lombardy as did the old *rector* of Susa and Maurienne. But it will do this in a new relationship and in a new way: its revenues go to support the Frankish host, its titular abbot is himself a Carolingian. Thus in the truest sense was Novalesa the heir of Abbo — it was the institutionalization and the continuation of all that he and his family represented in the service to the new masters of Europe.

BIBLIOGRAPHY

I. PRIMARY SOURCES

A. *Narrative Sources*

Ado archiepiscopus Viennensis. *De sex aetatibus mundi. PL* 123.23–138.

Annales laurissenses minores. ed. G. H. Pertz. *MGH SS.* I. Hannover, 1826. 112–123.

Annales marchianenses. ed. L. C. Bethmann. *MGH SS* XVI. Hannover, 1859. 609–617.

Annales mettenses priores. ed. B. von Simson. *MGH SS rer. Germ.* 10. Hannover, 1905.

Chronicon moissiacense. ed. G. H. Pertz. *MGH SS* I. Hannover, 1826. 280–313.

Chronicon novaliciense. ed. Carlo Cipolla. *Monumenta novaliciensia vetustiora* II. Rome, 1901.

Constantinus Prophyrogenitus. *Excerpta de legationibus Romanorum ad Gentes.* ed. Carolus de Boor. 2 vols. Berlin, 1903.

Fredegarius. *Chronicon.* ed. Bruno Krusch. *MGH SSRM* II. Hannover, 1888. 1–193. Book Four ed. J. M. Wallace-Hadrill. *The Fourth Book of the Chronicle of Fredegar with its continuations.* London, 1960.

Gregorius episcopus Turonensis. *Historia Francorum.* ed. Bruno Krusch and Wilhelm Levison. *MGH SSRM* I. Hannover 1937–1951.

Gesta SS patrum fontanellensis coenobii (Gesta abbatum fontanellensium). ed. F. Lohier and J. Laporte. Société de l'histoire de Normandie. Rouen, 1936.

Hariulf, *Chronicon.* ed. Ferdinand Lot. Collection des textes pour servir à l'étude et à l'enseignement de l'histoire 17. Paris, 1898.

Liber historiae Francorum. ed. Bruno Krusch. *SSRM* II. Hannover, 1888. 215–328.

Legerius. *Liber episcopalis viennensis ecclesiae* ed. L. Duchesne. *Fastes épiscopaux de l'ancienne Gaule.* I, 178–203.

Paulus Diaconus. *Historia Langobardorum.* ed. L. Bethmann and G. Waitz. *MGH SSRL.* Hannover, 1878. 1–187.

Priscus. *Excerpta e Prisci historia. Fragmenta historicorum Graecorum* 4. Paris, 1851. 69–110.

B. *Diplomata*

Cipolla, Carlo. ed. *Monumenta novaliciensia vetustiora.* 2 vols. Rome, 1898–1901.

Diplomata karolinorum: Die Urkunden Peppins, Karlmanns und Karls des Großen. ed. Engelbert Mühlbacher. *MGH Dip.* I.1. Hannover, 1906.

Diplomata regum francorum e stirpe merowingica. ed. G. H. Pertz. *MGH Dipl. imperii* I. Hannover, 1872.

Diplomata regum et imperatorum germaniae: Die Urkunden Otto des III. ed. Theodor Sickel. *MGH Dipl.* II, 2. Hannover, 1893.

Gallia Christiana novissima II Marseille; Valence. 2nd ed. Paris, 1899.

Guérard, B. *Cartulaire de l'Abbaye de Saint-Victor de Marseille.* Paris, 1857.

Lauer, Ph. and Samaran, Ch. eds. *Les diplômes originaux des mérovingiens.* Paris, 1908.

Marion, Jules. *Cartulaires de l'église cathédrale de Grenoble dits Cartulaires de Saint-Hugues.* Paris, 1869.

Meyer-Marthaler, Elizabeth and Perret, Franz, eds. *Bündner Urkundenbuch.* 2 vols. Chur, 1955.

Pardessus, J. M. and Bréquiny, L.G.O. *Diplomata chartae et instrumenta aetatis merovingicae.* 2 vols. Paris, 1849.

Poupardin, René. *Recueil des actes des rois de Provence (855–928).* Paris, 1920.

C. *Legal*

Capitularia regum francorum. ed. Alfredus Boretius and Victor Krause. *MGH Legum* II, 1 and 2. Hannover, 1883–1897.

Corpus Iuris Civilis. ed. Th. Mommsen, *et. al.* 3 vols. Berlin, 1911–1928.

Codex Theodosianus. ed. Th. Mommsen and Paul Meyer. 2 vols. in 3. 2nd ed. Berlin, 1954.

Formulae andecavenses. ed. Karl Zeumer. *MGH Legum* V. *Formulae.* Hannover, 1886. 1–25.

Formulae arvernenses. ed. Karl Zeumer. *MGH Legum* V. *Formulae.* Hannover, 1886. 26–31.

Formulae bituricenses. ed. Karl Zeumer. *MGH Legum* V. *Formulae.* Hannover, 1886. 166–181.

Fragmenta gaudenzia. ed. G. Vismara. *Ius Romanum medii aeui.* Milan, 1978.

Leges Burgundionum. ed. L. R. von Salis. *MGH Legum* I. *Legum nationum Germanicarum* II. Hannover, 1892.

Leges Visigothorum. ed. Karl Zeumer. *MGH Legum* I. *Legum nationum Germanicarum* I. Hannover, 1902.

Lex Salica. ed. Karl August Eckhardt. *MGH Legum* I. *Legum nationum Germanicarum* IV, II. Hannover, 1969.

Marculfi Formulae. ed. Karl Zeumer. *MGH Legum* V. *Formulae.* Hannover, 1886. 32–112.

D. *Hagiography*

Ado archiepiscopus viennensis. *Martyrologium.* PL 123.139–456. Dubois, Jacques and Renaud, Geneviève. eds. *Edition pratique des martyrologes de Bède de l'anonyme lyonnais et de Florus.* Paris, 1976.

Gregorius episcopus Turonensis. *Liber in gloria martyrum.* ed. Bruno Krusch. *MGH SSRM* I. Hannover, 1884. 484–561.

Miracula S. Dionysii. ed. Bruno Krusch. *Neues Archiv.* 18 (1893), 601–602.

Passio Ragneberti martyris Bebronensis. ed. Bruno Krusch. *MGH SSRM* V. Hannover, 1910. 207–211.

Vita Aigulphi. AASS Sept. I. 743–747.

Vita Amandi episcopi I. ed. Bruno Krusch. *MGH SSRM* V. Hannover, 1910. 395–449.

Vita Amandi episcopi II. auctore Milone. ed. Bruno Krusch. *MGH SSRM* V. Hannover, 1910. 450–483.

Vita Ansberti episcopi Rotomagensis. ed. Wilhelm Levison. *MGH SSRM* V. Hannover, 1910. 613–643.

Vita Sancti Arnulfi. ed. Bruno Krusch. *MGH SSRM* II. Hannover, 1888. 426–446.

Vita Audoini episcopi Rotomagensis. ed. Wilhelm Levison. *MGH SSRM* V. Hannover, 1888. 536–567.

Vita Boniti episcopi Arverni. ed. Bruno Krusch. *MGH SSRM* VI. Hannover, 1913. 110–139.

Vita Sanctae Consortiae virginis. AASS Iuni IV. 248–254.

Vita Desiderii Cadurcae urbis episcopi. ed. Bruno Krusch. *MGH SSRM* IV. Hannover, 1902. 547–602.

Vita Fursei abbatis Latiniacensis. ed. Bruno Krusch. *MGH SSRM* IV. Hannover, 1902. 423–451.

Vita Galli confessoris triplex. ed. Bruno Krusch. *MGH SSRM* IV. Hannover, 1902. 229–337.

Vita S. Hugonis episcopi Gratianopolitani auctore Guigone. *AASS Aprilis* I, 37–46.

Vita Landiberti episcopi Traiectensis vetustissima. ed. Bruno Krusch. *MGH SSRM* VI. Hannover, 1913. 353–384.

Vita Richarii sacerdotis Centulensis primigenia. ed. Bruno Krusch. *MGH SSRM* VII. Hannover, 1920. 438–453.

Vita Richarii confessoris Centulensis auctore Alcuino. ed. Bruno Krusch. *MGH SSRM* IV. Hannover, 1902. 381–401.

Vita S. Rictrudis auctore Hucbaldo. *AASS Mai* III, 81–89; *PL* 132.827–848.

Vita Rusticulae sive Marciae abbatissae Arelatensis. ed. Bruno Krusch. *MGH SSRM* IV. Hannover, 1902. 337–351.

Vita Walarici abbatis Leuconaensis. ed. Bruno Krusch. *MGH SSRM* IV. Hannover, 1902. 157–175.

E. *Miscellaneous*

Agobardus archiepiscopus lugdonensis. *Epistolae*. ed. Ernst Dümmler. *MGH Ep*. V. Hannover, 1899. 153–239.

Autenrieth, Johanne, Geuenich, Dieter, and Schmid, Karl. *Das Verbrüderungsbuch der Abtei Reichenau. MGH Libri memoriales et necrologia*. nova series I. Hannover, 1979.

Breggi, J. F. *Le polyptique de l'abbaye Saint-Victor de Marseille, essai de réédition*. Thèse de Droit, Université de Paris. Paris, 1975.

Isidorus episcopus hispalensis. *Etymologiarum sive originum libri XX*. ed. W. M. Lindsay. 2 vols. Oxford, 1911.

Le Blant, Edmond. *Recueil des inscriptions chrétiennes de la Gaule antereiurs au VIIIe siècle*. 2 vols. and supplement. Paris, 1856 and 1892.

Origo Francorum duplex. ed. Bruno Krusch. *SSRM* VII. Hannover, 1920. 517–28.

Regino abbas Prumiens. *Epistola ad Hathonem*. ed. Fredrich Kurze. *MGH SS rer. Ger*. Hannover, 1890.

Schmid, Karl, et. al. *Die Klostergemeinschaft von Fulda im früheren Mittelalter*. Münstersche Mittelalter-Schriften 8. Munich, 1978.

II. SECONDARY SOURCES

Abadal y de Vinyals, Ramón de. "El paso de Septimania del dominio godo al franco a través de la invasión sarracena 720–768." *Cuadernos de historia de España*. 19 (1953), 5–54.

Amargier, Paul. "La capture de S. Maïeul de Cluny et l'expulsion des Sarrazins de Provence." *Revue Bénédictine*. 73 (1963), 316–323.

– "La Provence au miroir des monumenta de la Novalaise." *Provence historique*. 27 (1977), 251–256.

Baratier, E., Duby, G., Hilde-Sheimar, F. *Atlas historique de la Provence*. Paris, 1969.

Barroul, Guy. *Les peuples préromains du sud-est de la Gaule: Étude de géographie historique. Revue archéologique de narbonnaise* suppléments I. Paris, 1969.

Becker, Alfons, and Lohrmann, Dietrich. "Ein erschlichenes Privileg Papst Urbans II. für Erzbischof Guido von Vienne (Calixt II.)." *Deutsches Archiv*. 38 (1982), 66–111.

- *Papst Urban II* vol. I *Herkunft und kirchliche Laufbahn. Der Papst und die lateinische Christenheit.* Schriften der *Monumenta Germaniae Historica,* 19, I. Munich, 1964.

Benson, Robert L. *The Bishop-Elect: A Study in Medieval Ecclesiastical Office.* Princeton, 1968.

Bergmann, Werner. "Untersuchungen zu den Gerichtsurkunden der Merowingerzeit." *Archiv für Diplomatik.* 22 (1976), 1–186.

Beumann, Helmut and Schröder, Werner, eds. *Aspekte der Nationenbildung im Mittelalter. Nationes: Historische und philologische Untersuchungen zur Entstehung der europäischen Nationen im Mittelalter,* 1. Sigmaringen, 1978.

- "Die Bedeutung des Kaisertums für die Entstehung der deutschen Nation im Spiegel der Bezeichnungen von Reich und Herrscher." *Aspekte der Nationenbildung,* 317–365.

- Ed. *Karl der Große.* 1 *Persönlichkeit und Geschichte.* Düsseldorf, 1965.

Bligny, Bernard. *L'église et les ordres religieux dans le royaume de Bourgogne au XIe et XIIe siècles.* Grenoble, 1960.

Bloch, Marc. *Les caractères originaux de l'histoire rurale française.* 2nd ed. 2 vols. Paris, 1960–61.

Blumenthal, Uta-Renata. *The Early Councils of Pope Paschal II, 1100–1110.* Toronto, 1978.

Böhmer, J. F. *Regesta imperii* I. *Die Regesten des Kaiserreichs unter den Karolingern 751–918* neu bearbeitet von Engelbert Mühlbacher, 2nd ed. Innsbruck, 1899.

Borgolte, Michael. "*Felix est homo ille, qui amicos bonos relinquit:* Zur sozialen Gestaltungskraft letztwilliger Verfügungen am Beispiel Bischof Bertrams von Le Mans (616)." *Festschrift für Berent Schwineköper zu seinem siebzigsten Geburtstag.* ed. Helmut Maurer and Hans Patze. Sigmaringen, 1982. 5–18.

- "Freigelassene im Dienst der memoria: Kulttradition und Kultwandel zwischen Antike und Mittelalter." *Frühmittelalterliche Studien.* 17 (1983), 234–250.

Bosl, Karl. *Die Grundlagen der modernen Gesellschaft im Mittelalter: eine deutsche Gesellschaftsgeschichte des Mittelalters.* 2 vols. Monographien zur Geschichte des Mittelalters 4, 1–2. Stuttgart, 1972.

- *Franken um 800. Strukturanalyze einer fränkischen Königsprovinz.* Munich, 1969.

- "Freiheit und Unfreiheit: Zur Entwicklung der Unterschichten in Deutschland und Frankreich während des Mittelalters" Bosl, Karl. *Frühformen der Gesellschaft im mittelalterlichen Europa.* Munich, 1964. 180–203.

Boys, Albert du. *Vie de saint Hugues, évêque de Grenoble.* Grenoble, 1837.

Bresslau, Harry. *Handbuch der Urkundenlehre für Deutschland und Italien.* 2 vols. 2nd ed. Berlin, 1912–31; reprinted Berlin, 1958.

- "Zur Lehre von den Siegeln der Karolinger und Ottonen." *Archiv für Urkundenforschung.* 1 (1908) 255–370.

Broens, M. "Le peuplement germanique du la Gaule entre la Méditerranée et l'océan." *Annales du Midi.* 68 (1951), 17–38.

Brown, Peter. "Eastern and Western Christendom in Late Antiquity: A Parting of the Ways." in *Society and the Holy in Late Antiquity.* Berkeley, 1982. 166–195.

- "Mohammed and Charlemagne by Henri Pirenne" *Society and the Holy.* 63–79.

- "Relics and Social Status in the Age of Gregory of Tours" *Society and the Holy.* 222–250.

Brunner, Heinrich. *Deutsche Rechtsgeschichte.* 2 vols. 2nd. ed. Berlin, 1906, reprint, Berlin, 1961.

Brunner, Karl. "Der fränkische Fürstentitel im neunten und zehnten Jahrhundert." Herwig Wolfram, ed. *Intitulatio II: Lateinische Herrscher- und Fürstentitel im neunten und zehnten Jahrhundert. MIÖG* Erg. Bd. 24. Vienna, 1973. 179–327.

- *Oppositionelle Gruppen im Karolingerreich.* Veröffentlichungen des Instituts für österreichische Geschichtsforschung 25. Vienna, 1979.

Buchner, Rudolf. *Beiheft: Die Rechtsquellen.* Wattenbach-Levison *Deutschlands Geschichtsquellen im Mittelalter: Vorzeit und Karolinger.* Weimar, 1953.

– *Die Provence in merowinger Zeit: Verfassung – Wirtschaft – Kultur.* Arbeiten zur deutschen Rechts- und Verfassungsgeschichte 9. Stuttgart, 1933.

Buckland, W. W. *A Text-Book of Roman Law from Augustus to Justinian.* 3rd ed. revised by Peter Stein. Cambridge, 1966.

Bullough, Donald A. "*Leo qui apud Hlotharium magni loci habebatur* et le gouvernement du Regnum Italiae à l'époque carolingienne." *Le Moyen Age,* 67, 4e série, t. 16 (1961), 221–245.

Chaume, Maurice. *Les origines du duché de Bourgogne.* 2 vols. Dijon, 1925–32.

Cipolla, Carlo. *Notizia di alcuni codici dell'antica biblioteca novalicense.* Memorie della reale accademia della scienze di Torino serie seconda tomo 44. Torino, 1894.

Clavadetscher, Otto P. "Churrätien im Übergang von der Spätantike zum Mittelalter nach den Schriftquellen." in Joachim Werner and Eugen Ewig, eds. *Von der Spätantike zum frühen Mittelalter: aktuelle Probleme in historischer und archäologischer Sicht.* Vorträge und Forschungen 25. Sigmaringen, 1979. 159–178.

– "Die Einführung der Grafschaftverfassung in Rätien und die Klageschriften Bischof Viktors III von Chur." *Zeitschrift der Savigny-Stiftung für Rechtsgeschichte, Kanonistische Abteilung.* 39 (1953), 46–111.

– "Zur Verfassungsgeschichte des merowingischen Rätien." *Frühmittelalterliche Studien.* 8 (1974), 60–70.

Cognasso, F. "Attorno alla fondazione della Novalesa." *Bollettino storico bibliografico subalpino.* 58 (1960), 362–64.

Colardelle, Michel. *Des Burgondes à Bayard: Mille ans de moyen âge: recherches archéologiques et historiques.* Grenoble, 1981.

Contamine, Pierre. *La guerre au moyen âge.* La nouvelle Clio 24. Paris, 1980.

Coville, A. *Recherches sur l'histoire de Lyon du Veme siècle au IXeme siècle (450–800).* Paris, 1928.

Crozet, René. "Le voyage d'Urbain II et ses négociations avec le clergé de France 1095–1096." *Revue historique.* 179 (1937), 270–310.

Daim, Falko. "Das 7. und 8. Jh. in Niederösterreich." *Germanen Awaren Slaven in Niederösterreich: Das erste Jahrtausend nach Christus.* Vienna, 1977. 88–102.

Demians d'Archimbaud, Gabrielle. "Ceramique médiévale en Provence." *Archeologia,* 72 (1974), 37–49.

Dhont, Jan. *Etudes sur la naissance des principautés territoriales en France (IXe–Xe siècles).* Bruges, 1948.

Didier, Noël. "Étude sur le patrimoine de l'église cathédrale de Grenoble, de la fin du Xe au milieu du XIIe siècle." *Annales de l'Université de Grenoble.* 13 (1936), 5–87.

– "Notes sur la fortune immoblière de l'église cathédrale de Grenoble du Xe à la fin du XIIe siècle." *Annales de l'Université de Grenoble.* 22 (1947), 9–49.

Doehaerd, Renée. *Le haute moyen âge occidental: Economies et sociétés.* La nouvelle Clio 14. Paris, 1971.

Dolbeau, F. "Le dossier hagiographique de S. Amé, vénéré à Douai, Nouvelles recherches sur Hucbald de Saint-Amand." *Analecta Bollandiana,* 97 (1979), 90–110.

Dopsch, Alfons. *Die Wirtschaftsentwicklung der Karolingerzeit vornehmlich in Deutschland.* 2 vols. third, augmented edition Darmstadt, 1962.

Du Cange, Carlo du Fresne. *Glossarium mediae et infimae latinitatis.* revised by Léopold Favre, 9 volumes Niort, 1883 reprinted Bologna, 1971.

Duby, Georges and Le Goff, Jacques. eds. *Famille et parenté dans l'occident médiévale.* Rome, 1977.

Duchesne, L. *Fastes episcopaux de l'ancienne Gaule*. 3 vols. in 2, 2nd ed. Paris, 1907–17.

Duff, Arnold Mackay. *Freedmen in the Roman Empire*. Cambridge, 1958.

Duprat, E. "Essai sur l'histoire politique d'Avignon pendant le haut moyen âge." *Memoires de l'Academie de Vaucluse*. 2eme serie t. 8 (1908), 27–58.

— "La Provence dans le haut moyen âge. I. Le couloir austrasien du VIe siècle." *Institut historique de Provence. Mémoires et bulletins*. 20 (1943–44), 36–65.

— "La Provence dans le haute moyen âge." *Encyclopédie des Bouches-du-Rhône*. 2. Marseille, 1923. 261–272.

Dupraz, Louis. *Contribution à l'histoire du Regnum Francorum pendant le troisième quart du VIIe siècle (656–680)*. Fribourg, 1948.

Ebling, Horst, Jarnut, Jörg, Kampers, Gerd. "*Nomen et gens:* Untersuchungen zu den Führungsschichten des Franken-, Langobarden-, und Westgotenreiches im 6. und 7. Jahrhundert." *Francia*. 8 (1980), 687–745.

— *Prosopographie der Amtsträger des Merowingerreiches von Chlothar II. (613) bis Karl Martell (741)*. Beihefte der Francia 2. Munich, 1974.

Eckhart, Karl August. *Studia Merovingica*. Bibliotheca rerum historicarum studia II. Aalen, 1975.

Ewig, Eugen. "Die fränkischen Teilreiche im 7. Jahrhundert (613–714)." in *Spätantikes und fränkisches Gallien,* 1, 172–230.

— *Spätantikes und fränkisches Gallien: Gesammelte Schriften (1952–1973)* ed. Hartmut Atsma, Beihefte der Francia 3/1–2. Munich, 1976–79.

— "Die fränkischen Teilungen und Teilreiche (511–613)." in *Spätantikes und fränkisches Gallien,* 1, 114–171.

— *Die mittelalterliche Kirche, erste Halbband: Vom kirchlichen Frühmittelalter zur gregorianischen Reform.* in Hubert Jedin, ed., *Handbuch der Kirchengeschichte.* Freiburg, 1966.

— "Saint Chrodegang et la reforme de l'église franque." in *Spätantikes und fränkisches Gallien*, II, 232–259.

— "Volkstum und Volksbewußtsein im Frankenreich des 7. Jahrhunderts." in *Spätantikes und fränkisches Gallien*, I, 231–273.

Falkowski, Rudolf. "Studien zur Sprache der Merowingerdiplome." *Archiv für Diplomatik*. 17 (1971), 1–125.

Febvre, Lucien. "De Linné à Lamarck et à Georges Cuvier." in *Combats pour l'histoire*. 2nd ed. Paris, 1965. 318–336.

Fischer, J. *Der Hausmeier Ebroin*. Bonn, 1954.

Fleckenstein, Josef. "Fulrad von Saint-Denis und der fränkische Angriff in den süddeutschen Raum." *Studien und Vorarbeiten zur Geschichte des großfränkischen und frühdeutschen Adels.* ed. Gerd Tellenbach. Forschungen zur oberrheinischen Landesgeschichte 4. Freiburg i. Br., 1957. 9–39.

— "Über die Herkunft der Welfen und ihre Anfänge in Süddeutschland." *Studien und Vorarbeiten.* 71–136; 101–102.

Fliche, A. "Le voyage d'Urban II en France." *Annales du Midi*. 49 (1937), 42–69.

Fournial, Etienne. *Histoire monétaire de l'occident médiéval*. Paris, 1970.

Fournier, Gabriel. "L'esclavage en basse Auvergne aux époques mérovingienne et carolingienne." *Cahiers d'histoire*. 6 (1961), 361–375.

Frezza, Paolo. "Giurisprudenza e prassi notarile nelle carte italiane dell'alto medioevo e negli scritti di giuristi romani." *Studia et documenta historiae et iuris*. 42 (1976), 197–245.

— *L'influsso del diritto romano giustinianeo nelle formule e nelle prassi in Italia.* Ius romanum medii aevi. pars I,2, c ee. Milan, 1974.

Fustel de Coulanges, Numa Denis. *Histoire des institutions politiques de l'ancienne France.* 6 vols. 4th ed. Paris, 1924–27.

Fürst, Carl Gerold. *"Ecclesia vivit lege Romana?" Zeitschrift der Savigny-Stiftung für Rechtsge-schichte, Kanonische Abteilung.* 61 (1975), 17–36.

Ganshof, François Louis. *Feudalism.* tr. Philip Grierson. New York, 1961.

– "Les avatars d'un domaine de l'église de Marseille à fin du VIIe et au VIIIe siècle." *Studi in onore di Gino Luzzatto.* vol. l. Milan, 1950. 55–66.

– "Les bureaux du tonlieu de Marseille et de Fos. Contribution à l'histoire des institutions financières de la monarchie franque." *Etudes historiques à la mémoire de Noël Didier.* Paris, 1960. 126–133.

– "L'origine des rapports féodo-vassaliques." *I problemi della civiltà carolingia.* Settimane di studio del centro italiano di studi sull'alto medioevo. I. Spoleto, 1954. 27–69.

– "Note sur les ports de Provence du VIIIe au Xe siècle." *Revue historique.* 183 (1938), 28–37.

– "Quelques aspects principaux de la vie économique dans la monarchie franque au VIIe siècle." *Caratteri del secolo VII in occidente.* Settimane di studio del centro italiano di studi sull'alto medioevo. V. Spoleto, 1958. 73–101.

Gaudement, J. "Survivances romaines dans le droit de la monarchie franque du Vème au Xème siècle." *Revue d'histoire du droit.* 23 (1955), 149–206.

Geary, Patrick J. "Un fragment récemment découvert du *Chronicon moissiacense." Bibliotheque de l'Ecole des chartes.* 136 (1978), 69–73.

Gockel, Michael. *Karolingische Königshöfe am Mittelrhein.* Veröffentlichungen des Max-Plank-Instituts für Geschichte 31. Göttingen, 1970.

Goffart, Walter. *Caput and Colonate: Toward a History of Late Roman Taxation.* Toronto, 1974.

– "From Roman Taxation to Mediaeval Seigneurie: Three Notes." *Speculum.* 47 (1972), 165–187; 373–394.

– "Old and New in Merovingian Taxation." *Past and Present.* 96 (1982), 3–21.

Gordon, Mary L. "The Freedman's son in Municipal Life." *Journal of Roman Studies.* 21 (1931), 65–77.

Grahn-Hoek, Heike. *Die fränkische Oberschicht im 6. Jahrhundert: Studien zu ihrer rechtlichen und politischen Stellung.* Vorträge und Forschungen, Sonderband 21. Sigmaringen, 1976.

Gulli, Luciano. "Abbone." *Dizionario biografico degli italiani.* I. Rome, 1960. 42–43.

– "A proposito della più antica tradizione novalicense." *Archivio storico italiano.* 117 (1959), 306–318.

Heidrich, Ingrid. "Südgallische Inschriften des 5.–7. Jahrhunderts als historische Quellen." *Rheinische Vierteljahrsblätter.* 32 (1968), 167–183.

– "Titulatur und Urkunden der arnulfingischen Hausmeier." *Archiv für Diplomatik.* 11/12 (1965/66), 71–279.

Heinzelmann, Martin. *Bischofsherrschaft in Gallien: Zur Kontinuität römischer Führungsschichten vom 4. bis zum 7. Jahrhundert. Soziale, prosopographische und bildungsgeschichtliche Aspekte.* Beihefte der Francia 5. Munich, 1976.

– "L'aristocratie et les évêchés entre Loire et Rhin jusqu'à la fin du VIIe siècle." *Revue d'histoire de l'église de France.* 62 (1975), 75–90.

– "Les changements de la dénomination latine à la fin du l'antiquité." *Famille et parenté.* 19–24.

Herlihy, David. "Church Property on the European Continent 701–1200." *Speculum.* 36 (1961), 81–105.

– "Land Family and Women in Continental Europe 710–1200." *Traditio.* 18 (1962), 89–120.

– "The Agrarian Revolution in Southern France and Italy 801–1190." *Speculum.* 33 (1958), 23–41.

– "The Carolingian Mansus." *Economic History Review.* 13 (1960), 79–89.

– "The History of Rural Seigneury in Italy, 751–1200." *Agricultural History.* 33, 2 (1959), 58–71.

Higham, John, ed. *Ethnic Leadership in America.* Baltimore, 1978.

Hlawitschka, Ed. *Franken, Alemannen, Bayern und Burgunder in Oberitalien.* Freiburg i. Br., 1960.

Irsigler, Franz. *Untersuchungen zur Geschichte des frühfränkischen Adels.* Bonn, 1969.

Isajiw, Wsevolod. *Definitions of Ethnicity.* Toronto, 1979.

Jarnut, Jörg. "Beiträge zu den fränkisch-bayerisch-langobardischen Beziehungen im 7. und 8. Jahrhundert (656–728)." *Zeitschrift für bayerische Landesgeschichte.* 39 (1976), 331–352.

— "Untersuchungen zu den fränkisch-alemannischen Beziehungen in der ersten Hälfte des 8. Jahrhunderts." *Schweizerische Zeitschrift für Geschichte.* 30 (1980), 7–28.

Kaiser, Reinhold. *Bischofsherrschaft zwischen Königtum und Fürstenmacht. Studien zur bischöflichen Stadtherrschaft im westfränkisch-französischen Reich im frühen und hohen Mittelalter.* Pariser historischer Studien 17. Bonn, 1981.

Kajanto, Iiro. *Onomastic Studies in the Early Christian Inscriptions of Rome and Carthage.* Helsinki, 1963.

— *The Latin cognominia.* Helsinki, 1965.

— *Supernominia: A Study in Latin Epigraphy.* Helsinki, 1966.

Kaser, Max. *Das römische Privatrecht.* II *Die Nachklassischen Entwicklungen. Rechtsgeschichte des Altertums im Rahmen des Handbuchs der Altertumswissenschaft.* III Teil, III Bd., II Abschnitt. Munich, 1971.

Keller, Hagen. "Fränkische Herrschaft und alemannisches Herzogtum im 6. und 7. Jahrhundert." *Zeitschrift für die Geschichte des Oberrheins.* 124 (1976), 1–30.

Kienast, Walther. *Studien über die französischen Volksstämme des Frühmittelalters.* Stuttgart, 1968.

Kiener, Fritz. *Verfassungsgeschichte der Provence.* Leipzig, 1900.

Kurth, G. *Etudes franques.* 2 vols. Paris, 1919.

Latouche, Robert. *Les origines de l'économie occidentale.* L'évolution de l'humanité. 2nd ed. Paris, 1970.

Latrin, P. "L'influence colombanienne à l'abbaye de Moroeuil en Artois." *Mélanges colombaniennes.* Paris, 1950. 243–46.

Levi, Ernst. *Pauli Sententiae: A Palingenesia of the Opening Titles as a Specimen of Research in West Roman Vulgar Law.* Ithaca, N. Y., 1945.

— *Weströmisches Vulgarrecht: Das Obligationenrecht.* Weimar, 1956.

— *West Roman Vulgar Law: The Law of Property.* Philadelphia, 1951.

Lewis, Archibald R. *The Development of Southern French and Catalan Society, 718–1050.* Austin, 1965.

— "The Dukes in the *Regnum Francorum,* A. D. 550–751." *Speculum.* 51 (1976) 381–410.

Lombard, Maurice. "Mahomet et Charlemagne: Le problème économique. "*Bedeutung und Rolle des Islam beim Übergang vom Altertum zum Mittelalter.* ed. Paul Egon Hübinger. Wege der Forschung 202. Darmstadt, 1968. 160–177.

Lopez, Robert S. "Mohammed and Charlemagne: A Revision." *Bedeutung und Rolle des Islam.* 65–104.

Lühe, W. *Hugo von Die und Lyon, Legat von Gallien.* Breslau, 1898.

Luppi, Bruno. *I saraceni in Provenza in Liguria e nelle Alpi occidentali.* Bordighera, 1952.

Manteyer, G. de. *La Provence du Ie au XIIe siècle.* Paris, 1926.

Margin, Paul Edmond. *Etudes critiques sur la Suisse à l'époque mérovingienne 534–715.* Geneva, 1910.

Ménager, L. R. "Considérations sociologiques sur la démographie des grands domaines ecclésiastiques carolingiens." *Etudes d'histoire du droit canonique dédiées à Gabriel Le Bras.* Paris, 1965. II, 1318–1335.

Morin, D. G. "Le testament de S. Césaire d'Arles et la critique de M. Bruno Krusch." *Révue Bénédictine.* 16 (1899), 97–100.

Moyse, Gerard. "La Bourgogne septentrionale et particulièrement le diocèse Besançon de la fin du monde antique au seuil de l'âge carolingien (Ve–VIIIe siècles)." *Von der Spätantike zum frühen Mittelalter: Aktuelle Probleme in historische Sicht.* ed. Joachim Werner and Eugen Ewig. Vorträge und Forschungen 25. Sigmaringen, 1979. 467–488.

– "Les origines du monachisme dans le diocèse de Besançon (Ve–Xe siècles)." *Bibliothèque de l'Ecole des chartes.* 131 (1973), 21–104 and 369–485.

Nehlsen, Hermann, "Aktualität und Effektivität der ältesten germanischen Rechtsaufzeichnungen." *Recht und Schrift im Mittelalter.* ed. Peter Classen. Vorträge und Forschungen 23. Sigmaringen, 1977. 449–502.

– *Sklavenrecht zwischen Antike und Mittelalter.* Göttingen, 1972.

Nonn, Ulrich. "Merowingische Testamente. Studien zum Fortleben einer römischen Urkundenform im Frankenreich." *Archiv für Diplomatik.* 18 (1972), 1–129.

Oexle, Otto Gerhard. "Le monastère de Charroux au IXe siècle." *Le Moyen Age.* 76 (1970), 193–204.

Penco, Gregorio. "Tradizione mediolatina e fonti romanze nel *Chronicon novaliciense.*" *Benedictina.* 12 (1958), 1–14.

Percival, John. "Seigneurial aspects of Late Roman estate management." *The English Historical Review.* 332 (1969), 449–473.

Pirenne, Henri. *Mahomet et Charlemagne.* Paris, 1937.

– *Medieval Cities.* Garden City, s.d.

Poly, Jean-Pierre. *La Provence et la société féodale, 879–1166.* Paris, 1976.

– "Régime domanial et rapports de production 'féodalistes' dans le midi de la France (VIIIe–Xe siècles)." *Structures féodales et féodalisme dans l'occident méditerranéen (Xe–XIIIe siècles): Bilan et perspectives de recherches.* Collection de l'École française de Rome 44. Rome, 1980. 57–84.

– and Bournazel, Éric. *La mutation féodale, Xe–XIIe siècles.* Nouvelle Clio 16. Paris, 1980.

Prinz, Friedrich. "Bayerns agilolfingische Kloster- und Adelsgeschichte und die Gründung Kremsmünsters." *Die Anfänge des Klosters Kremsmünster.* ed. Siegfried Haider. *Mitteilungen des oberösterreichischen Landesarchivs.* Erg. Bd. 2. Linz, 1978. 25–50.

– *Frühes Mönchtum im Frankenreich.* Munich, 1965.

– "Heiligenkult und Adelsherrschaft im Spiegel merowingischer Hagiographie." *Historische Zeitschrift.* 204 (1967), 529–544.

Quentin, Henri. *Les martyrologes historiques du moyen âge. Etude sur la formation du martyrologe romain.* Paris, 1908.

Reuter, Timothy, ed. *The Medieval Nobility: Studies on the ruling classes of France and Germany from the sixth to the twelfth century.* Europe in the Middle Ages: Selected Studies 14. Amsterdam, 1979.

Rigoir, Jacqueline. "La ceramique paléochrétienne sigillée grise." *Provence historique.* 10 (1960), 1–92.

– "Les sigillées paléochrétiennes grises et orangées." *Gallia.* 26 (1968), 177–244.

Roman, J.-H. *Abbon et Valchin. Etude sur un point controversé de l'histoire du VIIIe siècle.* Paris, 1885.

– *Legs faits par Abbon dans son testament dans les pagi de Briançon, Embrun, Chorges et Gap.* Grenoble, 1901.

Rouche, Michel. *L'Aquitaine des Wisigoths aux Arabes (418–781): Naissance d'une région.* Paris, 1979.

– "Les Aquitains ont-ils trahi avant la bataille de Poitiers? Un éclairage événementiel sur les mentalités." *Le Moyen Age.* 74 (1968), 5–26.

Scheibelreiter, Georg. *Der Bischof in merowingischer Zeit.* Veröffentlichungen des Instituts für österreichische Geschichtsforschung 27. Vienna, 1983.

Schieffer, Theodor. *Die päpstlichen Legaten in Frankreich vom Vertrag von Meersen (870) bis zum Schisma von 1130.* Berlin, 1935.

Schlesinger, Walter. "Hufe und mansus im Liber Donationum des Klosters Weißenburg." *Beiträge zur Wirtschafts- und Sozialgeschichte des Mittelalters: Festschrift für Herbert Helbig zum 65. Geburtstag.* ed. Knut Schulz. Cologne, 1976. 33–85.

— "Vorstudien zu einer Untersuchung über die Hufe." *Kritische Bewahrung: Beiträge zur deutschen Philologie: Festschrift für Werner Schröder zum 60. Geburtstag* ed. Ernst-Joachim Schmidt. Berlin, 1974. 15–85.

Schmid, Karl. "Welfisches Selbstverständnis." *Festschrift für Gerd Tellenbach.* Freiburg, 1968. 389–416.

— "Zur Problematik von Familie, Sippe und Geschlecht, Haus und Dynastie beim mittelalterlichen Adel." *Zeitschrift für die Geschichte des Oberrheins.* 105 (1957), 1–62.

Semmler, Josef. "*Episcopi potestas* und karolingische Klosterpolitik." *Mönchtum, Episcopat und Adel zur Gründungszeit des Klosters Reichenau.* ed Arno Borst. Vorträge und Forschungen 20. Sigmaringen, 1974. 305–395.

— "Zur pippinidisch-karolingischen Sukzessionskrise 714–723." *Deutsches Archiv.* 33,1 (1977), 1–36.

Sickel, Theodor von. *Acta regum et imperatorum Karolinorum digesta et enarrata. Die Urkunden der Karolinger, gesammelt und bearbeitet.* 2 vols. Vienna, 1867.

Sprandel, Rolf. *Der merowingische Adel und die Gebiete östlich des Rheines.* Freiburg i. Br., 1957.

— "Struktur und Geschichte des merowingischen Adels." *Historische Zeitschrift.* 193 (1961), 33–71.

Spreckelmeyer, Goswin. "Zur rechtlichen Funktion frühmittelalterlicher Testamente." *Recht und Schrift im Mittelalter.* ed. Peter Classen. Vorträge und Forschungen 23. Sigmaringen, 1977. 91–114.

Staab, Franz. *Untersuchungen zur Gesellschaft am Mittelrhein in der Karolingerzeit.* Wiesbaden, 1975.

Störmer, Wilhelm. *Früher Adel: Studien zur politischen Führungsschicht im fränkisch-deutschen Reich vom 8. bis 11. Jahrhundert.* 2 vols. Monographien zur Geschichte des Mittelalters 6, 1–2. Stuttgart, 1973.

Stouff, L. "Étude sur le principe de la personalité des lois depuis les invasions barbares jusqu'au XIIe siècle." *Revue bourguignonne de l'enseignement supérieur.* 4, 1 (1894), 1–310.

Stroheker, Karl Friedrich. *Der senatorische Adel im spätantiken Gallien.* 1948, reprint Darmstadt, 1970.

Tabacco, Giovanni. "Dalla Novalesa a S.-Michele della Chiusa." *Monasteri in Alta Italia dopo le invasioni saracene e magiare (sec. X–XII).* XXXIIo Congresso storico subalpino, Deputazione Subalpina di Storia Patria. Turin, 1966. 481–526.

— "I processi di formazione dell'Europa Carolinga." *Nascita dell'Europa ed Europa Carolingia: un 'equazione da verificare.* Settimane di studio del centro italiano di studi sull'alto medioevo 27, 1. Spoleto, 1981. 17–43.

Tellenbach, Gerd. *Königtum und Stämme in der Werdezeit des deutschen Reiches.* Weimar, 1939.

— "Über die ältesten Welfen im West- und Ostfrankenreich." *Studien und Vorarbeiten zur Geschichte des großfränkischen und frühdeutschen Adels.* ed. Gerd Tellenbach. Forschungen zur oberrheinischen Landesgeschichte 4. Freiburg i. Br. 1957. 335–340.

Thomas, H. "Die Namenliste des Diptychon Barberini und der Sturz des Hausmeiers Grimoald." *Deutsches Archiv.* 25 (1969), 17–63.

Van Der Essen, L. *Etude critique et littéraire sur les vitae des saints mérovingiens de l'ancienne Belgique.* Louvain, Paris, 1907.

Vehse, O. "Das Bündnis gegen die Sarazenen vom Jahre 515." *Quellen und Forschungen. Aus italienischen Archiven und Bibliotheken.* 19 (1927), 181–204.

Verhulst, Adriaan. "La genèse du régime domanial classique en France au haut moyen âge." *Agricoltura e mondo rurale in occidente nell'alto medioevo.* Settimane di studio del centro italiano di studi sull'alto medioevo 13. Spoleto, 1966. 135–160.

Verlinden, Charles. *L'esclavage dans l'Europe médiévale.* I. *Pénisule ibérique, France.* Bruges, 1955.

Vezin, Jean. "Une nouvelle lecture de la liste de noms copiés au dos de l'ivoire barberini." *Bulletin archéologique du comité des travaux historiques et scientifiques.* nouvelle série 7 (1971), 19–53.

Vregille, B. de. "Les origines chrétiennes et le haute moyen âge." *Histoire de Besançon.* ed. Claude Fohlen. Paris, 1964. I, 182–485.

Wallace-Hadrill, J. M. *The Long-Haired Kings.* New York, 1962.

Wataghin Cantino, Gisella. "Il valico del Moncenisio in età romana: dati archeologici e ipotesi di lavoro." *Le reseau routier en Savoie et en Piemont: Aspects historique et contemporain. Bulletin du Centre e'études franco-italien.* 8 (1981), 27–33.

— "Prima campagna di scavo nella chiesa dei SS. Pietro e Andrea dell'abbazia di Novalesa. Rapporto preliminare." *Archeologia medievale.* 6 (1979), 289–317.

— "Seconda campagna di scavo nello chiesa dei SS. Pietro e Andrea dell'abbazia della Novalesa. Rapporto preliminare: Le fasi premonaniche." *Atti del V Congresso nazionale di archeologia cristiana. Torino, valle di Susa, Cuneo, Asti, valle d'Aosta, Novara, 22–29 settembre 1979.* Rome, 1981. 1–10.

Wattenbach Levison. *Deutschlands Geschichtsquellen im Mittelalter: Vorzeit und Karolinger I. Die Vorzeit von den Anfängen bis zur Herrschaft der Karolinger.* Bearbeitet von Wilhelm Levison. Weimar, 1952.

Weinberger, Stephen, "Peasant Households in Provence ca. 800–1100." *Speculum.* 48 (1973), 247–257.

Wemple, Suzanne Fonay. *Women in Frankish Society: Marriage and the Cloister 500–900.* Philadelphia, 1981. 127–148.

Wenskus, Reinhard. *Stammesbildung und Verfassung: Das Werden der frühmittelalterlichen gentes.* Cologne, 1977.

— "Die deutschen Stämme im Reiche Karls des Großen." *Karl der Große.* 178–219.

Werner, Karl Ferdinand. "Andreas von Marchiennes und die Geschichtsschreibung von Anchin und Marchiennes in der zweiten Hälfte des 12. Jahrhunderts." *Deutsches Archiv.* 9 (1952), 402–463.

— "Bedeutende Adelsfamilien im Reich Karls des Großen." *Karl der Große: Persönlichkeit und Geschichte.* ed. Helmut Beumann. Düsseldorf: 1965. I, 83–142. Translated in Timothy Reuter, *Medieval Nobility.* 137–202.

— "Les nations et le sentiment national dans l'Europe médiévale." *Revue historique.* 244 (1970), reprinted in *Structures politiques du monde franc VI–XIIe siècles: Etudes sur les origines du la France et de l'Allemagne.* London, 1979.

— "Les Principautés périphériques dans le monde franc du VIIIe siècle." *I problemi dell'Occidente nel secolo VIII.* Settimane di studio del Centro italiano di studi sull'alto medioevo 20. (Spoleto, 1973). 483–514; 524–532.

— "Le rôle de l'aristocratie dans la christianisation du Nord-est de la Gaule." *Revue d'histoire de l'église de France.* 62 (1975), 45–73.

Werner, Matthias. *Adelsfamilien im Umkreis der frühen Karolinger. Die Verwandtschaft Irminas von Oeren und Adelas von Pfalzel.* Vorträge und Forschungen Sonderband 28. Sigmaringen, 1982.

— *Der Lütticher Raum in frühkarolingischer Zeit: Untersuchungen zur Geschichte einer karolingischen Stammlandschaft.* Göttingen, 1980.

White, Lynn. *Medieval Technology and Social Change.* Oxford, 1962.

Wolfram, Herwig. "Der heilige Rupert in Salzburg." *Salzburger Diskussionen: Frühes Mönchtum in Salzburg.* ed. Eberhard Zwink. Salzburg, 1983. 81–92.

– "Der heilige Rupert und die antikarolingische Adelsopposition." *MIÖG.* 80 (1972), 4–34.

– *Geschichte der Goten.* 2nd edition Munich, 1980.

– *Intitulatio I. Lateinische Königs- und Fürstentitel bis zum Ende des achten Jahrhunderts. MIÖG* erg. Bd. 21. Vienna, 1967.

– *Intitulatio II. Lateinische Herrscher- und Fürstentitel im neunten und zehnten Jahrhundert. MIÖG* erg. Bd. 24. Vienna, 1973.

– "*Libellus Virgilii:* ein quellenkritisches Problem der ältesten Salzburger Güterverzeichnisse." *Mönchtum, Episcopat und Adel zur Gründungszeit des Klosters Reichenau.* ed. Arno Borst. Vorträge und Forschungen 20. Sigmaringen, 1974. 177–214.

– "Vier Fragen an die Geschichte des heiligen Rupert." *Studien und Mitteilungen zur Geschichte des Benediktiner-Ordens.* 93 (1982), 2–25.

Zerner-Chardavoine, Monique. "Enfants et jeunes au IXe siècle: La démographie du polyptique de Marseille 813–814." *Provence historique.* 126. 356–384.

Zöllner, Erich. *Die politische Stellung der Völker im Frankenreich.* Vienna, 1950.

INDEX

Abbelenus *comes* 104, 105 n. 23

Abbo, bishop of Metz 147

Abbo *rector* and probably *patricius, passim;*
estates 149–50, 96; offices 33–35, 96,
120–125; cooperation with Charles Martel
145–46; family 101–107, 115–119, 151

Abbo, abbot of Novalesa 120, 124

Abbo, bishop of Besançon 104

Adalbaldus 131–32, 134–38, 145–47

Adalgisel, testament of 28

Adalsendis, daughter of Rictrudis 128

Adaltruda, daughter of Bercharius 129, 135,
145

Adelaïde, queen, wife of Louis VI 15

Ado of Vienne 108

Aegidii 8–9, 151

Aeochaldus (Eoldus), archbishop of Vienne
140

Agabertus, monk at Novalesa 21, 23, 38

Agiolfings 139, 141, 144

Agloaldus 74, 129

Agnaricus *patricius* 40, 129

Agobard, bishop of Lyons 108

Agracianis, possibly La Grave, Hautes-Alpes,
arr. Briançon 50

Agricola, praetorian prefect of the Gauls 101

agriculture 149

Aigulf, abbot of Lérins 140

Aigyna *dux* 113 n. 49

Aix-en-Provence 89

Albanatum Alberea or Alberedo, Piemonte
prov. Torino, cne. Venaus 42

Albarioscum Baratier, Hautes-Alpes, arr. Embrun 54, 117

Albiadis Albiez-le-Vieux or Albiez-le-Jeune, Savoie, arr. St. Jean-de-Maurienne 46

Albon, Count Guigo III of 18, 21

Alcherius, bishop of Grenoble 17

Alcuin 132 n. 23

Aldefredus *libertus* 58

Alemannia 126, 143, 152; Alemannians 4,
108

Allionicum unknown location 54

allodial property 31, 85

Alpes maritimae, Roman provence 1

Alpes-de-haute-Provence, département 1, 81

Alpes-Maritimes, département 1, 81

Alps, similarities across 122–123

Alsedis Aussois Savoie, arr. St.-Jean-de-Mau-
rienne can. Modane 46

Alsende 93

Altana Autannes, Drôme, arr. Nyon, cne. Ancelle 56

Alternetus unknown location 62

Amalbertus 120

Amalbertus *libertus* 56

Amalgarius *dux* 113 n. 49

Amalicionis Hermillon, Savoie, arr. St.-Jean-
de-Maurienne 48, 81

Amatus, bishop of Sion 132, 136

Ambel 89 see *Ambillis*

Ambertum Villarembert, Savoie, arr. St.-Jean-
de-Maurienne 46, 93

Ambillis Ambel, Hautes-Alpes, arr. Gap 64

Ambillis in Taraone Ambel-en-Trièves, Isère,
arr. Grenoble 70

Amblariacum Amblérieu, Isère, arr. Tour-du-
Pin 50

amita 115

ancilla 92, 97

Ancilla Ancelle, Hautes-Alpes, arr. Gap 56

Anglarias possibly Eyguières, Bouches-du-Rhône, cns. Senas 62

Annales Laurissenses minores 143

Annales Marchianensis 131, 136

Anneda unknown location 50

Ansfledis, wife of Waratto 129, 135–37, 140

Anstrudis, wife of Bercharius 129, 135, 138

Antener *patricius* 34 n. 89, 120, 126–27, 139,
145 n. 81

Aquisiana valley of the Guisanne, Hautes-Alpes 50–52

Aquislevas possibly Le Lauzet, Hautes-Alpes,
arr. Briançon 50

Aquitaine 3, 5, 106, 126–27, 129; Aquitai-
nians 108–109

Arauardum Allevard, Isère, arr. Grenoble can.
Allevard 48

Arbeo, bishop of Freising 144

Arc river 82

Arcia Arces, Isère, arr. Grenoble 68

Ardennes 5

Ardingus 150, 152, Carolingian agent (count?)
in Provence 34 n. 89

Ardulfus 50, 129

Aredius, bishop of Vaison 140

Aridius, testament of 28

Arinbertus *dux* 113 n. 49

Arlatinus pagus, Arelates, Arles 8, 62, 82, 85,
88, 101, 116, 118, 120, 122–28, 142, 152

Arly, river 1

Arnulf, bishop of Metz 147

Arnulfings 2, 116 n. 58, 120, 122, 124, 126,
128, 131, 136, 138, 144–46, 151

Arsilio in *pagus* of Grenoble 19

Artonoscum possibly Laragne, Hautes-Alpes,
arr. Gap. 58

Attaniscum unknown location 64

Attensis pagus Apt 64

Audoenus, bishop of Rouen 147

Auolus *presbyter* 58

Auriliana *liberta* 48

Austrasia 3–5, 37, 116 n. 58, 120, 131

Austrobertus, archbishop of Vienne 140

Austrualdus 46

Autun, synod of 16

Auvergne 103, 18

Auxerre, *Gesta episcoporum* 106

Avars 128 n. 9

Avignon 1, 127, Synod of 14

Avita, sister of St. Desiderius 147

Avitus, bishop of Vienne 103

Avoli 151

Avolus 117

Avolus *presbyter* 103

avunculus 115

Baccoriacum Criau, Isère, can. Chozéau 50,
129

Baio *ministerialis* 60

Balciacum 129

Baon 16

Baratier 87 see *Albarioscum*

Bardinus *capitolarius* 52

Barnuinus, archbishop of Vienne 16–17, 19

Baronta *libertus* (sic) 54

Barontus *dux* 113 n. 49

Barre des Ecrins 1

Barrum Bar, Piemonte prov. Torino, cne. Condove 42

Basciascum Baix, Isère can. St. Baudille 50

Bausetis Baussent, Savoie, arr. St.-Jean-de-
Maurienne can. Modane 48

Bautier, Robert-Henri 37 n. 3

Bavaria 5, 87, 126, 129, 139, 144, 152; Bavarians 108, 139, 143

beneficium 98, 150

Berbers 128 n. 9

Bercharius, *major domus* in Neustria 129,
135–36, 138, 145

Beroleos 74

Bertelinus 97

Bertelinus *seruus* 70

Bertildes *libertus* 58

Bertildus *liberta* (sic) 58

Bertille, Saint 132

Bertram, testament of 28–29

Besançon 92, 103, 104, 120

Bezaudon 92

Bicciatis unknown location 46

Bicorascum possibly Rubiana, Piemonte, province of Torino 44

bilingualism 109

Biriscum possibly Avrieux, Savoie, can.
Modane 46

Blaciacum Blet, Isère, cne. Porcieu-Amblagnieu
50

Bladonis unknown location 60

Blancolus *uerbicarius* 48

Blèone, river 1

Bobbio 23

Bodegisel 114

Bognoscum possibly Bramans, Savoie, can.
Modane 46, 93

Boneualus 58

Bonitus 146 n. 81

booty 151

Bordeaux 102; Bordelais 118

Boresium unknown location 54

Bornacum St. Pierre de Bournay, Isère, arr.
Vienne 50

Bosedo Bezaudun, Drôme, arr. Die 62

Bosl, Karl 5, 87, 93

Boso, king of Provence 17

Bossieu, in *pagus* of Grenoble 19

Bouches-du-Rhône, département 1

Bournazel, Eric 105–107; 112

Braccium Bras-d'Asse, Alpes de Haute-
Provence, arr. Digne 68, 70, 89

Bregis Brégoz, Savoie, arr. St.-Jean-de-Mau-
rienne can. Modane 46

Breme 20, 24

Breuil-sur-Lys 133, 136

Briantinus pagus Briançon 50, 118, 123, 20,
81, 85–86, 89 *vallis* 52

Bricoscis possibly Brigot, Savoie, can. St. Michel-de-Maurienne 48

Brigantinus pagus see *Briantinus pagus*

Brignoles 101

Brinticum unknown location 52, 117

Briord dép. Ain 142

Brosiolis Bruzolo, Piemonte, province of
Torino 44

Brown, Peter 7, 124, 128 n. 9

Brunner, Heinrich 110

Brunner, Karl 4

Buchner, Rudolf 9–10, 34

Bullone Ballons, Drôme, arr. Nyons 60

Burgundy 5, 88, 103, 111, 120, 123, 127,
138–39, 142–43, 145–46, 149; Burgundians 4, 101, 105–107, 110, 148

Byzance 8

Caesarius of Arles, testament of 25, 29

Cahors 118

Calaicum possibly Le Caire, Alpes-de-Haute-
Provence, arr. Sisteron 54

Camargue 2, 82

Cambis Champs, Isère, arr. Grenoble, can.
Vizille 48

Cammites superior et subterior unknown locations 44

Campannae unknown location 58

Campus unknown location 62

Camundis Chiomonte, Piemonte, province of
Torino 42

Capetians 148

Capitulare missorum 111

capitularii 95, 97, 99, 100

Carnacum Charnay-lès-Mâcon, Saône-et-Loire 50

Carolingians 2, 4–5, 24, 143, 146; see
Arnulfings; Pepinids

Carolmann 35, 125

cartulary of Grenoble 18–21, 36

Carusium flumen the Chéruis or the Bourbre,
Isère 50, 129

Cassaniola possibly St.-Jean-de-Chassagne,
Hautes-Alpes, com. Gap 72

Cassauda Montagne des Casses de Faudon,
Hautes-Alpes, arr. Gap 56

Cassies Cassières, Isère, arr. Grenoble 62

castellum 123

Catalonia 149

Cattoroscus possibly Cadarache, Bouches-du-
Rhône 62

Cauellicus pagus Cavaillon 64, 66, 118

Caux 136

Cavaillon 118 see *Cauellicus*

Celsebertus 68

Cenischia river 81; see *Cinisca*

Centronis St.-Tronc, Buches-du-Rhône, cne.
Marseille 62

cessio 85–86

Chagnericus vir illuster 50 see Agnaricus

Chairaardus dux 113 n. 49

Charles III the Fat 19

Charles Martel 3, 9–10, 26, 33–4, 40, 74,
86, 104, 112–114, 116, 120–27, 129–30,
140, 144–46, 148–52

Charles the Great (Charlemagne) 4, 10,
20–23, 25–26, 35–36, 38, 109, 121, 125,
144, 146

Chaudol, *villa*, dependency of St.-Victor of
Marseille 34 note 89, 150

Chaume, Maurice 131

Cheraonius vir nobilis 102

Childebert III 50 n. 77

Chilperic II Frankish king 141

Chlothar (Clothar) Frankish king 102, 104,
147

Chramlinus (Chramnelenus, Crammelinus)
103, bishop of Embrun 70, 104, 136, 139

Chramnelenus, *dux* 103, 112–113, 151

Chronicon moissiacense 128 n. 9

Chronicon novaliciense 22–23, 34–35, 38,
125

Chuonrat 143

Chur 120–122

Cicimianum Comiana, Piemonte, province of
Torino, cne. Mompantero 44

Ciconiola Sigoyer, Hautes-Alpes, arr. Gap 72

Cinicinum, possibly Senez, Alpes de Haute-Provence, arr. Castellane 72

Cinisca Cenischia River 42, 44

Cipolla, Carlo 36–37

Clavadetscher, Otto P. 121

Clementia, mother of Rusticula 102

Clotsendis, daughter of Rictrudis 128

Clovis, Frankish king 105

Clovis III, Frankish king 50 n. 77

Codex Justinianus 30

Codex Theodosianus 30

Cognasso, F. 27

coloni 91, 95 n. 85, 96 n. 87, 99

colonicae 6, 31–32, 86–91, 95, 96, 99, 129, 150

Columbus *libertus* 48

Comarium Saint-Georges-de-Commiers, Isère, arr. Grenoble 76

comes 121, 142

commerce, Mediterranean 8, 150

commutare 85

condoma 7

confiscations 129

conquirere 84

Constantius, bishop and *rector* of Chur 121

Corbie 141

Corennum Corenc, Isère, arr. Grenoble can. Grenoble 48

cortes 88–91, 150

Coruallicum Croaglie, Piemonte, province of Torino 42

Crammelinus see Chramnelenus

Crauasca Revoisse on the Dora Riparia near Esilles 42

Crauioscum possibly Chardavon 56

Critouis Crotte, Piemonte, province of Torino, cne. Susa 44

Cronia unknown location 62

Cronnum unknown location 60

Cumbulae unknown location 62

Curennum Curnier, Drôme, arr. Nyon 56

Dadinus 58

Dadinus *libertus* 60

Dagobert I, Frankish king 131–35, 137, 142, 145, 147

Darentasiensis vallis Tarantaise valley, Savoie, arr. Moutiers-en-Tarantaise 48

demesne 89, 91

Desiderius, bishop of Cahors 147

Dhondt, Jan 3

Diensis Die 64, 76, 86, 97, 118, 129 *pagus* 32, 62, 64, 76

Digne 89

Diubiasca vallis valley of the Dubbione, Piemonte, province of Torino 44

Dodina, grandmother of Abbo 29, 60, 64, 115–117, 149

Dodo *domesticus* 116 n. 58

Dodo, uncle of Abbo 84–85, 115–119, *parens* (same?) 54, 60, 62, 64

Doliana possibly Daulan or Dolan, Vaucluse, comm. Avignon 60

Donatus, bishop of Besançon 103

Donatus, Church of 16–17, 19

Dora Riparia, river 20, 81, 123

Douai, Church of St. Amand 131 n. 22; region 136–37

Douzère, monastery 141

Drôme, département 1

Drac, river 1, 81

Droctesenda liberta 66, 93

Drogo *dux* son of Pepin II 129, 135 n. 39, 138 n. 52, 145, 146 n. 81

Dumnulina liberta 58

Dunimius 44

Durance, river 1, 81–82, 85, 89, 116

dux 122–123, 139, 141–42

Ebasciacum Possibly Passy, Saône-et-Loire, arr. Mâcon 50

Ebling, Horst 106, 112–114

Ebredunensis pagus see Embrun

Ebroin, *maior domus* 104, 131–32, 134–36, 138–39, 145

economy 149

Eligius, bishop of Nyon (St. Eloi) 147

Embrun 81, 104, 117–18, 123, 139 *Ebredunensis pagus* 52, 54, 76, 129

Eptolena, aunt of Abbo 64, 115

Erchinoaldus *maior domus* 128, 131–32, 134–36, 145

Ermento *dux* 113 n. 49

Erminethrudis 94

Ernoldus, father of Rictrudis 128
Escussarius 60
Esturbatina possibly Durbon, Hautes-Alpes, arr. Gap 58
ethnic leadership 114; ethnic identity 101–114
Etonum Aiton, Savoie, arr. St.-Jean-de-Maurienne 76
Eudo *dux* of the Aquitanians 139
Eusebia, daughter of Rictrudis 128
Eusthacius, bishop, cousin of Abbo 115, 119–20
evindicare 85
Ewig, Eugen 4, 105, 106
Exoratiana possibly Eysserères, Hautes-Alpes, cne. Gap 50
Eygues, river 1

faber 97
Faido unknown location 42
Felix 102
Felix Ennodius (Magnus) 101
Felix Ennodius 101
Felix Ennodius, proconsul of Africa 101
Felix, bishop of Besançon 104
Felix, father of Abbo 30, 33, 40, 101, 115, 125
Felix, senator from Marseille 102
fideles 127, 150
Filibert, abbot of Jumièges 136
Flaochad 151
Flavius Felix 101
Fleckenstein, Josef 143
Fleury-sur-Loire 140
Folchiad 138
Fontana unknown location 46
Fontenoy battle of (841) 108
Forest Montiers 133
forest products 81
Fos 8–9, 141, 150–51
Fournial, Etienne 7
Franconia 5
Franks 3, 4, 101, 105–111, 116, 139, 144; Francia 87, 114, 116, 149, 151; Frankish Aristocracy 147–48; empire 129; kingdom 129
Freberga 58, 117
Fredeberga *liberta* 76

Fredegar, *Chronicon* 123, 127, 128, 135, 142
Frisia 3, 126
Frodoinus, abbot of Novalesa 21, 23, 38
Fulcradus *dux* 152
Fustel de Coulanges 93

Galiscum unknown location 56
Galisiaca possibly Galise Piemonte, province of Torino 44
Gallic monasticism 144
Gallionum Giaglione, Piemonte, province of Torino 42
Gallo-Roman Aristocracy 4, 101–105, 112–113, 126–27, 138, 144, 147
Ganshof, François Louis 6–7, 34, 86, 90, 150
Gap 9, 30, 32, 85–86, 89, 90, 92, 102, 118, 123; *Vuapencensis pagus* 32, 54, 56, 70, 74, 76, 129; ecc. S. Mariae 68, 70
Garmond, archbishop of Vienne 14
Gasca Queirazza, Giuliano 37
Gascons 109; Gascony 147
Gauioaldus *seruus* 64
Geneuensis pagus Geneva 58, 97, 102, 120, 149, 152
gens 107–109
Gerberta, mother of Adalbaldus (?) 128
Gerentonica vallis valley of the Gironde 52
Gerentonnis Vallouise Hautes-Alpes, arr. Briançon 52
Gertrudis, grandmother of Adalbaldus (?) 128
Ghyslemarus *comes palatii* 136–38, 145–46
Ghyslemarus *maior domus* in Neustria 129, 134–37, 145
Ghyslemarus *propinquus* of Maurontus 133–36
Gislarannus *libertus* 76
Gislarannus, monk at Novalesa 21, 23, 38
Gismundus 52
Glasia Glaise, Hautes-Alpes, arr. Gap 60
Glisio Glysin, Isère, cne. Pinsot 68
Goda, *parens* of Abbo 54, 60, 62, 64, 68, 84, 85, 115–117
Godo, abbot of Novalesa 120
Godobald, kinsman of Dodo *domesticus* 116 n. 58
Godobertus *libertus* 58
Goffart, Walter 6–7
Gondobertus 60

Gondobertus *eunucus, libertus* 66
Gontardus, bishop of Valence 15
Gotfrid, *dux* of the Alemannians 139
Goths 101, 105–111
Gradosa possibly Gresse, Drôme, arr. Nyons
    60
Grande Casse 1
Grande Chartreuse 1
Gratauuna unknown location 48
Gratinopolitanus Grenoble 12–20, 24,
    31–33, 36, 85–86, 89, 103, 118, 123, 129,
    152; *pagus* 48, 66, 76
Gregorian reform 12–15
Gregory of Tours 112
Gregory VII, pope 14
Grenoble see *Gratianopolitanus*
Grionde river 87 see *Gerentonica flumen*
Grosseau *Grasellus* monastery 140
Grummum Grimordo, Piemonte, province of
    Torino, cne. Giaglione 42
Guido of Burgundy, archbishop of Vienne,
    then Pope Calixtus II 14–20, 33
Guido, bishop of Geneva 15
Guigo III, count of Albon 18
Guil, river 1
Gulli, Luciano 26–27
Guntello, wife of Riculfus 142
Guntramn, Frankish king 102
Gylippus 108
habere 85, 97–98
habitus 109
Hadoindus, testament of 28–29
Haerchemfreda, mother of St. Desiderius 147
Haldetrud, mother of Dagobert I 131
Harioldus, *nepos* Walana 44
Hariulf 133
Hautes-Alpes, département 1, 81, 116
Heilwig 143
Heinzelmann, Martin 142
Helena *liberta* 66
Hemma 143
Hermillon see *Amalicium*
Herstal 139
Hildebertus *libertus* 56
Hirsch, Ernst 37
Honorata *liberta* 95, 129
Honorata, cousin of Abbo 29–31, 64, 115,
    117–118

Honoria *liberta* 74
Honorius *libertus* 52
Hucbaldud of St. Amand 132–33 n. 23
Hugo of Châteauneuf d'Isère, bishop of
    Grenoble 12–21, 23–24, 31, 33
Hugo of Die, apostolic legate 14, 16, 19
Hugo, son of Charles the Great 125
Huns 107–108
Hytbertus 27, 40

impensio 31, 98–99
imperial aristocracy 3–5
infidelitas 76, 129–30, 136
ingenui 91
inheritance, 118–119
inscriptions 28, 142
Iocos, harpist *(lerator)* 68, 91
Iohannes *ministerialis* 44
Iohannes *libertus* 58
Irofrankish monasticism 140, 144
Isaac, bishop of Grenoble 19
Isajiw, Wsevolod W. 114
Isarnus, bishop of Grenoble 16–17, 19
Isère, département 1, 81; river 1, 81
Italy 111, 149
iudex 30–31
Iustebertus *libertus* 58
Iustina *liberta* 58
Iustinus *libertus* 60

Jactadus *praeses* 121
Jarnut, Jörg 113
Jews 151
Jumièges 135, 139 abbot: Filibert
Jura 104

Kalares La Motte-du-Caire, Alpes de-Haute-
    Provence, arr. Sisteron 56, 85
Kampers, Gerd 113
Kremsmünster 22 n. 23

Löwe, Heinz 27
La Salle *coris* 89 see *Sallaris*
Laciomaus see *Latiomaus*
Lagny 135
land, acquisition of 84–87
Landbertus, abbot of St.-Wandrille 141
Landricus, bishop of Mâcon 15

Langobardorum regnum, fines 44, 123, 125
language 109
Laquaticum possibly Eygalayes, Drôme, arr. Nyons 58
Lastadio Stagno, Piemonte, province of Torino, cne. Mompantero 42
Latiomaus possibly Laye, Hautes-Alpes, arr. Gap 60
Lauarioscum cortis Lavars, Isère, arr. Grenoble 56, 64, 72
Laurentius *uerbicarius* 54
Lavars *cortis* 89 see *Lauarioscum*
law and ethnicity 110–111; see *lex*
law, Alemannic 110
law, Bavarian 110
law, Burgundian 30, 88, 109–110
law, Frankish 109–110
law, Roman 8–9, 27–31, 96, 110, 114, 118, 147
Le Blant, E. 142
Le Cointe, Carlo 36
Leibulf *comes* 152
Lenonius possibly Ligagnau, Bouches-du-Rhône, cne. Arles 62
Leo, Carolingian supporter in Italy 146 n. 88
Leudebertus *dux* 113
Leudesius *maior domus* 128, 136
Leudunensis pagus Lyon 50
Leutsind, wife of Erchinoaldus 128
lex 108, 110–11; see law
lex de ingratis et contumacis libertis 30, 66
lex Falcidia 30, 64, 66
Liber historiae Francorum 135
Liber pontificalis 22
Libertatus, son of Iohannes 44
liberti 91–99, 150; obligations of 94
Licentiacum unknown location 72
Lichia, mother of Rictridus 128
Liliola, abbess of St. Caesarius of Arles 102
Limoges 102
lingua (language and identity) 108–110
Lisola fons Font-Douille, Bouches-du-Rhône, arr. Aix 62
Liutprand, king of the Lombards 128
Liège 116 n. 58
locella 89–90
locus 86
Lombards 108; see *Langobardorum fines* 123, 125

Lothar I, Emperor 22, 150
Lotharingians 108
Louis the Blind, king of Provence 17, 19, 20
Louis the Pious, Emperor 22, 109, 143, 151
Lucianum unknown location 60
Lugdunensis see Lyon; ecclesia S. Petri 44
Lupolina *mancipium* 56, 92
Luxeuil, monastery 147
Luxomonis Lisimonte, Piemonte, province of Torino, cne. Gravere 42
Lyonnais 127, 142
Lyon 17–18, 28, 86, 102, 103, 105, 108, 142, 146
Lérins monastery 140

Mühlbacher, Engelbert 10, 25–26, 36
Maastricht 116 n. 58
Mabillon, Jean 36
Mabin, Mount 81
Macitha Massette, Isère, cne. St. Guillaume 64
Mâcon 93; Mâconnais *Matascensis pagus* 50, 81, 118
Maconianum Maconin, Isère, can. Chanignieu 48
Magafredus, father of Frodoinus 38 n. 2
Magnabertus *uir clarissimus* 78
Magnebertus *libertus* 48
Magnibertus *libertus* 58
Magnum possibly Les Magnis, Savoie, arr. St.-Jean-de-Maurienne 46
maior domus 139, 147
Maiorianus *faber* 50, 129
Malencianum unknown location 70
Mamers 104
mancipia 88, 91, 92, 96, 97, 100, 150
manere 92, 97, 99
manor, structure of 6, 150
mansus 6–87, 99
manumission 94
Maorongos *abbas* 122, 130
Marabertus 60
Marchiennes 131–32, 134
Marcianus *seruus* 54
Marculfi formulae 28, 90
Marion, Jules 36–37
Marius *libertus* 54
Marius *uerbecarius* 52
Marne river 135

Maroaldus *libertus* 58, 97

Maroeul 132 n. 22

Marro, grandfather of Abbo 70, 104, 115

Marseille 8–9, 81–82, 85, 88, 102, 112, 116, 118, 126, 128, 141–42, 150–51

Massif Pelvoux 1

Massilia Marseille 60

Matanatis region of Matésine, Isère 74

Matarellus *libertus* 56

Matascensis pagus see Mâcon

matertera 115

Maurengus 151

Maurengus *clericus* 74, 105 n. 23, 129–30, 140, 144, 146

Maurienne 9, 32–33, 96, 118, 123, 130, 152; ecclesia. St. Johannes 70; valley of Maurienne *(Maurigenica vallis)* 42, 46, 86

Maurinus, grandfather of Abbo 29, 64, 115, 117, 149

Maurontus 151

Maurontus, abbot of Breuil-sur-Lys 128, 132–38

Maurontus, abbot of Forest Montiers 134–36

Maurontus, abbot of St.-Florent-le-Vieil 134

Maurontus *archidiaconus* 141

Maurontus, bishop of Marseille 146

Maurontus *dux* 105 n. 23, 113, 123–24, 127, 130–31, 141–42, 145–48

Maurouila Méreuil, Hautes-Alpes, arr. Gap 60

Maurus 58

Maximus *libertus* 54

Mediterranean 123, 149

Memiana St.-Antoine-de-Ménémènès, Vaucluse, cne. Isle-sur-Sorgue 70

Merovingian family 2, 4, 138, 140, 147; Merovingian society 152

Metz 138

Milan 17, 20

ministeriales 91, 98, 100

Misicasiana unknown location 48

Misiottanum Modane, Savoie, arr. St.-Jean-de-Maurienne 46

Missorianus Mizoën Isère, arr. Grenoble can. Bourg-d'Oisans 48

mixed marriages 111

Moccensis vallis 54, 117 see *Occensis vallis*

monasticism in Rhone valley 140–41

Mont Cenis 1, 86, 92

Mora *ancilla* 60

Morenzo, monk at Fulda 143

mores 108–109

Moslems in Rhône Valley 127–128; see Saracens

Moulon, Mme 37

Muccunaua unknown location 60

Mullinaricus Molines-en-Queyras, Hautes-Alpes, arr. Briançon 52

Mumolane *libertus* 94

munera 94–95

Namenmode 106, 113

names 151

Nanctilda, wife of Dagobert I 133

Nanosces (St.-Julienne-de-Maurienne ?) 46, 93

Narbonensis II Roman provence 1

Neustria 3–5, 129–143, 145–147

Nonn, Ulrich 26–29

Notitia de servitia monasteriorum 125

Novalesa monastery of St. Peter, *passim* 1, 92, 97, 115, 124–26, 129, 144, 152; foundation of 9; destruction of 24; necrology 125; see *Chronicon novaliciense*

Nyons 85–86, 104

Obliciacis unknown location 46

obsequium 31, 90, 94–95, 98–99

obvenire 84

Occensis vallis Ubayette valley 52

officeholding 119–125

Oise département 136

olive cultivation 82

ollae 149

Olonna Meylans Isère, comm. Meylans 48

Opaga cortis Upaix, Hautes-Alpes, arr. Gap 56

opera 94

Optilonicus 68

Orbanum Urbiano, Piemonte, province of Torino, cne. of Mompantero 44

Orbanus *libertus* 46, 93

Orbicianus *seruus* 64

Orcières 117

Otto III 23, 25

Ottonians 148

Ouvèze, river 1

pactum 30
Paganum unknown location 66
pagus 31
Pancrasius, Saint 46, 112
Pannutia, wife of Gismundus 52
Pardessus, J. M. 36
Parelianum unknown location 76
Paris 147
Pascal II, pope 15, 18
pasturage 81
patricius 8, 26, 34–35, 113, 116, 122–124,
    139, 142, 147, 152; see Abbo; Agnaricus;
    Willibadus
patrocinium 90, 93, 98; monastic 144
patronus 94
patruus 115
Paulus libertus 58
Pavia 23
Peccianum unknown location 64
peculium 98
Pentus unknown location 60
Pepin II maior domus 3, 34, 126–27, 129,
    131, 135, 138 n. 52, 139, 145, 148, 151
Pepin III Frankish king 125
Pepinids 138; see Arnulfings; Carolingians
Perret, André 37
Persa 56, 86
personality of law 109
Perum unknown location 60
pervenire 85
Peter siricarius 62, 91
Petracaua unknown location 42
Piacenza, council of 17, 20
Piemonte 1, 81
Pinianum Biviers, Isère, comm. Biviers 48
Pinum La-Tour-du-Pin, Isère 66
Pirenne, Henri 7–8, 10
Plancianus Plaisians, Drôme, arr. Nyons 60
Poilonicus libertus 98
Poitiers, battle of 127
poletica (polyptychs) 6, 80, 84
Poly, Jean-Pierre 105–107, 112
Pontius II, bishop of Grenoble 14
Pontius, bishop of Belley 15
portio 90, 118
potestas 125
pottery 149
praeses 121

Pratalio unknown location 62
Prinz, Friedrich 140, 144, 147
Priscus 107–108
Promacianum unknown location 42
Protadius fidelis 74
Protadius, bishop of Besançon 104
Protadius dux 104
Protadius, fidelis of Abbo 32, 104, 105 n. 23
Provence 96, 106, 115–116, 118, 126,
    138–41, 145–46, 149; revolt 34, 86, 124,
    126–48; society 151
Pseudo Fredegar 104
pégau 149
Péronne 135–36

Quincieux Isère, arr. St.-Marcellin 20, 33, 48
Quonaona possibly Cairanne, Vaucluse, arr.
    Orange 60
Quossis unknown location 64

Radbertus ingenuus 68, 93
Radulfus, dux of the Thuringians 139
Raetia 121, 152
Ralis possibly Realon, Hautes-Alpes 52
Ramnulfus, son of Maiorianus faber 50, 129
Raudenouilianum unknown location 44
recipere 85
rector 8–9, 34, 94, 113, 120–23, 130, 152;
    see Abbo; Constantius
Regensis pagus pagus of Riez 32, 62, 68, 72,
    118
Regino of Prüm 108–110
Reichenau Verbrüderungsbuch 38 n. 2, 143,
    146
Remigius, testament of 28–29
Rhineland 5
Rhône, river, communication 123; valley, pas-
    sim 149, 151; relations with Neustria
    138–143; passim Rhône valley 149, 151;
    revolt in 126–28, 139
Riacioscum Riossard, Isère, arr. Grenoble 64
Richarius, Saint (St. Riquier) 132 n. 23, 133,
    135
Rictrudis, Saint, mother of Maurontus 128,
    132, 134–35, 147
Ricuberga 58, 119
Ricuberta Deo sacrata femina 72

Riculfus son of Rodulfus, "rebel" 54, 74, 76,
    129–30, 141, 142, 144, 145
Riez 118, 89 see *Regensis pagus* 32
Rigaberga 54, 85, 117–118
Rigomagensis pagus pagus in the Ubaye 54
Rigouera *ingenua* 46, 93
Riguberga see Rigaberga
Rodanonis Rosans, Hautes-Alpes, arr. Gap 60
Rodbaldus son of Rodulfus, "rebel" 54,
    129–30, 141–42, 144, 146
Rodis unknown location 54
Rodulfus, father of Riculfus and Rodbaldus
    74, 129–130, 141, 145
Rogationis unknown location 44, 89, 90
Rollières 87 see *Ralis*
Roma Romette, Alpes-de-Haute-Provence, cne.
    Gap 58
Romano-Ostrogothic constitution 151
Romans 3, 4, 105
Rosière, in *pagus* of Grenoble 19
Rouche, Michel 5, 127, 128 n. 93
Rouen 136–37
Ruadpreht 143
Ruarmum unknown location 70, 89
Rudolf, king of Burgundy 146
Rule of Benedict 144
Rule of Macarius 140
Rule of St. Benedict and Columbanus 140–41
Rupert archbishop of Salzburg 138–39, 141,
    143
Rupertiners 138
Rustica, mother of Abbo 33, 40, 58, 60, 64,
    84, 97, 102, 115, 117, 125
Rusticiu *mancipium* 56, 92
Rusticius *uir clarissimus* 78, 102 n. 10
Rusticula, abbess of St. Caesarius of Arles 102
Rusticus, brother of St. Desiderius 147
Rusticus, bishop of Geneva 102

Salliaris curtis La Salle, Hautes-Alpes, arr.
    Briançon 52
salt production 82
Salvus, father of St. Desiderius 147
San'Andrea di Torino 125
Sanctitilda *liberta* 66
Saracens 9, 15, 19–20, 24–25, 126, 151; *gens
    sarracenorum* 76
Sauina 54

Sauinus *libertus* 58
Savel 91 see *Seuelis*
Savoie, département 1, 81
Saxons 108
Schlesinger, Walter 88
Schmid, Karl 4, 145–46
Scythians 107–108
Segucium ciuitas Susa 42, 129; *vallis* 70, 74
Seine river 140, 141
Seine-Maritime département 136
Selina, sister of St. Desiderius 147
Semforianus, bishop of Gap, uncle of Abbo
    30, 32, 56, 58, 68, 70, 89, 103, 115, 119,
    120
Semphorianus *uir clarissimus* 78
Semmler, Josef 124–25
Semprugnanum possibly Savournon, Hautes-
    Alpes, arr. Gap 74, 129
Sendebertus *liberta* (sic) 48
Sendibertus *libertus* 58
Septimania 111
Sergi, Giuseppe 37
Sermorens, pagus, archdeaconry 15–18
serui 31, 91, 92, 96, 98; *casati* 92
Seuelis Savel, Drôme, can. Roman et Sauel 58
Seuorium Saboire, Isère, h. cne. St. Savin 50
Siagria 46, 48–50, 54, 56, 62–64, 70, 72, 76,
    84, 85, 92, 103, 118–119
Siagrius, brother of St. Desiderius 147
Siagrius, bishop of Autun 102
Sicualdus *libertus* 54
Sicuberga 68
Sicufredus *libertus* 66
Sicumarus *libertus* 66
Sigestericus pagus Sisteron 32, 60, 72
Sigilina *liberta* 66
Sigiricus *libertus* 66
Sigualdus *libertus* 52
Sigusina vallis Susa Valley 40, 42, 68
Sion 139 bishop: Amatus
Sippe 145–46
siricarius 97
Siseberga *liberta* 58
Sisteron 82, 89, 118; see *Sigestericus pagus*
slavery 92
slaves 7, 100
Solia possibly Mont-Soeil, Hautes-Alpes, arr.
    Embrun 54

Somme département 136; river 135
Spreckelmeyer, Goswin 25
St. Bonnet 86
St. Maurice, monastery 140
St. Riquier *Chronicon* 133
St. Stephen, Church of at Lyon 19
St. Victor of Marseille 34, 84, 126, 146, 150
St.-Denis, monastery 141
St.-Jean-de-Maurienne 81–82, 97, 123; see Maurienne
St.-Wandrille 135
St. Fermin 85–86
Störmer, Wilhelm 5, 87
Staab, Franz 5
Stroheker, Karl Friedrich 101
Subtus ripas Souribes, Alpes de Haute-Provence, arr. Sisteron 56
Suevs 108
Sulpitius, bishop of Bourges 147
Susa 9, 20, 26, 33–34, 40, 81, 85, 89, 122–123, 130, 152
Syagrii 8–9, 103, 118, 151; see Siagrius; Syagria

Tabacco, Giovanni 26
Talarnum cortis Tallard, Hautes-Alpes, arr. Gap 54, 89
Tannoborgonis Borgone, Piemonte, province of Torino, cne. Bruzolo 44
Taraonis St.-Jean, Alpes-de-Haute-Provence, cme. Volonne 58
tariffs 151
Tasculfus 76
Tassilo III, *dux* of the Bavarians 22 n. 23, 128 n. 9, 144
Tellenbach, Gerd, 3–4, 143
Tello, bishop of Chur 121
Tenegaudia Le Than, Isère, cne. Mens 64
Tercia unknown location 52
Terraneo, Gian Tommaso 36
Tersia *liberta* 32, 74, 95, 97, 129
testaments, late Roman and Merovingian, 27–29; testament of Abbo *passim*
Teudaldos 74, 129
Teutcarius *Alamannus* 38 n. 2
Theodo, *dux* of the Bavarians 139
Theodoric the Great, Ostrogothic king 23, 101–102

Theudaldus *libertus* 44
Theuderic II, Frankish king 104
Theuderic III, Frankish king 104, 131, 134, 136, 141
Theuderic IV, Frankish king 26, 74, 95, 129, 140, 148
Theudoaldus *libertus* 52
Thodure in *pagus* of Grenoble 19
Thucydides 107–108
Thuringia 3; Thuringians 139
Tollatecus Talucco, Piemonte, province of Torino, cne. S. Pietroval Lemina 44
Tolonensis pagus The Toulonnais 62
Torino 24, 125
Torridum possibly Les Tourretts, Vaucluse, cne. Apt. 64
Toulon 82, 88
Transjura 149
Trebocis Trebot, Piemonte, province of Torino, cne. Meana 42
tribunus 121
Trier 34
Trojan origins of Franks 139 n. 56
Tétry, battle of (687) 135

Ubaye, river 1
Ultan, abbot of Péronne 136
Upaix *cortis* 89 see Opaga
Urban II pope 15–18, 20

Vaison 102–103, 118
Valence 14, 17
Valenciennes 136
Valerianus 64, 86, 103
Valerianus, father of Rusticula 102–103
Valerianus *vir illustrissimus* 103
Valerignaca cortis Valernes, Alpes-de-Haute-Provence, can La Motte 58, 89
Valucis possibly Valgioie or Balgioie, Piemonte, province of Torino 44
Var, département 1
Variates unknown location 64
Vasensis pagus Vaison 60
Vaucluse, département 1
Vauellicus pagus Cavaillon, Vaucluse 64
Velentium unknown location 30, 54, 76
Venantius Fortunatus 102–103
Venasque 104, 118

Venator 56

Venauella possibly Vaumeilh, Alpes-de-Haute-Provence, arr. Sisteron 54

Venauis Venaux, Piemonte, prov. Torino 70

Vendanum Le Veyer, Hautes-Alpes, arr. Briançon 52

Vendascinus pagus The Venaissin 60

Vera liberta 58

Veranus, bishop of Cavillon 112

Veranus, bishop of Vence 42, 112

verbicarii 97

Verdo flumen Verdon river 1, 64, 89

Verhulst, Adriaan 6–7, 86

Verissimus libertus 58

Verona, Diet of 109

Vianensis pagus see Viennensis

Victor, bishop of Chur 121

Victor libertus 58

Victor praeses 121

Victoriden 120–122

Viennaticum Vinay, Isère, arr. St.-Marcellin 48. See Vinay

Vienne 118, 122, 126

Viennensis pagus 129, Vienne 48–50

Viennensis, Roman provence 1

Vigilius, bishop of Chur 121

Vigilius tribunus 121

Vilidiacus (Vélizy) 140

villae 86–87, 90, 150

Vinay, Isère, arr. St.-Marcellin 20, 33, 48

viniculture 81–82

vir inluster 113, 142

Virgilia 32, 70

Visigoths 128 n. 9; Visigothic law 99

Vita Boniti 146 n. 81

Vita Ermenlandi 134

Vita Richarii primigenia 132–134

Vita Rictrudis 136

Vita Walarici 133

Vitalis capitularius 52

Vitalis uir clarissimus 78

Viu possibly Viougue, Bouches du Rhône, cne. Salon 62

Viuarius unknown location 62

Vnebertus libertus 64

Vobridium Ubrieux, Drôme, arr. Nyons 58

Voconcium unknow location 44, 68, 70, 89

Vuala liberta 76

Vuapencensis pagus see Gap

Vuidbertus uir clarissimus 78

Vuilla Vitola Villevieille, Hautes-Alpes, Arr. Briançon 52

Walana 44

Walchunus episcopus 124–125, 72, 74

Waldebertus 103, 151; presbyter 85; episcopus 54, 72, 104

Waldelenus dux 103, 107, 112, 114; kin 115, 120, 123

Waldericus dux 113

Wandalbertus 103

Wandalbertus abbas 60, 104, 115, 117–120

Wandalmarus, dux 112, 113 n. 49

Wandelbertus, bishop of Besançon 104

Waratto maior domus in Neustria 129, 131, 135–138, 140, 141, 145

Wardacelis Varages, Var, arr. Brignolles 62

Welfs 143, 146

Wenskus, Reinhard 107–108

Werner, Karl Ferdinand 4, 103–104, 108, 120, 123, 145–46

Werner, Matthias 5

Widegunda 52, 60, 66, 72, 85, 118

Widerad, testament of 28

Wilihari, dux of the Alemanni 139

Willelmia, countess of Maurienne 14–15

William the Liberator, count of Provence 25

Willibadus patricius 113 n. 49, 123, 151

Willicarius, archbishop of Vienne 140

Wolfram, Herwig 107, 138, 141

Worms 139

Yüsuf, Ibn Abderaman, wali of Septimania 126–27

Zöllner, Erich 108

Zacco, praeses 121

THE MIDDLE AGES
Edward Peters, *General Editor*

Christian Society and the Crusades, 1198–1229. Sources in Translation, including The Capture of Damietta by Oliver of Paderborn. Edited by Edward Peters

The First Crusade: The Chronicle of Fulcher of Chartres and Other Source Materials. Edited by Edward Peters

Love in Twelfth-Century France. John C. Moore

The Burgundian Code: The Book of Constitutions or Law of Gundobad and Additional Enactments. Translated by Katherine Fischer Drew

The Lombard Laws. Translated, with an Introduction, by Katherine Fischer Drew

From St. Francis to Dante: Translations from the Chronicle of the Franciscan Salimbene (1221–1288). G. G. Coulton

The Duel and the Oath. Parts I and II of Superstition and Force. Henry Charles Lea. Introduction by Edward Peters

The Ordeal. Part III of Superstition and Force. Henry Charles Lea

Torture. Part IV of Superstition and Force. Henry Charles Lea

Witchcraft in Europe, 1110–1700: A Documentary History. Edited by Alan C. Kors and Edward Peters

The Scientific Achievement of the Middle Ages. Richard C. Dales

History of the Lombards. Paul the Deacon. Translated by William Dudley Foulke

Monks, Bishops, and Pagans: Christian Culture in Gaul and Italy, 500–700. Edited, with an Introduction, by Edward Peters

The World of Piers Plowman. Edited and translated by Jeanne Krochalis and Edward Peters

Felony and Misdemeanor: A Study in the History of Criminal Law. Julius Goebel, Jr.

Women in Medieval Society. Edited by Susan Mosher Stuard

The Expansion of Europe: The First Phase. Edited by James Muldoon

Laws of the Alamans and Bavarians. Translated, with an Introduction, by Theodore John Rivers

Law, Church, and Society: Essays in Honor of Stephan Kuttner. Edited by Robert Somerville and Kenneth Pennington

The Fourth Crusade: The Conquest of Constantinople, 1201–1204. Donald E. Queller

The Magician, the Witch, and the Law. Edward Peters

Daily Life in the World of Charlemagne. Pierre Riché. Translated, with an Introduction, by Jo Ann McNamara

Repression of Heresy in Medieval Germany. Richard Kieckhefer

The Royal Forests of Medieval England. Charles R. Young

Popes, Lawyers, and Infidels: The Church and the Non-Christian World, 1250–1550. James Muldoon

Heresy and Authority in Medieval Europe. Edited, with an Introduction, by Edward Peters

Women in Frankish Society: Marriage and the Cloister, 500 to 900. Suzanne Fonay Wemple

The English Parliament in the Middle Ages. Edited by R. G. Davies and J. H. Denton

Rhinoceros Bound: Cluny in the Tenth Century. Barbara H. Rosenwein

On the Threshold of Exact Science: Selected Writings of Anneliese Maier on Late Medieval Natural Philosophy. Edited and translated by Steven D. Sargent

Miracles and the Medieval Mind: Theory, Record, and Event, 1000–1215. Benedicta Ward

The Chronicles of Theophanes: An English Translation of anni mundi 6095–6305 (A.D. 602–813). Translated, with an Introduction, by Harry Turtledove

The English Medieval Landscape. Edited by Leonard Cantor

Dante's Italy and Other Essays. Charles T. Davis

Maurice's Strategikon: Handbook of Byzantine Military Strategy. Translated by George T. Dennis

The Republic of St. Peter: The Birth of the Papal State, 680–825. Thomas F. X. Noble

Pope and Bishops: The Papal Monarchy in the Twelfth and Thirteenth Centuries. Kenneth Pennington

The Origins of Courtliness: Civilizing Trends and the Formation of Courtly Ideals, 939–1210. C. Stephen Jaeger

Aristocracy in Provence: The Rhône Basin at the Dawn of the Carolingian Age. Patrick J. Geary